SHADOWS FROM LIGHT
UNAPPROACHABLE

Praise For...

SHADOWS FROM LIGHT UNAPPROACHABLE
Marking the Twenty-fifth Year of
Anglican Frontier Missions (AFM)

Millions of people do not get a chance to hear about the good news of Jesus Christ because they are ignored by most Christians and Christian mission ministries. The harvest is plentiful but the laborers are indeed few. Allow the Lord to speak to you through this book; allow him to let you see his heart.

Archbishop Foley Beach
Anglican Church in North America

Since its beginning, Anglican Frontier Missions continues to grow into its original vision and call. This 25th anniversary book, *Shadows from Light Unapproachable*, is not just a celebratory recounting of significant moments in the history of AFM, but is also a helpful missiological text, beginning with Bishop Michael Nazir-Ali's Foreword and ending with Rev. Chris Royer's conclusion on the continued vision of AFM, 'to mobilize the Church to pray for and send missionaries to the largest and least-evangelized people groups and geographical regions...' I heartily endorse this book.

The Rev. Canon Dr. John A. Macdonald, Director
Head, Department of Pastoral Theology
Trinity School for Ministry

AFM is truly at the frontier of missions today, as it has been for some time. Anglicans need to know the path-breaking work of Anglican missions in the past and the exciting opportunities they have today. Veteran missionary Chris Royer and the other authors provide us with an eminently readable and intriguing account of both these things.

Gerald R McDermott
Anglican Chair of Divinity
Beeson Divinity School

Thanks be to God that he willed into existence Anglican Frontier Missions, to call and challenge his Church to go to ethnicities where the Gospel of Kingdom has not yet reached in any significant measure. May God use this 25th anniversary publication to raise up much prayer, support, and workers as we enter into what must surely be the final phase of the completion of world evangelization.

Bp. Kuan Kim Seng
Director of Missions
Assistant Bishop
Diocese of Singapore

SHADOWS FROM LIGHT UNAPPROACHABLE

MARKING THE TWENTY-FIFTH YEAR OF ANGLICAN FRONTIER MISSIONS

Edited by
TAD DE BORDENAVE

**Northumberland
Historical Press**
NHP

Northumberland Historical Press
Heathsville, Virginia 22473

Unless otherwise noted, biblical quotations are from the
English Standard Version.

Cover photo provided by the Anglican Diocese of Singapore.
Cover design by Sue Carlson

ISBN: 978-0-9979846-3-7
Library of Congress Control Number: 2018930938

Printed in the United States of America

CONTENTS

Part Four
**ANGLICANISM, THE GREAT TRADITION,
AND FRONTIER MISSION**

FOREWORD

Anglicans are often seen as springing from the established Church of England, with all its paraphernalia of gilded abbeys and splendid vestments. In fact, what has made Anglicanism a worldwide movement is none of these external manifestations but its rootedness in Scripture as authoritative, and its title deeds, the *Book of Common Prayer* and the *Articles of Religion*. The first reminds us immediately of God's universal purposes in choosing a people to reveal himself and in coming as man to redeem his creation. This should lead to taking the Great Commission seriously and to try and reach the *panta ta ethne* or all the world's people groups with the good news of what God has done in Jesus Christ. The *Book of Common Prayer* and the Articles remind us that this good news, and its consequences in worship, prayer and public liturgy, need to be expressed in the idiom and the thought forms of the culture that is being reached (*Articles of Religion*, 24 and 34). Some cultures are practically minded (the Chinese?). Others are more speculative and philosophical (the Indian?) and yet others are rule bound (the Islamic world). Each has to be engaged with in its own way.

On its Silver Jubilee, Anglican Frontier Missions (AFM) is to be congratulated for its commitment to both of these evangelical tasks. It is unashamedly Anglican in its loyalty to the Great Tradition: Many of the people groups to be reached—for example in the Middle east and further Asia—value structured worship (not be confused with mere ceremony). They also value spontaneity, the feasts and fasts of the Church, and disciplined prayer and Bible reading.

In the past this was recognized, for example, in the creation of the Nippon Sei Ko Kai (Holy Catholic Church in

Japan) and the Chung Hua Sheng Kung Hui (Holy Catholic Church in China) but needs fresh expression today. At the same time, AFM takes culture and a people's spiritual journey seriously in providing for forms of ministry, ways of worship, and programs of discipleship. It is true, of course, that dangers of syncretism, of blending a biblical world view with falsehood, abound, and the missionary, pastor, or overseer has to be ever careful that enculturation does not lead to syncretism. In particular, the sacraments cannot be seen simply as "functional substitutes" for previous religious or superstitious practices but as channels of grace, conveying Christ's lifegiving presence to believers.

Culture includes a people's customs, music, poetry, sagas, literature and patterns of work and leisure. It also includes their religious traditions, beliefs and values arising from these. It is here that there may be scope both for authentic enculturation but also for compromise and syncretism. On the one hand, those who are turning *to* the truth of the Gospel are also turning *away* from whatever they now see as false and even harmful. On the other, affirming the deep spiritual aspirations of people, and sometimes even using the existing vocabulary for such aspirations, can lead to a more profound understanding and expression of the Gospel in such situations. We need to recognize a proper *praeparatio evangelica*, or preparation for the Gospel, among a people. Thus not forgetting the past, but translating it into the present.

Interfaith dialogue can be useful just to discover what people believe but it can also be an occasion for sharing spiritual experience, as well as asking hard questions about common citizenship and a commitment to fundamental freedoms. It need not be and should not be syncretistic, whether by intention or accident but it can lead to the discovery of an appropriate vocabulary for effective witness.

AFM has been marked not by a spirit of rivalry but by a spirit of cooperation with all who are seeking to fulfill the Great Commission. This is wholly admirable. Pioneering mission work is international and mission is now, more than ever, "From Everywhere to Everywhere." It is important that no energy is wasted in interagency competition. It is also crucial, however, that we should be discriminating in knowing who is engaged in bringing the whole gospel to people and where it is being distorted by the missionary's own cultural attachments. It is also necessary to learn from one another. As pointed out in the book, temptations for competition are best thwarted by keeping in mind similar temptations among Western missionaries in the nineteenth and twentieth centuries.

Many, even then, resisted the lures of imperialism and colonialism but not all. Also, it is humbling to note how often it is the *departure* of the foreign missionary that leads to explosive growth in the Church and to a commitment to cross cultural mission itself.

The desire to see churches which are locally led, pastored and taught, and which themselves engage in cross cultural mission, sets limits to the missionary's task and presence amongst a people. AFM's loyalty to the vision of Anglican statesmen like Henry Venn and Roland Allen makes it unlikely that it will seek to perpetuate a presence that is not determined by partnership and participation in the life and mission of such churches. Mutual responsibility and interdependence will be for the sake of the whole mission of the Church which will include social action in empowering the poor, seeking justice for the oppressed and marginalized, as well as evangelism and church planting.

It is a glorious heritage and a wonderful calling but there are challenges in the way. Not the least of them is how to renew a biblically faithful Anglicanism so that it values its title deeds and does not jettison them for the 'mess of pottage' offered by the spirit of the age. The other is how to encourage Christians and churches all over the globe to engage in witness and service across barriers of language, customs, religions and ethnicity. I am sure that by God's grace AFM is well equipped on both of these fronts to offer a biblically faithful and authentically Anglican vision for the next twenty-five years and more. Amen, so be it!

+Michael Nazir–Ali

INTRODUCTION

by Chris Royer

I looked again. I saw a huge crowd, too huge to count. Everyone was there—all nations and tribes, all races and languages. (Revelation 7:9, The Message)

Yogi Berra, baseball hall-of-famer and slapdash philosopher, once remarked, "If you don't know where you're going, you'll wind up somewhere else." By the grace of God, Anglican Frontier Missions has known where it's going for the last twenty-five years. Our destination has never been nebulous or debatable—we've never wound up "somewhere else."

Over the decades, the word *missions* has accumulated a wide range of meanings, signifying an extensive spectrum of ministry activities. We have missional churches, mission organizations, local missions, national missions, global missions, social justice missions, personal mission statements, and short-, mid-, and long-term missions. In addition, I frequently hear statements such as, "My workplace (or school) is my mission field," and, "The Church doesn't need to go overseas to do missions anymore since America is now a mission field." But if everything is missions, then nothing is missions. Thus, the word loses all meaning.

The Reverend Chris Royer served for sixteen years in Turkey doing evangelism and church planting. After returning to the U.S., he served as a parish priest for six years before becoming the third director of AFM in 2014. Chris is married and has two daughters in university.

1

So what then does AFM understand by the word *missions*, and what is distinctively missional about Anglican Frontier Missions? In short, where have we been and where are we heading?   The word *missions* comes from the Latin root "missio" (to send). One way to understand the big picture of missions (the view from thirty-five thousand feet) is Harold Fuller's alliterative four relational phases of missions.[1]

<u>P</u>ioneer	Foreigner enters new culture, and individuals from indigenous culture accept Christ.
<u>P</u>aternal	Foreigner trains locals.
<u>P</u>artnership	Foreigner ministers as equal with locals.
<u>P</u>articipation	Foreigner ministers only by invitation of locals.

When missionaries take the gospel for the first time into regions and to peoples without a viable and visible church, they are *pioneer* (and frontier) missionaries in the truest sense of the word. That is, they are doing something that has never been done before: birthing a new community of Christ followers (a church) where Christians and churches are not yet present.

The apostle Paul—theologian, pastor, mentor and ecclesiastial leader—was passionate about the Pioneer Phase of missions: "It has always been my ambition to preach the gospel where Christ was not known, so that I would not be building on someone else's foundation" (Romans 15:20).

After Paul planted churches in Asia Minor, Thrace, Macedonia and Achaia, he could have easily settled into any one of these localities. Why not Ephesus, which possessed a great climate, a sophisticated urban culture, and a thriving

---

[1] Ralph D. Winter and Steven C. Hawthorne, eds. *Perspectives on the World Christian Movement: A Reader* (Pasadena, CA: William Carey Library, 1992), 8-37 Revised Edition.

church that he himself had planted? He could have served at Ephesus as the senior pastor or the theologian-in-residence for years to come. Or he could have mentored future church planters from Ephesus, making it a strategic center for training and theological education.

But Paul did not (and could not) do this because Paul's primary call was as apostle to the nations (in Greek, *ethné*, which denotes ethnolinguistic nations and not political nation states). Therefore, Paul was always plodding and pioneering to new areas totally devoid and untouched by the gospel.

In 1995 God called my wife and me to move to a city in Turkey with one million Muslims and just a handful of scattered Christians. Not one single Protestant church existed in the entire city. Muslims desiring to learn about Jesus could not go to church because there were no churches for miles around.

Try to imagine what the cities of Indianapolis or Jacksonville (populations of about one million) would be like without one single church. Today, thousands of churches reach hundreds of thousands of people in these two metropolises; they disciple, teach, evangelize, serve, and pray for people at every stage and phase of life. Churches in these cities, as in all American cities, are the salt and light of American society, the hands and feet of Jesus. But today, sixty-seven generations after the resurrection of Christ, 29% of the world is still without a Church witness; 29% of the world remains in the Pioneer Phase of missions.

As my wife and I settled into pioneer mission work, we started to make friends and, within a year, a few of our Muslim friends put their faith in Christ! When the reality of God's love and indescribable peace, which comes from walking in the Spirit, became one new believer's reality, she asked me this haunting question: "Why haven't any

Christians come to our city and told us about this Jesus before?"

The Pioneer Phase of missions is the "ends of the earth" part of Acts 1:8. Being Christ's beautiful feet (Romans 10:15), we take the gospel to people groups and regions where Christ is still not known *and not knowable* because of the complete absence of Christians and churches.

The second phase of missions is the Paternal Phase (discipleship). When Christ's followers go to regions and people groups in complete darkness and shine Christ's light, hearts are inevitably opened, worldviews inescapably challenged, and destinies eternally changed. But after conversion, the hard work of discipleship begins. Paul often depicts discipleship as a father-child relationship: "For though you have countless guides in Christ, you do not have many fathers. For I became your father in Christ Jesus through the gospel" (I Corinthians 4:15).

Paul's point is that individual Christians do not reach spiritual maturity apart from godly leaders, mentors, and friends. Just as a toddler needs an engaged father and mother to become a balanced and well functioning adult in life, so also first generation believers coming out of animist, Buddhist, atheist, Hindu, and Islamic cultures need spiritual fathers and mothers to help them reach maturity in Christ.

In the Turkish language, the word *Abi* means "older brother" and *Abla* "older sister." These words are used not only within families but also as terms of respect and endearment to elders. Although my wife and I were younger than some of the ex-Muslim Christians in our small church, they nonetheless called us Abi and Abla because they recognized our spiritual parenthood. Even though we were foreigners not fully adept in the Turkish culture or language (and we spoke with an accent!), we were nonetheless their spiritual mother and father in Christ. The best parents begin with the end in mind, acknowledging that the end goal is for their children to become mature and autonomous adults. So also, the pioneer missionary, who disciples those whose hearts the Lord has opened, aims not for a perpetual Paternal Phase (a spiritual parent-child relationship), but partnership, which is the third relational phase of missions.

In the Partnership Phase, the picture is the indigenous believer and the foreign missionary walking side by side, shoulder to shoulder, doing ministry together as equals. Jesus slowly nurtured the twelve disciples into a partnership relationship with himself. But in the beginning of his ministry, Jesus was content to let the disciples observe him as he ministered. Only as time passed did Jesus increasingly call them to do what he did and practice what he preached.

For instance, Jesus called his disciples to co-labor with him in the harvest: "And he called the twelve together and gave them power and authority over all demons and to cure diseases, and he sent them out to proclaim the kingdom of God and to heal" (Luke 9:1-2). Jesus' disciples encountered many successes during this Partnership Phase. After their second itinerant preaching tour, we read that they returned with joyful hearts, saying, "Lord, even the demons are subject to us in your name" (Luke 10:17).

But we also know that the twelve disciples walked through experiences of spiritual failure, especially during Jesus' final hours alive on earth. They denied him, betrayed him, and failed him. They experienced fear, doubt, and brokenness. But Jesus restored them after his resurrection. And then, after the descent of the Holy Spirit on Pentecost, the disciples no longer needed the physical presence of Jesus Christ because his Spirit now indwelled them. Jesus, the archetypal missionary, was able to return home to his Father in heaven. Amazingly, he stressed that his departure would be advantageous because each disciple would "do the works that I do; and greater works than these will he do, because I am going to the Father" (John 14:12).

On the mission field, the goal of the foreign missionary is to spiritually nurture disciples from the father-son or mother-daughter relationship into a full and vibrant partnership. The missionary and those he has led to Christ are now walking side by side, doing ministry together; the missionary, gradually and intentionally, begins to relinquish responsibility to indigenous believers. The ultimate goal for the missionary is for the indigenous church to become self-evangelizing, self-governing, self-financing, and self-theologizing.

In fact, a missionary's continued presence (and unwillingness to empower indigenous believers) can actually stunt church growth by mitigating opportunities for them to lead their own church, walk by faith, make mistakes, and learn from these experiences. In short, there comes a time when it is actually better for the missionary to depart from the mission field and return to it only by invitation to *participate* (Phase 4) in the work God is doing.

In 2015, the chairman of AFM Nigeria, Bishop N.N. Inyom of the Diocese of Makurdi, invited me to teach at the Samuel Crowther Seminary in Abeokuta, Nigeria, and at his diocesan retreat for ordination candidates. His invitation stemmed not from the lack of qualified Nigerians to teach at these venues, but his desire for AFM U.S. to deepen its participation in the ministry of AFM Nigeria and vice versa. Participating in ministry with Christians across borders and cultures is glorious; I am a deeper Christ follower for having ministered in Nigeria.

Two billion people (29% of the world's population) are still waiting to hear the good news, even though it has been almost two thousand years since Jesus Christ gave the Great Commission! One in four people are waiting for a frontier missionary (Pioneer Phase) to visit them, learn their language and culture, share Christ with them, model the Christian walk for them (Paternal Phase), and lead them into Christ-like maturity to become equal partners in the Gospel with them (Partnership Phase).

God's call upon AFM and our vision over the last twenty-five years have never changed. In Yogi Berra-speak, "We've always known where we are going." Our destination and call have been the Pioneer, Paternal, and then Partnership Phases of missions in areas where the viable and visible Church simply doesn't exist. I'm not sure if AFM's founder, Tad de Bordenave, had this alliterative and relational progression of four P's in his mind in 1993 when he launched AFM. Nonetheless, Tad was indisputably committed to starting churches in frontier fields, areas untouched with the gospel.

HOW TO READ THIS BOOK

This twenty-five-year anniversary book is not primarily a timeline or historical account of prominent AFM people or events over the years. Due to the multidirectional, multifaceted, and diverse nature of missions, we have refrained from attempting to produce an exhaustive account of the history of AFM. Accordingly, although we recommend that you read this book sequentially, we've asked our authors to write so that every chapter can, in fact, stand alone, illuminating a particular component of missions or segment of mission history.

Our goal is to draw attention to God's promise to draw individuals from every tribe, tongue, people, and language into a relationship with himself. Jesus' Great Commission is insuppressible, flowing toward completion, and will one day consummate around the throne of glory: "I looked again. I saw a huge crowd, too huge to count. Everyone was there— all nations and tribes, all races and languages" (Revelation 7:9, *The Message*). Our hope is that as you, the reader, progress through the chapters, you do not lose focus on the great story of Scripture: God redeeming all the peoples of the world.

Tad de Bordenave, our founder and first executive director, kicks off the book by describing the establishment of AFM and its early years, as well as the challenge of taking the gospel to unreached peoples. Tad was truly a light in the darkness during the 1980s and 1990s, one of the few Episcopalian priests crying out for an Episcopalian response to the needs of unreached people groups. Tad also lays some theological and missiological groundwork for the rest of this book.

Bishop N.N. Inyom of the Diocese of Makurdi in the Anglian Province of Nigeria is our next author. He has partnered with AFM U.S. for over two decades and is passionate about going to unreached peoples within and around Nigeria. Bishop Inyom will share how AFM Nigeria is reaching some of the least reached and most resistant peoples with the gospel of Christ.

Rev. Canon Patrick Augustine writes about AFM's early years in Pakistan. From his years under the strong missions presence in the Pakistani church, he draws key observations about keeping the fire of missions lit in his new land, the United States.

In the next section, we turn to the people who serve as church planters among the least evangelized peoples. First we'll hear from the Reverend Canon Norman and Beth Beale (AFM missionaries, 1992-1999). They will share how God not only birthed a church through their ministry in Nepal but also an entire Anglican Deanery.

Two AFM missionaries, Andrew and Phoebe Johnson (alias names), write about the Strategy Coordination model and about doing business as mission. They were the first two Westerners to settle sixteen years ago among an unreached people group of 1.3 million people. Individuals from this people group continue to turn to Christ—God is blessing their ministry abundantly.

The final chapter in this section comes from Rev. Canon Dr. Pete and Dr. Shirleen Wait, shepherds to AFM's cross cultural workers since 2000. They share stories from their lives as they interacted with the lives of AFM missionaries and how the message of missions knows no age limit. Both Pete and Shirleen are now in their eighties, and their fires have never burned brighter!

The book then moves to four great missional challenges for world evangelization confronting the Church in this century—Southeast Asia, China, Islam and India.

First, I've asked a dear friend and International AFM Advisor, Bishop Kuan in the Diocese of Singapore, to write about the challenge of reaching Southeast Asia. Bishop Kuan Kim Seng has walked beside us from our earliest days, and the Anglican Diocese of Singapore has boldly, yet judiciously, proclaimed Christ in Vietnam, Thailand, Nepal, Cambodia, Laos, and Indonesia for twenty-five years.

The Reverend Dr. Julian Linnell, second executive director of AFM (2008-2014), describes the growth of the church in China and how the global church can partner with the Chinese church in missions. AFM has had a missionary presence in China for many years.

I've asked the Reverend Dr. Duane Miller to write about the challenge of Islam. Duane and his family have been serving in the field with AFM since 2005. Duane will highlight the historically unprecedented movement of Muslims coming to Christ and its implications in the coming years, especially for the Western Church. Duane is fluent in Arabic and has lived in the Middle East.

The Rev. Canon George Ivey, AFM board member and Canon for Missions in the Anglican Diocese of the South, describes the astounding movement of God in India, the world's largest democracy and second-largest populated country. AFM has ministered in and prayed for India from our founding. India has more unreached people groups than any other nation, and so any discussion of world missions without including India is incomplete.

The next two articles are by two Indian leaders, Prem James of Partners International and S.D. Ponraj of Bihar Christian Church. Prem James has been a strong advocate for collaboration and networking. He brought together consultations for church planting among the Marwari of Rajasthan. Tad and Constance de Bordenave worked closely with Prem during those consultations. The wisdom of networking in frontier missions is forcefully explained in Prem's article.

S.D. Ponraj built a key church planting movement in Bihar State (sometimes called "the graveyard of missions"), sustained by multiple structures of support for evangelism and discipleship. These are well described in his chapter. One of the principal ministries was that of strategy coordinator, clearly resembling the approach of AFM as described by Andrew and Phoebe Johnson earlier in the book. The legacy of the Bihar Outreach Network (BORN) continues and thrives.

The fourth section of this book contains apologetic material for fulfilling the Great Commission, *Anglicanly.* I begin by sharing part of my "Canterbury Journey" and my conviction that Anglicanism's liturgical and sacramental distinctives make it surprisingly contextualizable, transferable, and applicable for discipling and nurturing believers from Islamic, Hindu, Buddhist, and animist worldviews.

The Reverend Joshua Wu then describes his journey into Anglicanism, which occurred while serving in China. He contends that the Anglican tradition is a "gateway" that can uniquely bridge the past and the future for Chinese believers, enabling them to be "both wholly indigenous, yet radically 'catholic,' " that is, connected to the worldwide Church.

Finally, we hear from Rev. Canon Yee Ching Wah, the Anglican Dean of Thailand and Assistant Director of Missions in the Diocese of Singapore. He describes the prin-

The Reverend Canon Tad de Bordenave, Founder and First Director of AFM; The Rt. Reverend N.N. Inyom, Chairman of AFM Nigeria; The Reverend Chris Royer, Current Director of AFM in Abeokuta, Nigeria in 2016.

ciples and practices that the Diocese of Singapore has attempted to express in the planting of the one holy, catholic and apostolic Church in its deaneries, and how Anglicanism's distinctives affect their approach to discipleship.

I wrap up our silver anniversary book by sharing AFM's vision for the next quarter century. Although we're thankful for the unreached peoples God has touched through us in our first twenty-five years, we know that God's heart continually yearns and longs for other least evangelized peoples to have an opportunity to call him Lord, to kneel at his feet, and to receive him in faith.

As you work through the following pages, it is my earnest hope and prayer that God will bless you, and that his Spirit will reveal to you how you should respond to God's call to make disciples of all nations. "For from him and through him and for him are all things. To him be the glory forever! Amen!" (Romans 11:36).

PART ONE

ANGLICANISM IN FRONTIER MISSIONS

1. The Passion and the Path of AFM

2. The Birth of AFM Nigeria

3. Mission Ignited!

1

THE PASSION AND THE PATH OF AFM

by Tad de Bordenave

The passion of AFM is the humble and amazed awe before the slender glance we have of the love of God. The direction of our path is to those who do not yet know of this love.

In telling my part of the story of AFM, you have to know that the story includes many people whom God has used to put the organization together and, more importantly, to keep it moving forward. My part of the story describes living under the influence of a strong dose of God's anesthesia. That's the best way to tell how I took this up: I just didn't notice the risks that others saw. I wasn't bothered by leaving a fine church, having no guaranteed income, and moving into an unknown theatre of operation. As I looked into what I could see of the future, it all looked kind of inviting, an adventure that I was happy to undertake.

One of my mentors was the daffy cartoon hero, Alfred E. Newman, whose simple philosophy was, "What, me worry?" Well, I did worry, but with the support of my wife Constance

---

The Rev. Canon Tad de Bordenave has authored two books on St. Paul and his advocacy of frontier mission. He is affiliated with the Diocese of Makurdi, the Anglian Province of Nigeria, where he serves as Canon at All Saints Cathedral. He and his wife, Constance, live in Richmond, Virginia.

and believing all those stories in the Bible about God taking care of people, I stepped out.

PERSPECTIVES ON THE WORLD CHRISTIAN MOVEMENT

To get inside the motivation and operation of AFM, let me give a short overview of three categories that reinforce the passion and path of AFM: *the nations* as heaven's vision of the world; *the call* of the Church to all the nations; and *the resistance* of the Church to this call.

The Nations

When we picture the world God loves, we must not have an image of masses of people, a huge crush of individuals. This is not the biblical picture. The more precise image is well-defined throngs, each one differentiated from all others. Each has distinctive cultures, its own language, unique social norms, and a rich legacy of legends addressing life's questions. In the terminology of cultural anthropology, these are ethno-linguistic people groups. In the Bible these are "the nations." God deeply and dearly loves all the nations of the world. There are roughly seventeen thousand nations in the world today.

The Call

The Tower of Babel demonstrates the arrogance of the world and the rejection of God. It also shows the origins of one nation becoming distinct from another. In the biblical record immediately following this account, God inaugurated a way for the nations to return to him and gain entrance into his kingdom. The history of salvation is the history of the return of the nations.

Abraham, "the father of all nations," was the first person God appointed to this mission. God described to Abraham the fundamental outline of how he would bring salvation to the world:

> Now the LORD said to Abram, "Go from your country and your kindred and your father's house to the land that I will show will make of you a great nation, and I will bless you, and I will make your name great, so that you will be a blessing. I will bless those who bless you, and him who dishonors you I will curse, and in you all the families of the earth shall be blessed." (Genesis 12:1-3)

This vision God repeated through Moses just before the Hebrew people crossed the Red Sea:

> [God said], "You yourselves have seen what I did to the Egyptians, and how I bore you on eagles' wings and brought you to myself. Now therefore, if you will indeed obey my voice and keep my covenant, you shall be my treasured possession among all peoples, for all the earth is mine; and you shall be to me a kingdom of priests and a holy nation."(Exodus 19:4-6)

The apostle Peter picked up these very words from Moses, reminding the Church that to be God's priests and holy nation brings with it a divine purpose. This role was not a static posture but a purpose driving us beyond ourselves to show God's glory to the world:

> But you are a chosen race, a royal priesthood, a holy nation, a people for his own possession, that you may proclaim the excellencies of him who called you out of darkness into his marvelous light. (I Peter 2:9)

The history of the world is the history of kingdom expansion into new territories. But we have paused at the borders. At present there are over twenty-two hundred nations without their own disciples of Jesus, who do not know of the birth of the Son of God and his redeeming death and resurrection. Another five thousand ethnic groups have a few disciples but do not have a church thriving enough to reproduce. These all await the Church's emissaries to tell them the power of the gospel that brings light from death and darkness.

And the Resistance

A cursory reading of the early chapters of Acts gives exciting vignettes of miracles and extraordinary events among the small band of the first followers of Jesus Christ. But looking below the surface, we get hints of considerable dissension. A riveting controversy was emerging. At the center of the controversy was the question of who was included in Christ's company. It was challenging enough that Christians made room for the Greek speaking Jews, even though they did not live in the epicenter of Judaism—Jerusalem. But then, some had the nerve to make the case for including Gentiles also, even Roman gentiles. This controversy—the central focus of the first fifteen chapters of Acts—is nothing less than the archetypal controversy that the Church has been grappling with ever since.

The early resistance is easy to understand. For centuries the Jews had been an occupied people, and the occupiers treated the Jews atrociously. Although the prophets called Israel to be "a light to the nations," the overruling sentiment of the day was to protect God's beleaguered people and preserve their particular blessings. As to the Gentiles, they were polluted and pagan. They were the ones heaping oppression on the Jews. They—if anyone!—should be banned from proximity to God and access to his grace.

That reaction reflected the ingrained sentiment of the era. It persisted even after Pentecost, when they heard Christ's call again: "You will receive power when the Holy Spirit has come upon you, and you will be my witnesses in Jerusalem and in all Judea, Samaria, and to the end of the earth" (Acts 1:8).

The first three territories—Jerusalem, Judea, and Samaria—received successful inroads fairly easily, though the Spirit's presence among the Samaritans did need special verification.

Then the controversy sharpened over the Gentile nations, those at "the ends of the earth." Did God really mean for the Gentiles to receive the invitation to his kingdom? There were strong voices on both sides. For some, going outside the boundaries to people like the Romans was a call too far. The Jews were, after all, the elect of the only and true God. Outside were the pagan and the polluted. For others, however, they saw no boundaries in the grace of God. If grace was extended to sinners apart from any qualification, then the logic forced the conclusion that the invitation was for all. "All sinners" meant Jew and Gentile sinners.

Putting these three pieces into a mission philosophy, we discern a clear scenario that has continued throughout history. It goes like this: The world is divided by *nations*, ethnic people groups who have their own unique history and characteristics. God calls his believing people to teach and baptize new Christians, who will, in turn, teach and baptize others. This continues until there are disciples in each and every nation. The agency of God's redeeming work is the Church. The Church is the holy agent that God calls, disciples, and sends to these nations. But therein hangs the rub. Though the Church is to be God's witness to the nations, the Church has shown—and still shows—an unwillingness to go to unharvested fields.

The apostle Paul was the advocate whom God appointed to be the protagonist for the universal boundlessness of his grace. He had been the foremost defender for preserving the sacred status of the Jews and rejecting the inclusion of the Gentiles. Then Paul encountered the deacon Stephen in the Synagogue for the Cilicians and later at Stephen's trial before the Sanhedrin. He heard Stephen make powerful arguments for the removal of all restrictions on the kingdom. He was deeply challenged by Stephen's incisive argument for the nations. The seeds planted by Stephen took root. When Paul encountered the Lord on the road to Damascus, Christ gave him the commission to be the apostle to the nations. The universal contours of God's grace and kingdom broke through and reshaped Paul's understanding. Here is how he forcefully articulated how God designated him to defend the inclusion of the nations and to establish churches among the Gentiles.

> This is God's plan: Both Gentiles and Jews who believe the Good News share equally in the riches inherited by God's children. By God's grace and mighty power, I have been given the privilege of serving him by spreading this Good News. I was chosen to explain to everyone this mysterious plan to everyone. (Ephesians 3:6,7,9, New Living Translation)

Till his dying breath this two-fold commission absorbed Paul's energy, wisdom, and effort. He faced persecution from both Jew and Greek. The Gentiles perceived the gospel as a threat to their livelihood; the Jews opposed the inclusion of Gentiles. Some of these Jews were fellow believers in Christ who simply stood against the notion of grace for non-Jews. To the end, he was "faithful to the heavenly vision," as he testifies in his final letter to Timothy:

> The Lord stood by me and strengthened me, so that through me the message might be fully proclaimed and all the Gentiles might hear it. (2 Timothy 4:17)

"PERSPECTIVES" AND MISSION TO THE FRONTIERS

The Church has always needed to hear again and again the call to those tribes and nations that have no disciples. In our recent history, a trumpet call came in 1974 when Ralph Winter addressed a large gathering of mission leaders at the

Lausanne Mission Conference. He spoke of "the people in hidden nations," over twelve thousand ethnic groups living outside the borders of Christian mission. This news was stunning to the mission world. Most had never heard these facts presented so clearly and had not put the unreached into their mission strategy. Ever since, Winter's revelations have provoked uncomfortable and challenging soul searching. They have also brought a new mission emphasis on those at the ends of the earth.

Ralph Winter was a man of energy and vision, consumed by passion for the world's hidden people. He drew together these twin foci: 1) the call to go to all nations, and 2) the neglect of a large number of nations. From this he designed a course to explore and expand the Church's mission, titled "Perspectives on the World Christian Movement," but it is better known simply as the "Perspectives Course." The goal of the course is to show the biblical theme of the call of the Church to make disciples of each and every nation. The course traces the history of Christian expansion, the present status of that thrust, and the strategic and cultural lessons for further progress.

I took the course in 1988. It proved to be a very moving experience in two ways. First, it changed my view of missions, of the Bible, and of the Church. Second, it moved me from serving St. Matthew's Episcopal Church to founding Anglican Frontier Missions.

I was not a stranger to world mission. A short-term mission trip to Japan introduced that reality into my life back in 1963. My father wasn't sure what to do with me during that summer. I was nineteen and had worked as a day laborer for several summers. That was an option, of course, but the chaplain at Virginia Tech told him of a trip for college students. He invited me to join an eight-week work camp at a church school in Japan under the sponsorship of the Anglican Province of Japan. Why not?

The night before departing by ship from San Francisco, I showed my spiritual colors of the time. I joined some friends at the city's Zen Temple for meditation. That was the preferred flavor of my religion. Within that religious posture, the work camp experience was mostly just a trip to another country.

One event did elevate the trip to a pilgrimage, one event that has stayed in my memory and influenced my life. The first missionary Bishop of Japan was Channing Moore Williams from Richmond. He was my uncle several times removed. His tombstone lay in a remote cemetery outside of Kyoto, near the Bishop Williams Seminary, which he founded. One day I parted from my work camp friends for a visit to his tomb. Bishop Williams was highly regarded by the Japanese Christians, and tales of his faith and mission became implanted in my soul. He was a missionary to the people at "the ends of the earth." He saw little fruit but persevered for the Lord's name. Even fifty years after his death, he was honored and revered for his life and legacy. I learned of the teachings and institutions that are the surviving fruit of his ministry. Later my wife and I were to name our firstborn for him. Clearly, that visit made more of an impression on me than I realized at the time.

Following my conversion to Christ in 1965, the way was cleared for ordination to the ministry of the Episcopal Church in 1969. A few years later, I joined the board of the first voluntary and independent missionary society of the Episcopal Church, the South American Missionary Society (SAMS), and soon was designated chairman-to-be. SAMS had been experiencing several internal changes, and I initiated a two-year process for setting in order the inner workings of the missionary society. The result of the process helped to stabilize that organization. More importantly for me, I became intimately acquainted with the inside workings of a missionary society and the marks of corporate health.

This proved to be great schooling for the setup of Anglican Frontier Missions.

TWO NEW REALITIES

Then came the Perspectives Course. Along with all the facts and history that I learned, the course forced me to grapple with two stunning concepts. At least, they were stunning to me: the number of nations without disciples, and the Church's role in mission.

The Number of Nations without Disciples

In 1990 the number was somewhere between twelve and sixteen thousand ethnic groups without their own church. The aggregate number of people in these groups was over one quarter of the world's population or more than 1.8 billion people. Accompanying those statistics were signs of mission imbalance. These signs reflected the emphatic tilt of attention to places where the Church was established already. The resources for nations with no churches were minuscule by comparison. Tools such as radio, training, correspondence courses, literature, evangelists, health personnel, and more—all these registered less than 5% of Church mission resources for the 25% of the world who knew nothing about Jesus Christ. I was left staggered by this picture of the world and the current status of mission.

The Church's Role

The second concept was God's clear and definite expectation of the Church to be his witness to these neglected nations. He declared that *through the Church* the gospel will go to the nations of the world. That declaration pointed to the most fundamental purpose of the Church—to be his light and witnesses to the ends of the earth. That, too, was an entirely new thought—me in my twenty-fifth year of parish ministry! Before the beginning of the Perspectives Course, I recall thinking that there might be some people who had not heard of Jesus Christ. Maybe they lived beyond the Amazon and around the Sahara. If so, God's plan for them would have been to use Southern Baptists and angels to carry the gospel.

Not after Perspectives. All too clearly I saw that God intended, and still intends, for the Church to be the agency that takes the gospel to all nations. And, yes, that does sound much like the parting instruction of our Lord to his disciples: Go and make disciples of *each and every ethnic group* (my emphasis and my distinct—but accurate—rendering).

THE ARRIVAL OF THE MAN UPSTAIRS

The paramount authority in the science of mission research was David Barrett, an Anglican researcher who had worked in East Africa and moved to Richmond in the late 1970s. The Foreign Mission Board of the Southern Baptists set the goal that everybody in the world would hear the gospel by the year 2000. After setting that goal, they invited Barrett to join them in preparing the research for fulfilling the vision.

I learned of David through the background work he had done for the Perspectives Course. I knew he had insights I wanted to pursue. In a short time, David became a close friend and an invaluable advisor to our vision. He and his staff, editors of *The Encyclopedia of World Christianity*, moved to our building, one floor above ours. Later, when I was working with AFM, I enjoyed referring to David as "the man upstairs." David and his office staff were to contribute to AFM in several meaningful ways—friendships, encouragement, and spotting nuances in mission talk. Of course, one of the lasting contributions came from the research they did. This they shared with us, accompanied by interpretation, caution, and guidance.

Once, on a study leave from St. Matthew's Church, I read the galleys for one of David's forthcoming books, *Our World and How to Reach It.*[1] In it he had a chart (Figure 1) with an ellipse showing the areas of the world with the heaviest concentration of missionary work. The territory inside the curve marked the densest locations of mission deployment. To my amazement, the ellipse covered only the most heavily Christianized lands and evangelized places. That stunned me. That could not be! Christ's mission priority was the nations without disciples—not to people already heavily evangelized. That is where the ellipse ought to have been located. I took that page and marched into David's office, declaring, "David, you have this all wrong." I then proceeded to point to the places where the ellipse belonged. David smiled, gave me my time, and then set the record straight. During that visit to David's office, "the iron entered my soul," as the expression goes.

Through David's influence I saw the value of research. It serves as the eyes of God. This separates conclusions from hunches and real data from what everybody else thinks. Research transforms strategy from simply going where everyone else is going to using detailed information about areas and peoples overlooked. It pinpoints the critical needs and hard facts for meaningful strategies to reach the nations. Through this science, we track essential findings, such as: nations lacking the Bible in their own language, pastoral and leadership training requirements, health care needs, educational needs, and house church locations. Then we search throughout the world for the people who can respond to the needs.

---

[1] David Barrett and Todd Johnson, *Our World and How to Reach It* (Pasadena, CA: William Carey Press, 1990).

EVANGELIZATION IN WORLDS A,B,C
(Vertical Scale of Figure 1 on Opposite Page)

A. THE UNEVANGELIZED WORLD
Present cost of Christian foreign missions: $0.1 billion a year
30 restricted-access (closed) countries (RACs)
3,000 foreign missionaries (1.0%)
No citywide evangelistic campaigns
30,000 full-time Christian workers
50,000 lay Christians residing abroad in closed countries
0.1% of all Christian literature
0.01% of all Christian radio/TV

B. THE EVANGELIZED NON-CHRISTIAN WORLD
Per capital income of non-Christians: $1,350 p.a.
Present cost of Christian foreign missions: $1 billion a year
23,000 foreign missionaries (8.1%), 5,000 being in 50 RACs
200 cities per year have citywide evangelistic campaigns
200,000 full-time Christian workers, 50000 being in 50 RACs
0.9% of all Christian literature
0.1% of all Christian radio/TV

C. THE CHRISTIAN WORLD
Present cost of home Christianity: $140 billion a year
Foreign missions to other Christian lands: $7.5 billion a year
259,250 foreign missionaries to other Christian lands (90.9%),
4,000 in 39 RACs
1,100 cities per year have citywide evangelistic campaigns
4.0 million full-time Christian workers (95%) work in World C,
including 200,000 in 39 RACs
500 million lay Christians live in 39 RACs
99% of all Christian literature is consumed by World C
99.9% of all Christin radio/TV output is directed at World C

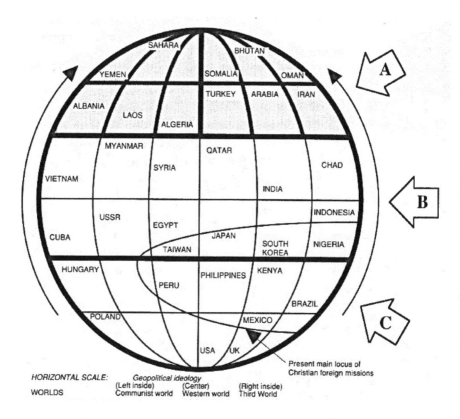

Figure 1
EVANGELIZATION IN WORLDS A,B,C
(Statistics on Opposite Page)

Barrett's research verified what the ellipse told: Less than 5% of the Church's mission resources went to those people—25% of the world—who had not heard of Jesus Christ. 90% went to those thoroughly familiar with Christ, and another 5% to places like Japan—well evangelized but not responding.

The implications of the ellipse tell the story. Inside the contours of it, where most mission goes on, are countries that already have massive amounts of resources and most missionary personnel. Outside the ellipse lie the people who rank as the least evangelized, the most overlooked by the Church's mission. These continue to receive almost none of the Church's mission resources. The resistance continues.

Current statistics continue to show the need for re-assessing priorities. Todd Johnson collaborated with David Barrett and continues his mission research with his associate, Gina Zurlo, at the Center for Study of Global Christianity located at Gordon-Conwell Seminary. Their work shows that 2.0 billion people remain unevangelized, or 29.3% of the world's population. The areas that receive the most missionaries per million are Oceana and the Caribbean, both of which have Christian majority populations. In contrast, the countries receiving the fewest missionaries per million have some of the least Christian populations.[2]

Through discussions with David, the readings he gave me, and the research he was doing, I began to grasp the essential elements about frontier missions and the Church's resistance. My understanding deepened as I discerned what feeds mission trends: I took in the statistics and their implications; I could see the paths that would lead to

---

[2] Todd Johnson and Gina Bellofatto, "Key Findings of Christianity in Global Context 1970-2020," *International Bulletin of Missionary Research 37,* no. 3 (2017): 157.

unharvested fields; I could spot the familiar reasons for staying away from them. The imbalance of mission and the people who were left out became more than a study for me; it was my preoccupation.

ANGLICAN FRONTIER MISSIONS

In the years following the Perspectives Course, one particular certainty was growing in my mind—that someone needed to take the lead for the Episcopal Church in frontier missions. The official policy of the Episcopal Church was to send a missionary to anywhere in the world...at the invitation of the local bishop. The problem was obvious: There were no bishops over most of the least evangelized world. So no missionaries were sent. For Jerusalem, Judea, and Samaria, the Church covered them well. But for those at the ends of the earth—the Marwari of Rajasthan, the Tajakant of Mauritania, the Zazas of Turkey, for example—the names and the locations were unknown, the avenues to them seemed nonexistent, and the mission concerns went elsewhere. I summed this up in the title I gave to the AFM newsletter, *Out of Sight, But Not Out of God's Mind.*

The movement toward a new missionary society did not happen in a vacuum. The Episcopal Church had a fairly close knit group of mission leaders. We met together at least annually, exchanged ideas, supported one another, and explored issues before the Church and the world. One of the issues we began to recognize was the unreached areas of the world and the need to respond. A cluster of interested persons met in St. Louis in 1989 to explore ways forward. I called a meeting in November of 1990 in Richmond to take explicit steps. This core group of people became the think tank who met together, prayed over the call, thought through the options, and gradually gave shape to the call.

Following the St. Louis meeting and the Richmond conference, this core group began meeting at Holy Comforter Church in Vienna, Virginia. Rev. Bob Denig was the rector and brought not only full support but wise counsel as we progressed. It was Bob who came up with our name. We put out several words and combinations of words. Bob observed that if we chose "Episcopal Frontier Missions," our initials would be the same as "Education for Ministry," so he suggested "Anglican Frontier Missions," and we concurred.

Of course there remained the person—someone to take the lead for our church's involvement in the frontiers—and I could see whom the Lord had in mind. In early 1993, after reading Stephen Neill's *History of the Christian Mission* and receiving my wife's support, I announced my resignation from St. Matthew's to become director of Anglican Frontier Missions. I officially began on the first of September in 1993 with $2,000 in the bank and a lot of good will from many sources.

At the time of taking the Perspectives Course, I was rector at St. Matthew's Episcopal Church in Richmond, Virginia, a fine place to minister with fine people growing in the faith— and still is. St Matthew's Church had been the garden where many of these seeds were planted or nourished. I served there a total of seventeen years, from 1976 until 1993, the last thirteen years as rector. I know rectors lead congregations, but rectors also grow and learn from those they serve. I took a lot with me from this congregation and drew on their resources and kindness for all my years at AFM.

After resigning from St. Matthew's, I moved the AFM operation to the basement of our home, a section of the house removed from our three children, who were also at home and still in school. All the papers and documents for AFM covered half a ping pong table. The following February, a heavy snow hit Richmond and closed down everything for several days, including schools. During those snow days, the basement got very crowded! That was when I decided I needed an office. After the snowstorm, all of AFM moved to the space of two rooms in mid-Richmond. Greg Mueffleman, AFM's first missionary, was working with a people group in Central Asia. He joined me in our first office with all of four hundred square feet. It was sheer luxury.

I was not courageous in founding Anglican Frontier Missions; I was confident. The purpose and calling were not of human derivation but of God's. He is the one who declared that there will be disciples in each and every nation. He is in absolute and uncontested control, so he will successfully fulfill his claim for them. I believed God and set about preparing AFM as one of many channels for the Holy Spirit to work in these neglected nations.

My model for accepting this call was Peter in the boat when Jesus came walking on the water. Peter did not say, "Lord, I am coming to you..." What he did say was, "Lord, if you call me, I will come to you" (Matthew 14:28-19). I believe God called me.

Frodo Baggins and I almost share birthdays. He is the heroic adventurer of J. R. R. Tolkien's trilogy, *The Lord of the Rings*. Frodo began the journey from his Shire on his fiftieth birthday. My fiftieth came two days later than his, in the same month that I left St. Matthew's on my AFM journey. Like Frodo, I was willing but hadn't a blessed clue as to what lay ahead. I only knew I would ever be nurturing a dependence on the Lord. My suitability had many ill-fitting aspects; probably the most noticeable was the Lord's sense of humor in choosing as spokesman one who is a life-long stutterer.

THE DUAL ROLES OF AFM

What did I know about running a missionary society? I had never been a missionary and inherited no organization or personnel for support. I did have that enlightening experience of dissecting the South American Missionary Society. I didn't take notes with AFM in mind, but the exercise was a text book case that I knew well.

I had a steep learning curve but also a diverse group of friends with missionary experience. I used to tell people that I would beg, borrow, and steal... while I was looking at them! That meant anything from mission ideas to how to equip the office.

Very soon I became aware that the telephone was not ringing off the hook. In fact, it hardly rang—be it from churches interested in the least evangelized or from people interested in serving with AFM. The penny dropped, and I soon became aware of something distinct about AFM: We were a curiosity. On many fronts and from many angles, AFM represented something new.

New is difficult. I soon developed an appreciation for how AFM was new and how difficult it is to conceptualize the new. This was not only a new missionary agency; we were addressing a field that was new to most Episcopal churches. Furthermore, our mission work resembled nothing in the traditional world of missions. Our training would draw on different disciplines, our goals had to be redefined, and our expectations were unlike those of traditional mission societies. Even our terminology was new.

True, there were fertile partnerships with churches and dioceses in other parts of the world, and many churches have had a significant impact in the areas of poverty, justice, and evangelism. But church planting among the tribes and nations that were Hindu or Muslim? That was outside their experience and their concept. This was new thinking, new territory, new methodologies, and new foundations.

In a short time, all this became clear, and with it came a new emphasis in my leadership. I became aware that the calling of AFM was precisely the two-fold ministry God called Paul to: a ministry of advocacy as well as a ministry of church planting where there had been no church. Let me elaborate on both.

Advocacy

The most surprising part of my ministry as director of a missionary society was my role as *advocate*. That meant speaking to churches, writing essays, publishing a newsletter, and getting the attention of clergy leaders. I thought I would be recruiting and sending people to unharvested nations, but not so. I remembered an image from one of my colleagues at the Southern Baptist Foreign Mission Board: The unreached have no voice to the Church, so they rely on advocates like me to speak on their behalf. My ministry took on the form of itinerant preacher. I used to say that I would draw up to a church, unfold the covers of my Conestoga wagon, and begin to sell my wares. I did a lot of that.

The important part of my presentation was in attitude—not to get exasperated, not to show impatience, not to roll my eyes at ignorance or neglect. By the grace of God, I didn't, and the reason was easy to spot. After all, I had my own experience of ignorance and neglect. In my ten years of involvement with SAMS, not once was I bothered by the lack of attention to the unreached people groups. Plus, I knew my audience and liked them.

I have grieved over the loss of the historical biblical teaching on marriage and the ambivalence toward the authority of the Bible and God's moral order. But I grieve more over the seemingly unending energy—the conferences, debates, books, DVDs, etc.—directed to these topics. All this, while conferences devoted to church planting among remote tribes are few and participation slim. Where is the scholarship devoted to our call to these people, the attention to this biblical mandate? I have often asked for merely a tithe of the energy given to marriage and sexuality to be turned to frontier mission. Clearly the primary purpose of the Church to be a light to the nations has been muted.

Today, the battleground is no longer the inclusion of Gentile nations, as it was with the earliest Church. Now the question is: Shall we move beyond where the Church already is established? Do we actually go to *all* the nations? Is it possible that the Church actually chooses not to keep advancing into new areas?

Expressed so boldly on paper, this may seem a preposterous possibility—refusing to go to the ends of the earth. Could it be? Well, there are many answers to that question. Some are understandable; others reflect resistance. Here are some of the answers:

- Reinforcements must go to the territories that have been evangelized. Advancing armies, after all, often become occupying armies.

- Many young or poor churches require additional support and resources as they gain strength.

- There is no way we can be culturally sensitive to people so unknown to us.

- The intensity of spiritual warfare is frightening. Satan is no slight adversary, and mission to the unevangelized nations is hand-to-hand combat, leaving many wounded and scattered.

- These nations are too far away and too hostile.

- They have not requested missionaries and Christian work, while millions of Christians have.

- Doing mission at home is all we can manage.

- Many churches choose not to spend energy on those pagan and "polluted" peoples.

The central hope of the Christian's faith is nothing other than grace. Grace properly understood, though, opens up to frontier mission. When we hold it dear that God's grace is intended for all, logic moves in an unexpected direction. The logic of that statement defeats all resistance to frontier mission. Embedded in grace is movement beyond ourselves, to those who could qualify but do not yet know that. Grace must shift from only being my hope for salvation to demanding the Church's sacrificial call to unharvested fields. If saving grace does not bust our boundaries of God's mercy and lift our sights to the unreached, grace has missed its place. Properly placed, grace brings to our ears what Jesus commanded, "Go and make disciples of each and every nation" (Matthew 28:19).

There is mission in other places, of course. I know that—massive resources and personnel sent to fields already established. Work there pushes back the darkness of cultures that have known Christian principles but whose populations are disconnected from the Word of God and his grace. Work in these Christianized areas often brings hardship and persecution. These are the places, after all, where the populations have heard it all before but with many hardened to the message. These fields need all that is sent to them and more.

But note, this deployment moves resources from one part of the Body of Christ to another part of the Body of Christ. We must and we can do better.

This reality leads me to this sobering conclusion: All will face judgment—we who know Jesus Christ and they who have never heard of him. But there is a difference. They will be judged on the basis of truth they have never heard; the

Church will be judged for obedience to the Commission we *have* heard.

Church Planting

Gradually, AFM began taking on the distinctive shape of mission to the least evangelized. One afternoon, I had two calls from people interested in learning more about AFM. I had begun thinking of an inquirers' conference before that, and by the second person's call I was convinced: We would be holding our first inquirers' conference in three months. That meant, of course, having clarity about what we expect of our missionaries and how we work.

The DNA of any missionary organization is held in its dominant strategy. After deliberation and research, we hooked ourselves to what is known as the Strategy Coordination (SC) model. SC was rooted in biblical principles and had a history to examine. The origins of SC go back to efforts for church planting behind the Iron Curtain. A group of mission leaders had confidence that God had ways to grow churches even behind that wall of atheism. They met, thought, prayed, and developed a strategy for the time and place. They knew there were believers within the Soviet dominions. Key Christians had contact with them, monitoring their needs and goals. This communication then went to sources and personnel who could respond to those particular needs. Gradually and carefully these resources made it inside the Iron Curtain to assist the efforts of planting churches there. Since the fall of the Soviet Union, the shape of SC was adjusted to fit other hostile and remote nations.

The structural bones of the SC are easily discerned. Consider the analogy of a construction trailer beside the construction site. Outside on the ground are the workers, the material, the tools, and the foremen directing what is being done when and by whom. Inside the trailer is a different scene. There, the workers are not wearing hard hats; their work is different. They don't have hammers and pliers; they have the architects' plans, lists of suppliers, and contacts for whatever is needed. They have e-mail, telephone, and other forms of communication. As the key planners, they know the master plan and make sure it is followed. They work the timetables for the arrival of supplies and listen to the needs expressed by foremen and workers. The collaboration of those inside with those outside is essential to the success of what is being built.

Our SC plan was similar. It depended on the occasional communication between the few Christians inside an ethnic group and agents or coordinators living outside. This allowed information to come out—prayer requests and information to fill specific needs at specific locations. The agent (or coordinator) on the outside had access to the worldwide network of the Body of Christ for bringing prayer support and the resources requested.

This is an obvious application of the teachings of 1 Corinthians 12 where Paul talks about the members of the Body of Christ working together. He refers to God's operation through this unified effort as well as the human distortions that can hamper the process. The motif fits the ministry of planting churches among the unreached.

Staying with the image of the Body of Christ, the mind of Christ is to see his disciples established in all the nations. Some members of his body take part in the effort with high profile roles, like translators. Others are more in the background, like those who go out to care for children. Both are essential and interconnected. But, as Paul pointed out, the symmetry can be overturned easily. There can be either too much assertiveness or not enough, too much ego or too much shyness. There can be too much ego (not everyone can be an eye like me!) or too much shyness (because I'm not an eye, I don't belong). But there the model is, and like most divine decrees with human involvement, it *mostly* works.

FIVE FOUNDATIONAL PRINCIPLES

The core group that was praying for this agency was also a study group. In our explorations and conversations with leaders in frontier missions, we developed these five foundational principles:

1. The opportunity for millions to hear the gospel of Jesus Christ;
2. Cooperation across every line in implementing the work;
3. The resources of the worldwide Body of Christ to meet the physical and spiritual needs;
4. The entrepreneurial skillset of the North American;
5. The presence of the Holy Spirit's power within the Church for frontier mission.

Like the wise use of a map, these principles held our attention and gave us direction. Let me expand on each.

1. For Millions to Hear

At an early meeting of the AFM board, we took a step that was audacious, bold, and yet also carefully assessed. Preceded by much prayer and then with careful study, we committed to church planting among the twenty-five largest and least evangelized people groups. The actual list came from the database of *The World Christian Encyclopedia*. The people groups were located between western Morocco and western China, each group with a population of over one million and with fewer than five agencies active among them.

By this, we were making two statements to the larger church—to whomever was paying attention to this wee group of evangelical Episcopalians meeting in our little domain. One statement was to call attention to the least evangelized world. As far as we knew, ours was the only agency in the Anglican Communion that concentrated exclusively on the least evangelized world. The number of those who had not heard the gospel was almost two billion people. The aggregate number of those among our twenty-five groups would have been well over seventy-five million, a number far in excess of the fields of other mission agencies.

The second statement was just as straightforward. If we could take steps toward church planting among groups of over one million, then anybody could—and should! Of course, with the shift from traditional methods and fields to the SC concept and the least evangelized, we needed to accept a number of new realities for this mission:

- AFM would not be exclusive to Episcopalians and Episcopal churches; our personnel should be multi-denominational.

- North Americans would have an offstage role.

- The numbers of converts would be infinitesimal for a long time.

- Cooperation and coordination would hold the center and the future for the work.

We were building upon the biblical virtues of cooperation, research, and analytical tools for strategizing development of the mission. Efforts by our missionaries would build teams diverse in denomination, race, homeland, and gifts—a tangible diversity of Christ's Body in mission.

2. Cooperation

Only a train track separated our office from the world's largest missionary organization. That would be the Southern Baptist Foreign Missionary Board (FMB). One afternoon, David Barrett mischievously pointed across to the FMB and said that they were the largest agency. Then he said what he needn't have observed. Pointing up to our three windows, he said, "And you are the smallest."

David got me into the president's office of the FMB more than once. During one conversation with Dr. Keith Parks, the president, he told me that he would make the full resources of the FMB available to our missionaries. The impact of that struck me forcefully. Here was the president of the FMB, with unimaginable (to me) resources, history, and experience, offering us whatever our workers might need.

I have been flippant about his comment, saying that I missed the opportunity to say, "And we, Keith, offer you our full resources." I didn't. But what did occur was that the board of AFM inserted the virtue of initiating cooperation as one of our five principles. We did not say that we would welcome cooperation but that we would *actively initiate* it. That came from the example of Dr. Parks and the FMB.

3. Resources of the Worldwide Body of Christ

Participating in this strategy encourages an outward push toward an ever expanding company of workers. Under a Spirit-led imagination, there is always room for more in the Body of Christ. With sensitive leadership, people with varying expertise can be folded into the larger picture. Knowing the particular gift of each member and making everyone cognizant of their role in the forward movement, increases the depth of the planted seed of the gospel.

4. The Entrepreneurial North American

The resources and personnel for the varying operations are scattered around the world and through the Internet. The role of a North American missionary, especially one who is white, is critical to get right. Too often and too easily, such missionaries can get into a position that discourages healthy development of the local church, obstructs maturing of national leadership, and confuses issues of contextualizing the gospel in the other culture. Other than that...!

One strong temptation for Westerners is paying too much attention to praise and flattery, which negatively affects the progress of mission. The lure can come from flattery by nationals, advanced technology, or the evident ability to tap into rich resources.

The image I used of a Strategy Coordinator (SC) was that of an offstage conductor. That is, the essential contributions that the SC makes are important to the forward movement of strengthening the young church. But these contributions can be done one or two or three steps removed from the active leadership of the church. There are times, of course, when specific expertise and training should move the Westerner to a high profile role, and these should not be resisted. But ordinarily, especially with the SC's frequent contact in the world beyond the frontiers, these contributions can be done in the background.

5. The Unlimited Power of the Holy Spirit

We have looked unto the hills for our help: Our help does not come from computers, databases, networks, and funds. Our utter confidence is in the unlimited power of the Holy Spirit, the missionary arm of the mighty God. The underlying dynamic of this vision brings forth facts, information, data, and analysis. The impact of technology on the operation dazzles and seems to constantly improve. But we know the source of power.

As the Holy Spirit is a dynamic power, we also knew that being fluid was essential. Any really good strategy can be stretched, adapted, reshaped, and reinvented to fit changing times and challenges. That is true of the Strategy Coordination approach. Just as it was first designed for church planting behind the Iron Curtain, we in the 1990s adjusted it to the needs of large numbers of ethnic groups that had virtually no mission activity. Now, thankfully, with the current attention focused on the least evangelized, fewer than one thousand people groups are totally without mission activity. That means that most groups with large numbers of people have some Christian mission presence. This presents a different scene for engagement from what we faced in 1993. The way the SC operates today is altered, as it should be, for today's different circumstances.

There are many ways to implement AFM's founding principles, depending on the personalities and backgrounds of the SCs. The fields of mission are never alike, and so the specific strategies do not resemble one another. Recognizing this flux allows the Lord to direct and overrule the methods and the mixture. How the SC functioned in the years of the Iron Curtain differed from how we operated in the years I was with AFM. New circumstances ahead will necessitate new revisions and adjustments.

LAMBETH AND THE UNFOLDING FUTURE

In the Spring of 1998, the board asked what my plans were for the summer. I outlined the hammock, the crabs, and the fish I was going to enjoy. They said that I ought to be at the Lambeth Conference of the Anglican Bishops. So to Lambeth I went with an AFM booth.

We were allotted a booth in a very strategic position—right opposite the grand display of Almy Vestments. Our banner was to the point: "Yes, a missionary society," "Yes, for the Unreached." I also took along sixty pounds of a brochure drawn up by David Barrett, showing the statistical growth of the Provinces of the Anglican Communion over the past one hundred years. The booth and the brochure drew several hundred visitors. Our simple message for those interested was that we would work alongside any bishop who was committed to the least evangelized in or near the bishop's diocese. Seventy bishops, a good biblical number, signed up for more information.

Of the seventy, the most and the most eager were from Nigeria. And so I made my first trip to Nigeria in 2000, visiting the Rt. Rev. N. N. Inyom and the Ven. Zacchaeus Asun. Bishop Inyom became the chairman of AFM Nigeria, with Venerable Asun as secretary. The reach of frontier mission work in Nigeria has grown over the past twenty years; with its strong organization and leadership, AFM Nigeria is poised for a significant impact in the future.

Over the next ten years, AFM developed an extraordinary outreach. By the generosity of many, we in Richmond, Virginia, were able to send more than twelve bishops from Nigeria to Singapore, where they took a four-week training course on the Strategy Coordination model in a classroom under the Southern Baptists. The bishops returned home with the vision and the intent of raising up leaders to implement the SC strategy. Soon afterwards, we were able to expand that program to do training in Kenya and England for East African leaders. That was an unanticipated, unplanned development, the sovereign work of God. As he is the sovereign Lord of the harvest, such unanticipated new turns are nothing more than his favor and his continuation of the plan he gave to Abraham for the Church as his witnesses among the nations of the world.

A few weeks ago I listened to a pastor whose contract was about to end. We talked about what would be next, with concentration on the spiritual discipline of waiting. I esteem waiting as one of the most intense opportunities for seeing God at work. After all, by definition, nothing humanly speaking is brought to the table. All is in the hands of the God and Father of our Lord Jesus Christ. We wait and we watch. Along the way, we think of the titles that he has—Good Shepherd, Counselor, Rock, Lord of all, our Hope, our Maker, the One of Glorious Majesty. Are not those the very characteristics of the One we want to govern and guide us?

So it is and ever shall be with Anglican Frontier Missions. My successor, Julian Linnell, a former missionary to China, led the organization through the Great Recession and came out with the same vision, only clearer. Chis Royer is the third director, a missionary with over sixteen years' experience in Turkey. He brings the twin assets of passion and experience to his leadership of AFM.

The board has changed its makeup, people in the field have moved on, new ones have entered, and the world is changing almost monthly. Times don't stay the same, and neither should we expect the ways God works to stay the same. And so AFM continues always in the context of waiting. We know that apart from Christ we can do nothing; we also know God is always at work. We make it our aim to wait. We keep our eyes on the Lord, expectantly watching for his movements and eagerly shifting to where he is working. Over the past years our calling has paralleled that of Paul's, as he described the grace given him in Ephesians 3: to help the Church accept the inclusion of all the nations, and to plant churches among Gentile nations. As we move on, we are right to be confident—confident of his call to the Church, and confident that he will stoop down and use even us.

2

THE BIRTH OF AFM NIGERIA

by N. N. Inyom

The birth of AFM Nigeria began with the Lambeth Conference in 1998 at Kent University in Canterbury, UK, and a meeting with Rev. Tad de Bordenave, founder and first director of AFM. As is a normal tradition in conferences of such nature, Rev. Canon Tad de Bordenave erected a stand at the conference venue where many people came to sign up and pick up a brochure about AFM. I and many other bishops, both in and outside Nigeria, took turns to sign up as interested in learning more about AFM. Some bishops even had snapshots with the canon; I did not. My first contact with him was rather casual and not formal.

After the conference, Tad wrote letters to establish contacts with those who signed his attendance list. He sent me a photo, which he thought was of me, but, in fact, it was a picture of one of our bishops, Rt. Rev. Ugochukwu Uzouke, then bishop of Umuahia and the retired archbishop of Aba Ecclesiastical Province, and one other bishop from Kenya.

Bishop Nathan N. Inyom was a teacher in Nigeria until God called him to the ordained ministry. He has served in the Anglican Province of Nigeria as Bishop of Makurdi since 1996. He is a visionary leader of missions for Nigeria and serves as the Chair of AFM Nigeria.

Tad, Bishop Uzuoke, and the Kenyan Bishop

We maintained contacts through e-mails or sometimes via telephone calls. He kept contact with some bishops in the Communion both in Nigeria and elsewhere. Here in Nigeria, he maintained contact with the likes of Rt. Rev. Edmund Akanya, Rt. Rev. Joseph Akinfenwa, Rt. Rev. Emmanuel Mani, Rt. Rev. George Bako, Rt. Rev William Diya, and later Archbishop I. C. O. Kattey, among others. These contacts yielded positive results.

Apart from manning his stand, the gentleman from Virginia attended some sessions in the conference. He was also at the Mission and Evangelism session of our conference, where reports on the Decade of Evangelism from bishops across the globe were presented and discussed. There was great excitement about the growth of the Anglican Communion Worldwide. Tad also followed us during Nigeria Day, where bishops in the Missionary Dioceses of Nigeria presented reports about missionary enterprise and the expansion work in their dioceses due to activities of the Decade of Evangelism. Rev. Canon Tad was there at all these events, taking note of all that transpired at the Lambeth Conference and the great rejoicing over the growth of the Anglican Communion Worldwide.

In his statement and observation about the reports on the Decade of Evangelism, Tad noted thus: "While Bishops and the entire Conference reported great success in their work during the Decade of Evangelism, no one remembered to talk about the unreached and the least evangelized people of the world. Everyone was reporting about great work done within their areas of jurisdiction. There was no agenda for the frontier missions." In the mind of Rev. Tad, one thing was missing from the reports, *frontier missions.* His statement hit me like dynamite, and it sent a message to me and created a desire in me to know more about Anglican Frontier Missions and how my diocese could get involved.

TAD'S VISIT TO NIGERIA, YEAR 2000

In the year of the Lord two thousand, Tad visited Nigeria for the first time on my invitation. During this visit, he met with the former Primate of *All* Nigeria, the Most Rev. Peter Akinola, Rt. Rev. George Bako, Rt. Rev. William Diya and others. He also visited many places of interest and explored the possibility of working with the Church of Nigeria in order to expand the scope of Anglican Frontier Missions.

Tad expressed happiness and delight that the Church of Nigeria was moving forward in a positive direction and further observed that there is a need for the church to remain focused and direct her resources toward frontier missions. According to him, the church has enough resources, both human and financial, to reach out to the rest of Africa and beyond. He noted that the church has the spiritual and evangelical muscle to march forward and take over the lands. It is based on this conclusion that he later asked to join the

Church of Nigeria. Tad is now canon of the Cathedral Church of All Saints, Makurdi, Benue State, Nigeria.

FIRST STRATEGY COORDINATION COURSE IN SINGAPORE

After the visit to Nigeria, Tad and the AFM Board in the USA organized training for six bishops, including me. We had one month of intensive training on Strategy Coordination at Fortune Centre, Singapore (2000), which opened my eyes to the mission world and has kept my passion for frontier missions burning to this day. It was at that training that I was appointed chairman and coordinator of AFM Nigeria, saddled with the responsibility to ensure that AFM's vision spreads across Nigeria and beyond. From that beginning, AFM Nigeria has put on several training events. All of them have expanded the vision for the unreached and the call of our churches to work among them:

Training Organized by AFM Nigeria
With the AFM Board in USA

1st Singapore (2000): 6 participants, sponsored by AFM USA

2nd Singapore (2002): 8 participants, sponsored by AFM USA

3rd Abuja (2004): 12 participants, The Blessed 12, sponsored by AFM USA

4th Jos (2007): 36 participants, AFM Nigeria/NEMA Jos, supported by AFM USA

Seminars/Trainings on
Strategy Coordination Missions (SCM)

5th Agbara-Otor(2011): 153 Bishop's Retreat, Ibru Centre

6th Awka   (2012): 136 Clergy/Wives, Retreat at Emmaus
House, Awka

7th Agbara-Otor (2013): 236 Clergy/Wives Retreat,
Ibru Centre Agbara-Otor

8th Niger Delta North (2014): 126 Trained

Grand Total of Participants: 713

IMPACT OF AFM TRAININGS

Daniel 11:32b says, "...but the people who know their God shall stand firm and take action."

This scripture has proven to us as a people that God is ever faithful. There are times in ministry when one feels like giving up; even Jesus came to this point (Mathew 26:39). But glory to God, his faithfulness and mercy endure forever. Moses, while leading the Israelites, also felt like giving up on God in Exodus 32:32, but God forbids that we turn our back on the gospel. Like Paul said, we will run the race and get the prize (1 Corinthians 9:24-27).

AFM Nigeria is organized by the chairman and the bishop of the Anglican Diocese of Makurdi, where the office is currently coordinated by the administrative assistant to keep things going. Office personnel handle correspondence and ensure that activities are carried out as scheduled.

AFM is working with the Diocesan Mission Society to carry the gospel outside the shores of the land, e.g. the Baka Pygmies. AFM has impacted a lot of the people and has created awareness in the minds of even clergy about frontier missions. This aspect of mission has not been explored for a long time, that is, reaching the unreached and the least evangelized people groups. AFM Nigeria has been able to break open the conventional Sunday gathering of Christians, whose attention stays within the confines of the diocese.

One of the major channels of breakthroughs in AFM vision and mission in Nigeria is through training. Many of our trainees are doing exploits in missions. The training in Abuja 2004 has been called "The Blessing of the Twelve," for the twelve participants. They have gone to unreached places. Archbishop Kattey sent one of his mission stars, Deborah Mathias from Port-Harcourt, Nigeria. Deborah has been to Iraq, Iran, Libya, and Core Islamic areas. Right now she is in Sudan for missions. She got this fire burning in her due to the training she attended with the Blessing of the Twelve in Abuja. There are many others who have used the training to do missions fearlessly and extraordinarily within and outside their borders.

Most Rev. Segun Okubanjo went for the second Strategy Coordination course in Singapore (2002). After the course, he established a missionary school at Ibadan known as Inter-Cultural Missionary College, Onisa. The College is training missionaries even for the Church of Nigeria Missionary Society (CNMS) and for the entire West Africa sub-region.

Archbishop I. C. O. Kattey of Niger Delta North, an SC participant in Singapore 2000, in collaboration with the Church of Nigeria Missionary Society (CNMS), has sent many missionaries to different parts of the world: Madagascar, Cameroun, Indonesia and other countries. With the exposure and insight of AFM training, he has delved into reaching unreached people groups (UPGs) and doing very well in the countries mentioned.

We have the testimony of Pastor Umaru Suleymanne and many others, who are converts from Islam and now enjoying the dividend of Christ's salvation to mankind. Souleymane is one of the first trainees of AFM Nigeria, The Blessed Twelve among others, trained by Bishop Inyom in 2004 in Abuja. He accepted Christ and is already working on bringing salvation to his own people in Niger and his brethren (the Nomadic Fulani in the Northern part of Nigeria).

Souleymanne established the following schools after the training course in Abuja. These include: Madawa Mission Judah Tawa State Primary School, Brini Gaore Mission Judah Dosso State Primary School, and Santa Sons of Samuel, Raba Village. The vision of these schools according to him is to catch them young and bring them to the saving grace of Christ.

He was among the team of missionaries who went to Cameroon and faced heavy intimidation from the Cameroonian Police Authority on the borders. This strict border restriction caused the team undue hardship, but we understand that it was the forces of hell trying to resist the good news from penetrating the Baka Pygmies. Did we succeed? Yes, surely God gave us victory.

A Section of the Bakas after Worship and Sharing of the Gospel Led by Suleymanne

AFM Nigeria Missionaries Abraham Mtam, Peter Msule &
Suleymanne Umaru with a Cross Section of Bakas
May 2016

CHALLENGES FACING AFM NIGERIA

Challenges never mean impossibilities. The Bible records
that narrow is the road that leads to eternity (Mathew 7:13-
14). This means that the road is not smooth; it is not a bed
of roses. The road to our promised land has some obstacles
on it, but the confidence we have is in Christ Jesus, He is the
way, the truth and life. With him our destination is sure,
irrespective of the hurdles we encounter in our mission
fields. The leadership role of AFM Nigeria demands that we
squarely face issues within the Nigerian mission mindset,
issues, which if unchecked, can diminish the full potential of
the Nigerian church. These are the seven major places where
AFM seeks to bring a new vision:

1. Lack of Communication

Many leaders have had courses in training and are doing
great work in their areas, but they find it hard to give

feedback reports on work done. Therefore, it is difficult to coordinate future work and track down success stories.

2. Misinterpretation of Cross Border vs. Frontier Missions

The issue of cross border missions and frontier missions has been misconstrued by many. Some consider mission across a border as frontier mission, no matter that across the border there may be a healthy and strong church. It is not still clear to some church leaders about the differences between the two.

3. Money that Goes to the Spectacular

Big churches, highly recognized preachers, and outstanding church leaders do not comprehend frontier missions and how the gospel's power will harness the spread of the good news and the growth of the church. Huge sums of money are expended by preachers and evangelists on citywide crusades while frontier missions is neglected. Although frontier mission was not in sight, "Necessity *is* the mother of invention." I developed an interest in mission due to passion and challenges on the field.

4. Poor Execution

As we expected, the majority of the trainees have not put the training to effective use; they are like the steward who got a talent and hid it until the master returned. The ineffectual use of any knowledge hampers development. Unfortunately, these trainees do not even maintain contacts to give account of their stewardship, so they make their knowledge dormant and useless.

5. Little or Meager Participation in Mission and Evangelism

People still see mission and evangelism as an activity that only few can be engaged in while the rest sit and watch. This has created an unnecessary boundary among some believers and missionaries in the Body of Christ. Many people are too comfortable with the old traditional evangelism approach of crusade and deliverance services. Due to this fact, many are so busy with church programs and activities that they negate frontier missions. In this case, frontier mission is an alien, and they would not want to delve into what is not the usual thing they know. Churches are often more interested in projects than missions.

6. Funding

Funding of mission work has been challenging: About 95% of church funds go to local projects while there is little budget for missions in most cases. Many church members give very little to church work. The following statistics[1] show how church funds are utilized or appropriated:

- 95% of church spending goes into domestic projects.
- 4.5% of church spending goes into regular missions.
- 0.5% of church spending goes into frontier missions.

This explains the great imbalances in financing missions all over the world and over the ages. Though these statistics are from 1994, sadly the latest figures show little improvement.

---

[1] "Money and Missions: When Does It Corrupt Our Witness?" *Mission Frontiers* 16, no. 1-2 (1994): 28.

7. Personal Needs that Obscure Mission Needs

In most of the churches and prayer house meetings, people were praying only for personal needs; in none of the places visited was anybody praying for mission and evangelism. AFM, however, spreads the needs of the least evangelized, the names of our missionaries, and the stories that bring praise to God.

ANGLICAN DIOCESE OF MAKURDI AND THE BAKA PYGMIES OF EASTERN CAMEROON

From our training in 2000 at Fortune Centre Singapore, I researched the Baka Pygmies of Eastern Cameroon, and I have since adopted this group to reach them with the gospel. Over this period of time, we have been praying and networking, and we have visited the group twice. The present plan of AFM Nigeria is to carry out spiritual mapping, training of disciples, and church planting movements among the Baka Pygmies.

The Baka Pygmies of Eastern Cameroon. Who are they? There are different Pygmy peoples, e.g. the Bambuti, Batwa, Bayaka and Bagyeli. They live scattered over a huge area in Central and West Africa. They can be found in the Democratic Republic of Congo, Cameroon, Gabon, Central Africa Republic, Rwanda, Burundi, and Uganda. Each Pygmy group speaks a unique language, mostly related to those of neighboring non-Pygmy people. However, some few words are shared among even widely separated Pygmy tribes, suggesting that they have shared language in the past. About 150 thousand unreached Pygmies live in the region that stretches from Cameroon to Zaire in the Congo.

Pygmies are best known for their small size. Adults usually grow to be only three-to-four feet tall. *Pygmy* is derived from the Greek word *pyme*, which means "a cubit height." Pygmies are light-skinned, gentle, and peaceful people.

Rev. Remi with Two Baka People and a Missionary

Pygmies believe that a god named Tore created the world and is the *supreme being*. They are identified with the forest, since everything is dependent on it. They call upon Tore only during times of crisis. He is usually summoned by a trumpet blast, which is supposed to imitate his voice. Some groups believe that after creating the first humans, Tore was no longer interested in the affairs of the world, and so he withdrew to the sky. Other Pygmies believe that the forest spirits exert power over the soul of the dead.

The Efe believe that after the death of a Pygmy, their life is carried away from the body by a fly. It has been believed that the fly takes them to Tore.

Initiation process by a Baka Priest

A Baka Woman Making Her Tent/House

A Cross Section of the Bakas

NEEDS OF THESE PEOPLE

While the national government provides health and education services for some Africans, Pygmies are not included. Medical supplies as well as trained doctors are needed to work among them. Educational facilities and teachers are also needed.

Spiritually, the Pygmies are in dire need of missionaries. They must be told that there is a loving God who cares for them, who longs to make them part of his family with a Father who will never abandon them.

THE WAY FORWARD FOR AFM NIGERIA

As much as we can envision, this is our portion in the plentiful harvest. Frontier missions is looking beyond boundaries and tribes and people and religion (Revelation 5:9).

I want to recount the words of our former missionary to the Bakas, Rev. Remi Alumuna, who said there is water everywhere but none to drink. The UPGs are saying to the Church in our generation that there is church activity everywhere but none for them.

The aspect of frontier missions is alien in the understanding of most believers. They forgot the words of Jesus in Acts 1:8, "But you shall receive power when the Holy Spirit has come upon you; you shall be witnesses to me in Jerusalem and in *all* Judea and Samaria, and to the end of the earth" (New King James Version, emphasis mine).

Can you see the display of frontier mission as Jesus might have described it?

- Do not be satisfied telling the gospel to your household. Salvation is not for your household alone; that is your Jerusalem.

- Do not feel accomplished telling the gospel to your local church and your community; that is your Judea.

- Preaching the gospel within your country alone is not enough. Stretch out a little more; that is your Samaria.

- BUT take the message to the people who do not know what God looks like or is. That is frontier mission and the ends of the earth.

Remember, Jesus said in Luke 5:32, "*I have not come to call the righteous but sinners to repentance*" (emphasis mine). If we do not take the gospel to them, who will?

A current confrontation within Benue State shows the need for sacrificial love, overriding natural reactions of hate and revenge. Considering the trend of killings and maiming by the herders in Benue and other parts of the country by unevangelized and unreached (mainly Muslim) Fulanis, we have to evangelize this harvest field, too. Irrespective of the way the herders are treating Christians, through the eye of faith, see an opportunity to share the good news with them. We are highly encouraged by the statement of Souleymane at our Rural Churches Conference in Agasha, "Do not hate the Fulani herdsmen because of the killing, but love them to the extent of giving them the gospel." We are not deterred but are determined to go to them with the gospel because they have not heard about it. How will they know if they are not told? AFM Nigeria is already going through sessions of consultation with other mission agencies who are also burdened about the herders; we want to put our heads together and launch an entrance into these areas soon.

There have been reports on the proliferation of the Muslims and their intent to take over the world. We see this as an opportunity to gather many to the Lord. We might not stop them from procreating, but the more they grow, the more we send a good number of them to the kingdom of God. This is not just a harvest for Nigeria alone; it is a fruitful field for all believers, especially those in the frontier mission field.

Suleymanne marvels at the 100% cooperation that AFM Nigeria missionaries received from the Bakas and the possibility of future successes from their trip. In a statement, he said, "I wept at their desire to know that God exists, who is this loving divine being, having allowed the missionaries to leave their homes as far as Nigeria and Niger to visit them with the gospel." Certainly their long hunger for the gospel is a clear sign that we will continue to reach them with the good news.

People still see mission as an activity for just a few people in the Church. Therefore, we have the responsibility of continuous enlightenment and training to promote the essence of frontier missions.

As a result of the above, we have plans to organize an intensive strategic training course for the following: traditional leaders, interdenominational church leaders, evangelical movements, women and youth organizations, etc. In the future, we plan to deliver on this prospect. There is a need for more training on frontier missions for church leaders, such as bishops and presidents. There is an urgent need for constant training of apex church leadership in frontier missions. The following are other initiatives we plan to encourage:

- As a matter of urgency, training in frontier missions should be introduced in Bible and theological colleges throughout the world.

- We have been sensitizing people on the need for frontier missions and the limitations before us—insufficient financial resources. We have a target of one hundred fund raisers in the first quarter of 2018, with follow-up and commitment requests. Donors found through the fund raisers will be an alternative source of funding to aid the work of AFM Nigeria in reaching out to the unreached people groups.

- We plan to work in collaboration with Pastor Anthony Ishaya, who is an evangelist already making progress in reaching the Baka Pygmies. Considering his knowledge and exposure, we see him as a useful tool to achieve our goal of reaching the Baka Pygmies with the gospel of Christ.

- Reinvigorate the meeting of SCs and reawaken the AFM-Nigeria Newsletter.

- Organize a Consultation for Missionaries, and tap into their wealth of experience to move the vision and mission of AFM across the board.

- After the Consultation, we shall organize a Mission Conference targeting key mission agencies and major denominations in and outside Nigeria that intend to adopt UPGs.

- Adopt a mission strategy for the UPGs in West Africa and Africa at large.

- We shall organize a Strategic Resource Mobilization Seminar aimed at funding mission activities in our various mission fields.

- Organize short-term and long-term mission trips to selected UPGs across Africa, especially core North and Islamic North Africa.

The story of St. Paul in Acts 16:9 says, "And a vision appeared to Paul in the night: a man of Macedonia was standing there, urging him and saying, 'Come over to Macedonia and help us.' " From the aforementioned, it is clear to us that the year 2018 will be a year of divine explosion in frontier and strategic mission to reach the UPGs among the Baka Pygmies, Fulani, etc. We are calling on *all* mission agencies and partners, just as St. Paul saw in the vision beckoning him to come over to Macedonia and help.

PROPOSAL TO MOVE THE WORK OF AFM TO OTHER AFRICAN COUNTRIES AND THE WORLD

Pastor Umaru Orodji Suleymanne of Niger Republic, SC trainee, and a laborer indeed for the frontier mission, has desired to extend the tentacles of AFM to Niger for a wider scope of AFM. Recall that this man is keen for the salvation of souls, including the souls of nomads. His conversion story has been a potent tool for sharing the gospel. Born and brought up as a Muslim and from the linage of the Caliphate, he understood the challenges and bore much of them when he was determined to become a Christian. Indeed, God protected him despite all threats to life and rejection from his Muslim family and community. Being an AFM Nigeria active member, we see that Pastor Suleymanne could provide an avenue for birthing a new branch of AFM in Niger Republic.

The new bishop of Damaturu in Yobe State Nigeria, Rt. Rev. Yohana, received the training at Fortune Centre in Singapore. He has the pedigree for the unreached people groups of the Republic of Chad.

Pastor Ishaya Anthony, who is a Cameroonian but born and raised in Nigeria, is working along with AFM Nigeria to reach out to all of Central Africa, not Nigeria alone. He has established churches and understands the terrain of the Baka Pygmies.

CONCLUSION

There is actually a conflict of interest in church administration today. That conflict arises from the fact that some pastors seek their personal welfare, while some members are interested only in local church projects. Meanwhile, the main business of the Church, which is *mission,* suffers setbacks and neglect. This conflict is dramatically expressed in the overall representation of giving in the Church for missions, as shown in the statistics earlier in this chapter.

AFM has a distinctive message in mission. When I went to the Haggai Institute, I was struck with Haggai's observation of the "Buttoned up Approach to Evangelism." The implication is a willingness to be a follower of Christ but not a vocal witness. AFM is going to where the need is greatest, where the gospel has not reached before, focusing on the largest and least evangelized people in the world.

Have you ever considered that the Book of Acts is a story that has continued down through the Church's history? This is the reason—that we may continue in the work of the apostles of Christ. Actions of the apostles were documented in the Book of Acts, and we can say specifically that these are the acts of the apostle Peter, the acts of the apostle Paul, the acts of the apostle John, the acts of the Holy Spirit, and later the acts of people like Tad. Every believer's life is a script that will be read during their lifetime, after their lifetime, and even in heaven on the Day of Judgment. These acts are found written in the Book of Life as stated in Revelation 20:12. As unbelievers stand before the great white throne—alone, without a defense, and with no escape—John notes that "...the books were opened. Another book was opened, which is the book of life, and the dead were judged according to their works by what was written in the books."

All will be responsible for their actions and inactions, and note that all these actions will be documented in a book for future generations to see and learn from, or unlearn from. The inactions of a believer may lead to the destruction of unreached people; this is why we must urgently focus on and not relent in the salvation of unsaved souls.

Paul the apostle knew little about the effectuality of his letter to the Ephesians, Romans, and Corinthians. When God gave Rev. Tad the AFM vision, little did he know it was going to be in a book also for the benefit of future generations. This is not just a book that you read for information, but *The Acts of Anglican Frontier Mission Generals and Associates Until Jesus Comes.*

3

MISSION IGNITED!

Mission Fire in Pakistan and The United States

by Patrick Augustine

The Church exists by mission,
just as fire exists by burning.

That well known quote from Emile Brunner is as true now as when he wrote it in the early 1900s, and it is as true for the church in the West as for the church in my homeland, Pakistan. I grew up in a Christian family in Gojra, Pakistan, and experienced the fire of mission in that church. As an ordained priest in the church in the United States for the past thirty-five years, I have seen the struggle for reigniting mission in our church. I would like to draw on my life in the church in Pakistan to describe the fire of mission there and what has kept it ignited. I offer this with the hope that we here can see the flames of mission once again driving the church we love and serve.

The Very Reverend Canon Patrick Augustine, D. Min., D.D. served parishes in Virginia before moving to his present parish in Wisconsin. He has a ministry of encouragement to the persecuted churches in Africa and Asia, bringing them to the attention of the wider church.

When I became the associate rector at the Church of the Holy Comforter in Vienna, Virginia, in 1990, my rector was Father Robert Denig. He had a heart for world mission and soon had me involved in the mission efforts of the Episcopal Church.

There I also met a brother priest, Rev. Tad de Bordenave, then rector of St. Matthews Episcopal Church in Richmond, Virginia. He invited me into his prayer circle to pray that the Episcopal Church would reach outside the walls of our parishes and to the ends of the world with the gospel message. I was surprised by conversations going on in the early 1990s to close down the world mission department at the headquarters of the Episcopal Church in New York. An apologetic feeling had developed that the Church in the West should see other faiths as equally valid and salvific. The idea was that there are lots of ways to God, not just through Jesus Christ. I was not prepared for this shaky foundation for mission, for it was very different from what I had left.

THE STORY OF A HOME AND A CHURCH IN MUSLIM PAKISTAN

I have often wondered why I wasn't born in a Muslim family. After all, Pakistan is 95% Muslim. It's a mystery to me. I thank God for missionaries who brought the good news of the gospel of Jesus Christ to my great grandparents. My grandfather was a teacher and ordained Presbyterian minister who became an Anglican minister of the gospel in the 1920s. In 1929 my father graduated with a Bachelor of Arts degree from the Scottish Presbyterian Church, Murray College, Sialkot. He joined an Indian Ashram, started by Sadhu Sunder Singh based at Christ Church, Okara, Pakistan. He was an itinerant Indian Sadhu who carried a Bible and a *Book of Common Prayer* to teach, preach and heal as a Christian monk throughout the sub-continent of India.

The Anglican Bishop of Lahore encouraged my father to join the Lahore Divinity School. He was ordained and then became a parish priest in the early 1940s.

I was born into an Anglican household. In childhood, I watched my parents say the morning and evening Prayer Office from the *Book of Common Prayer.* We sang hymns in Punjabi, Urdu and a few in English too as part of our praise and prayer. We attended "the Great Litany" services every Wednesday afternoon in our church. I remember from my childhood some of the petitions from the Great Litany such as: "That it may please thee to send forth laborers into thy harvest, and to draw all mankind into thy kingdom." Every year in the month of October, we had a Christian convention for four days. Well known evangelists, missionaries and pastors from all over the country were invited to teach, preach and pray. Hundreds of people came for four days to hear the saving message of the gospel of Jesus Christ. The message of the gospel was broadcast on loud speakers throughout the city. Many Muslims came to hear the gospel, too. Christian literature was distributed as part of our effort to introduce our Muslim neighbors to Jesus.

My great grandparents had heard the good news of the gospel because men and women from the West had a heart to bring the light of the gospel to my ancestors. I heard many stories from Grandfather and Father about the hard labor and sacrifices of these people, who had dedicated their lives to love our people in the name of Jesus. It is because of their dedicated work that we have come to "the great new fact of our time,"[1] that the Christian church is now a global church. I learned early in my life that the call of Jesus to his disciples is to go forth into the world "...and make disciples of all nations, baptizing them in the name of the Father and of the

---

[1] Archbishop William Temple used this phrase in 1942 at his enthronement sermon at Canterbury.

Son and of the Holy Spirit, teaching them to observe all that I have commanded you. And behold, I am with you always, to the end of the age" (Matthew 28:20). I learned by heart the words of the Great Commission during my Sunday School class at St. John's Church, Gojra, Pakistan. As a baptized Christian, I was commissioned by Jesus to carry this message into the streets of Pakistan, to the United States, and, through my missional journeys, to the ends of the earth. When living in Pakistan I was part of a minority, discriminated against and occasionally persecuted. When I look back, I remember that we were never apologetic or embarrassed about sharing our faith with Muslim friends

While I understand that Jesus did not ask us to intrude insensitively on those who are not receptive to the Christian gospel, we still have the command to tell. The gospel is the good news for the downtrodden and rejects of society. It is a healing ointment. It brings peace and justice to unjust societies and gives dignity to our fellow human beings. I experienced this transformation in the subcontinent of India where masses of untouchables had no status or opportunities to have equal rights in their societies. In receiving the good news of the gospel, these people know they are not subhuman any more but now sons and daughters of the living God. Today, many of them are school teachers, nurses, doctors, engineers, bishops, priests, deacons, evangelists and lay leaders. The gospel of Jesus Christ not only transforms every single human who believes but has the power to bless whole nations. It is the ongoing miracle that Jesus continues in the twenty-first century to heal, bless, and enlighten the hearts of individuals and nations. But that is a far cry from what I found in my new home when I immigrated to the United States.

In 1983 I moved from Pakistan to the United States. I thought I was moving to a Christian country. I was amazed and shocked to find that many Christians in my new country of abode were apologetic about their faith. I heard directly from them that they are not supposed to impose their faith on anyone else. Religion is a private matter. I was told that missionaries who carried the good news of the gospel to foreign lands were stooges of the imperialists. They were named arrogant intruders on the culture and faiths of people living in Africa, Asia and other non-Western countries. It was a shock to me and my family. It was hard to find fellow Christians and brother priests in the United States who had the heart for mission to reach out to people of other faiths.

It was troublesome that the World Missions Department of the Episcopal Church would be closed. The name of the Episcopal Church registered in the USA as a corporation is "Domestic and Missionary Society." The Rev. Walter and Louise Hannum came to visit Rev. Robert Denig at the Church of the Holy Comforter in Vienna, Virginia, in the early 1980s. Father Denig introduced Rev. Walter Hannum as the father of the World Missions Department in the Episcopal Church. He was looking for partners to join him in a campaign to keep the department open and vote to increase funding at the next General Convention. Rev. Robert Denig, Rev. Tad de Bordenave and I joined the Hannums to organize a conference, New Wineskins, in North Carolina in 1994, prior to the General Convention. Six hundred Episcopalians came to attend the New Wineskins conference and passed a resolution to keep open the World Missions Department in New York. Later, at the General Convention, this resolution was overwhelmingly passed and funding increased.

Nevertheless, in most Episcopal churches, there was no hunger or desire for mission. It was obvious that our church had lost her vision as the bearer of the missional responsibility in the world. Mission activities were confined to short-term visits to other Anglican churches in developing nations. Most of our churches had come to envision the Church simply as a "place where certain things happen."

Increasingly, this view of the Church as a "place where certain things happen" locates the Church's self identity in its organizational forms and its professional class, the clergy who perform the Church's authoritative activities. Popular culture captures it well: You go to church in the same way you might go to a store. You attend a church the way you attend a school or theater. You belong to a church as you would to a service club with its programs and activities.[2] It is an enormous challenge to motivate our churches to reach the 1.6+ billion people with the gospel of Jesus Christ.

It was a natural and not unexpected turn of events that I should have been involved in Anglican Frontier Missions from the beginning. In the early 1990s while I was in Virginia, I started participating in prayer and Bible study meetings with Rev. Robert Dening, Rev. Tad de Bordenave, and a few other people from Episcopal Churches in Fairfax, Virginia. Tad had just taken a fifteen-week class called "Perspectives on the World Christian Movement." He shared his vision of reaching out to the unreached people groups in the world with the gospel of Jesus Christ. Tad was then also serving as chairman of the World Mission Committee in the Diocese of Virginia.

After two years of prayer and sharing, Rev. Tad de Bordenave resigned as rector of St. Matthews Episcopal Church in Richmond, Virginia. He was then only forty-nine years old. His children were still in high school. After he resigned from the rector's position, he had no budget or financial support. He took this giant step of faith, trusting the Lord to provide financial resources and personnel to form Anglican Frontier Missions, a new mission society. I was one of the original board members, joining in 1994.

---

[2] Darrel L. Guder, *Missional Church* (Grand Rapids, MI: William B Eerdmans Publishing Company, 1998), 79-80.

LESSONS FOR THE WEST

While AFM has been an instrument of reigniting missions in the Episcopal/Anglican world, I would like to suggest some general ways of supporting mission. From my background in the Anglican Church in Pakistan and then life here in the United States, let me offer five observations about reigniting missions and keeping the fire lit.

1. The Nature of the Church as God's Witness to the World.

The first thing is our purpose. God has called into existence a people to participate with God in the accomplishment of his mission. "Mission arises from the heart of God himself, and is communicated from his heart to ours. Mission is the global outreach of the global people of a global God."[3] We are "gospel people" and sharing the gospel in all possible ways is the essence of the mission of God's people. The mission of God's people is to bring good news to a world where bad news is depressingly endemic.

Darrell Guder sums up the connection of the Trinity, the Church, and mission:

> Missional fervor for the Church is not optional to pick and choose when circumstances may allow or we can spare our time for such an activity. Mission [is] understood as being derived from the very nature of God. It [is] thus put in the context of the doctrine of the Trinity, not of ecclesiology or soteriology. The classical doctrine of the *missio Dei* is God the Father sending the Son, and God the Father and the Son sending the Spirit [and is] expanded to include yet another 'movement': Father, Son, and Holy Spirit sending the Church into the world."[4]

---

[3] John Stott, *The Contemporary Christian: An Urgent Plea for Double Listening* (Downers Grove, IL: Intervarsity Press, 1992), 335.

[4] Darrell L. Guder, *Missional Church, A Vision for the Sending of the Church in North America* (Grand Rapids, MI., William B. Eerdmans Publishing Company, 1998).

2. Our Past Mission Roots

On December 2, 1993, the new mission society, Anglican Frontier Missions in the Anglican Communion, was inaugurated in the chapel of the Diocese of Virginia in Richmond. It was the feast day of Channing Moore Williams, the missionary bishop in China and Japan in 1910. Bishop Williams was also the great uncle of Rev. Tad de Bordenave. The Rt. Rev. Peter James Lee, Bishop of Virginia, presided over the inaugural service as the first patron of this new mission society. In his homily, Bishop Lee elaborated on Bishop Williams as representative of many who went out from the Diocese of Virginia. He was like many others who left their homes in the States to go to foreign lands so the inhabitants there could hear the gospel. These men and women sailed to Brazil and Chile, to Japan and China, and to many parts of Africa. Many of them died in the lands where they went to serve. Grace Church in New York City helped to found Hephzibah House as a staging home for the men and women who were in the city, awaiting their boats to take them to the mission fields. We have an awesome mission history!

3. The Historic Teaching of the Church

While I was at Lahore Divinity School in Lahore, Pakistan, in 1972-1976, I read the following statement of Emil Brunner, which made a great impact on me:

> Mission work does not arise from any arrogance in the Christian Church; mission is its cause and its life. The Church exists by mission, just as a fire exists by burning. Where there is no mission, there is no Church; and where there is neither Church nor mission, there is no faith. It is a secondary question whether by that we mean Foreign Missions, or simply the preaching of the Gospel in the home Church. Mission, Gospel preaching, is the spreading out of the fire which Christ has thrown upon

the earth. He who does not propagate this fire shows that he is not burning. He who burns propagates the fire. This 'must' is both things – an urge and a command. An urge, because living faith feels God's purpose as its own. "Woe is unto me, if I preach not the gospel," says Paul.[5]

This is also known as "Amazing Grace." John Newton was a slave trader who terrorized his slaves. In 1747 as captain of *The Greyhound*, a Liverpool ship, he was on his homeward journey from Africa. He had a full load of slaves chained and kept in the worst possible conditions on his ship. As he was reading Thomas Kempis's *The Imitation of Christ,* he was converted, and surrendered his life to Christ. The biggest change in his life was that now that he was promoting the "life of God in the soul" to both his crew and his African cargo. He experienced the grace of God in his own personal life and wrote this beautiful hymn:

> Amazing grace, how sweet the sound,
> that saved a wretch like me.
> I once was lost, but now am found,
> Was blind but now I see.

4. True Anglicanism is Missional!

We know that the beginning of the Anglican Church is the story of fulfilling of the Great Commission. In 596 A.D., Augustine set out nervously from Rome for England with forty equally fearful monks. He had not gone very far, when murmuring among the team and his own fears of that hostile and savage country, Britain, overwhelmed him. The party turned back to Rome, but Gregory the Great would not

---

[5] Emil Brunner, *The Christian Doctrine of God* (Eugene, Oregon: Wipf and Stock Publishers, 2014).

sympathize with their timidity.[6] He reminded them that they were called to a life of prayer and that they must have faith in the passionate commitment they shared: to witness to the claims of Christ. If they were loyal, he told them, they need not fear the "barbarous, fierce and pagan" warriors of Britain.

According to the historian, the Venerable Bede,[7] Gregory wrote to the party, "My very dear sons, it is better never to undertake any high enterprise than to abandon it when once begun...with the help of God you must carry out this holy task which you have begun. Be constant and zealous in carrying out this enterprise which, under God's Guidance, you have undertaken. Then you will not be remembered as Angles but as Angels!" The origin of the Anglican Church is through the work and ministry of scared, weak and frail human beings, but in the end, they were obedient to their call to be missionaries to the native Britons.

6. Stories of Anglican Mission and Missionaries: Lambeth, Nepal, Kashmir

Lambeth. In 1998 the Most Rev. George Carey, Archbishop of Canterbury, invited the bishops of the worldwide Anglican Communion to the Lambeth Conference in Kent, United Kingdom. AFM was invited with other mission societies to be present in the exhibit area. Myra Augustine and Charles LaFond went as volunteers to assist Rev. Tad de Bordenave. AFM was the only missionary organization to present the case of 1.6+ billion unreached people groups before the bishops of the Anglican

---

[6] Eugene H. Merrill, Mark E Rooker, Michael, A. Grisanti, *The Word and the World: An Introduction to the Old Testament* (Nashville, TN: B&H Publishing Group, 2011), 108.

[7] Bede, *The Complete Works of the Venerable Bede* (United Kingdom: Delphi Classics, 2015).

Communion. I was also present at that Conference as an advisor to the Archbishop of Canterbury. We held meetings with Anglican bishops during lunch breaks to advocate the case of the unevangelized. AFM Nigeria came into being through these interactions at the Lambeth Conference.

Nepal. Our first missionary there was Rev. Norman Beale, who traveled with his family to Nepal. In 2014, I had an opportunity to travel with Rev. Chris Royer, executive director of AFM, to attend a mission conference held at St. Andrews Church in Singapore. The Anglican Diocese of Singapore is committed to taking the gospel to people groups not yet in the Body of Christ. They are entrusted with the propagation of the gospel, and Anglican ministry and mission, in six countries in Asia: Cambodia, Indonesia, Laos, Nepal, Thailand, and Vietnam. It is a region of 450 million people with diverse cultures and languages. In these countries, less than 5% of the population are Christians. During the conference, we met three Nepalese, and AFM missionary Norman Beale was the first person to teach them about Jesus Christ. The Diocese of Singapore is continuing that work in partnership with AFM.

Kashmir. Ifraim Matthews is a fellow laborer in Pakistan. Let me share with you the following story about his ministry in Azad Kashmir. Ifraim shared this with me on October 25, 2014.

It was a pleasant morning of late spring in the year 2002. My telephone rang early in the morning. Rev. Patrick Augustine was on the other end of the line telling me to get ready immediately for a long trip to Azad Kashmir; we were to attend an emergency meeting at a refugee camp in Azad Kashmir. I was used to this kind of travel, and ever since my college days, I had wanted to take a trip to Muzzafarbad in Azad Kashmir. I hurriedly got ready and preceded to the meeting point. It took us three hours, passing through scenic views of the valley, to reach our destination. Upon arrival at the refugee camp, we found several people waiting for us, and they gave us a warm welcome.

Rev. Patrick immediately went into a meeting conducted by the camp dwellers on bare wooden benches. I preferred to mingle with the young lads sitting a short distance away, curiously watching the folks at the meeting. These young boys had nothing to do as it was vacation time in the local school. In response to my inquiry, they showed me their school, a 10x15-wide room with only a mattress to sit on. The boys were keen to study, but they had no books. As I carry books to give away, I searched my bag and found two copies of the New Testament, along with seventeen copies of the *Book of Proverbs* in the Urdu language. I distributed the books among them, and soon they spread out in the woods and absorbed themselves in reading. Their eagerness to read was amazing.

After an hour or so, when Rev. Patrick was done with his business, we were led to a place for lunch. These young boys literally begged me to promise to return to them with more books. We finished the lunch and headed back for another three-hour return journey through night.

On our way back, we stopped at the town of Kohala, situated right on the bank of the Jhelum River, a natural boundary between Pakistan and the State of Azad Jammu and Kashmir. We were stopped by the guards at the Khohala Bridge. The old bridge was narrow and could accommodate one-way traffic only. Amazingly, there was a long queue of vehicles waiting for the "go" signal on both sides of the bridge. While waiting for our turn, Rev. Patrick and I dismounted the vehicle to take a little stroll. I shared with Rev. Patrick my concerns. He listened intently to what I had to say, sighed deeply, and then said in a wishful tone, "I wish someday we could baptize the people of Kashmir in this water of the Jhelum River." Little did I know that this was a prophetic utterance: I believed that our Lord was going to grant me the honor of baptizing several Kashmiris and establishing a Kashmiri-speaking Church in Azad Jammu and Kashmir.

Kashmir, henceforth, became the focus of our prayer attention. The Lord miraculously opened the door for us by shaking the whole land on October 8, 2006. A huge earthquake took place. It was an unprecedented tragedy in the history of the country, but Christians were the first ones to respond and take relief goods to the far flung areas of Azad Kashmir. Three years later in April 2010, Potohar Fellowship, in cooperation with Adaila Evangelical Congregation, conducted the first Easter service in the small town of Dadyal in the house of the late Babu Samuel.

IN CONCLUSION

We are all part of the global family of human beings. We need to learn, respect, and honor other people's faiths, while seeing their errors and insufficiencies. Knowing the current affairs of our world, we learn that "the whole creation has been groaning as in the pain of childbirth right up to the present time" (Romans 8:22, New International Version). It is the first and foremost call of the Church to bring healing and the light of Christ to a world caught by the darkness of sin, hatred, racism, and terrorism. The world is in dire need of the gospel of Jesus Christ. It is a loving action of the Church to take the gospel to the ends of the world. We are reminded of the phrase, *extra Ecclesiam nulla salus,* which means, "Outside the Church there is no salvation."[8] This is not a pompous claim of the Church; it is based on Holy Scripture. "And there is salvation in no one else, for there is no other name under heaven given among men by which we must be saved" (Acts 4: 12).

---

[8] This expression comes from the writings of Saint Cyprian of Carthage, a bishop of the 3rd century.

This is the heart of the story of mission in my native country of Pakistan. The missional threads of Anglicanism are alive and well there. What is true of Christ's Church in Pakistan is just as true of his church in the West.

We know, however, that fires burn out. The embers can lose their heat, leaving nothing but ashes and remnants of what once burned brightly. We see that danger throughout history and in parts of the West today. Fires need fresh wood and people who keep them burning. That has been the role of Anglican Frontier Missions for this past quarter century. It has brought to the Church's vision for the first time the millions who have never heard of Jesus Christ. It has shown how mission to them can go forward. The concentration that AFM brings to people who have been overlooked strengthens the witness of the Church. Its voice and its call will keep the mission fire burning.

PART TWO

THE PEOPLE OF
ANGLICAN FRONTIER MISSIONS

4

REACHING THE
TAMANG PEOPLE OF NEPAL

by Norman Beale

Before our time in Nepal and ever since our first trip there in 1986, my wife Beth and I had prayed for and later observed the varied peoples of Nepal, seeking to discern which ethnolinguistic people group God might be calling us to serve. This search was the focus that we had for all of our years in Nepal. As we prayed and meditated on the Holy Scriptures, we asked God at every step, and especially when we reached Baddichaur and encountered the Magar people of western Nepal, "How are you calling us, O Lord? Are these Magar people the ones that we are to serve and are these the unreached peoples that we should be focusing on?"

UNREACHED PEOPLE GROUP FOCUS

Beth and I first became interested in unreached people groups in 1979 through Trudi Gates, a friend of ours at

---

The Very Reverend Norman Beale is a Chaplain in the Jurisdiction of the Armed Forces and Chaplaincy and Abbot of the Order of St. Marin of Tours, Anglican Church in North America. Beth teaches English at Passaic County Community College in the metro New York City Area. He and his wife, Beth, did pioneer work in Nepal with the result of the founding of the Anglican Church in Nepal. They now live in New Jersey.

Grace Episcopal Church in Manhattan. Trudi was a member of our parish and mentioned to us at a Missions Committee meeting that she was interested in unreached peoples. The first few times she used that expression, we had no comprehension of what she was talking about whatsoever. As she explained it to us over time, the new concept seeped into our consciousness.

Beth and I got to know Trudi pretty well. I ran the New York City marathon together with her and several other friends, for three years. We would see each other at church every Sunday and at Missions Committee meetings. Slowly, this new concept seeped into our consciousness, and we began to grasp the enormity of what she was saying.

Here is a brief definition: An unreached people group is an ethnolinguistic group of people among whom there is no indigenous community of believing Christians with adequate numbers and resources to evangelize this people group without outside assistance. Another way to say this is that the people of an unreached ethnicity have never heard about Jesus Christ, and there are few people who can tell them about Jesus Christ in their own language.

In 1982-83, when we first began to learn and study all of this, a persistent and disturbing question kept coming to us: How could it be that Christians have not fully understood and sought to fulfill the command of Jesus to go into all the world and preach the gospel to every nation (Matthew 28.18-20)? How could it be that his command has never been fully completed and obeyed in twenty centuries? While we kept asking the question, we had a very personal sense as a couple that we wanted to be part of doing something about addressing this pressing matter. Soon, events transpired in our lives that got us very much involved in seeking to be part of the solution to this conundrum.

COMING TO FAITH OURSELVES

I came to faith in Jesus Christ as my Savior and Lord in 1969 at the age of seventeen in Montreat, North Carolina. At about the same time, hundreds of miles to the north in New Jersey, Beth Haberer, who later became my wife, also came to faith in Jesus Christ through the outreach ministry of a Christian coffee house in 1970. We first met in 1978 in New York City. In our first months together, as we got to know each other, we shared how each of us had first come to faith in our late teen years and then had a sense of a calling to serve God as missionaries. As it turned out, neither of us had ever really known what to do with that sense of call. Consequently, neither of us had done anything about it.

Just before we were married at Grace Episcopal Church in 1980, we joined the Missions Committee. In the first year of our marriage, we were still wondering how we might become involved in missions. We got involved in various events that the Missions Committee of our parish sponsored in 1981. The next year, our Missions Committee invited three young women, who were seminary students at Gordon-Conwell in Massachusetts, to come and speak to us at Grace Church. That Sunday afternoon, as we sat and listened to them describe their experience with Mother Theresa in Calcutta, India, we were moved to tears. At that point in my life, tears were a rare event, and I knew that something significant was happening. I sensed in my heart a stirring and moving by God's Holy Spirit. It seemed like a reactivation of God's call on my life during the period 1969-1972. I asked my wife, Beth, if we might be alone in the hallway for a moment because I had something I wanted to talk with her about. We stepped out into the hall, and I said to her that I sensed the Holy Spirit was speaking to me, and saying, "You are to serve me as a missionary." She looked at me then, smiled, and said, "Oh, I'm so relieved. Me too!" We laughed and shared our excitement.

It was an exciting time. In the subsequent days, we told our Missions Committee members about our sense of call. We asked them what we should do next and how we might answer this call. They were as perplexed as we were about next steps. So together, we approached the vestry (the ruling body) and the rector of our parish. We were all left scratching our heads, uncertain what to do. Later, Cook and Martha Kimball, leaders of our Missions Committee, together with the rest of committee, recommended that we contact Walter and Louise Hannum, who were in charge of the Episcopal Church Missionary Community, with offices in Pasadena, California. Perhaps they would know what to do.

Walter and Louise had been to our parish a number of times at the invitation of our Missions Committee to speak about missions, and we remembered them. We gave them a call and asked them if they had any counsel for us about what we ought to do next. They suggested that we should do some study and preparation before we headed anywhere to serve as missionaries. They also suggested that we go out to California to the U.S. Center for World Mission and to the Missions Program at Fuller Seminary, both in Pasadena. There we might study missions and take the course called "Perspectives on the World Christian Movement," the same course Trudi had described to us. The Perspectives Course, still offered today, is about unreached people groups. It would be difficult to exaggerate how exciting and fascinating this course turned out to be.

We were not the first people to have this kind of call within our church. Other people in our parish had gone to serve as missionaries doing community work in South Africa and Liberia, but as far as we knew these people weren't supported by the parish as missionaries of the church. We were asking the church what to do. We wanted them to assist us in discerning the direction in which God wanted us to go. What steps should we take to become missionaries? Where should we go? We were later told that we were the first missionaries of Grace Church to be sent out by the parish and supported by the parish financially and through prayers. The parish ended up supporting us continuously over the next eighteen years.

We prayed about all of this, discussing and exploring as best we could what would be the best way forward. In prayer, we asked God to guide us. We decided that we wanted to follow the advice that the Hannums had given us: We would move to California to prepare for missionary service through study.

It was a huge leap into the unknown to close up our apartment in Manhattan, put our things in storage, and travel out to California. We had no idea what was next. We enrolled in the four-week Perspectives Course, travelled out to Pasadena, and got settled in. Our class started right away; it was an intensive course, meeting all day, Monday through Friday, and some evenings. While taking this course, the reality, the complexity, and the common characteristics of unreached people groups became much clearer to us. We learned that at the time, the summer of 1983, there were approximately 1.8 billion people in the world who were in this category of never having heard the gospel. We were shocked.

As we began to think about next steps and eventualities, we discussed going to Uganda or Kenya. We had many long talks with Walter and Louise Hannum in their home in Pasadena. One Sunday afternoon, Louisa and I said hello at the library, and were walking down the sidewalk together, back toward our respective homes. While we were walking, Louise asked me why we were interested in going to Uganda or Kenya. I explained that we had heard a number of bishops from those countries who had preached at our parish in New York, and that they had invited us to come and serve in

Africa. We felt such a warm and vital connection with them that this seemed to be the way to move forward—a way based on relationships and invitations. Louise asked me how this was connected to unreached people groups, as much of the population of both Kenya and Uganda at least had had opportunities to hear the gospel. "Isn't there anywhere else you've ever been interested in going to?" she asked me.

I replied that from 1973 to 1976, I had thought about going to Nepal as a missionary, as I had learned about it through my rock climbing and mountaineering experiences. I recalled how climbing Mount Everest was every rock climber's dream and that the mountains of Nepal represented one of the world's great mountaineering challenges. I wanted to climb Mt. Everest, and when I first began to think and plan about how I might get involved in missions, I realized that I could go to Nepal, be a missionary, *and* climb mountains.

I described how several years later, in 1976, while praying about missions and what to do after graduating from my university studies, the Holy Spirit gave me a moment of sharp clarity: I realized that I had not given a moment's thought about the people of Nepal or how I might share the love of Jesus Christ with them. I had not made the slightest effort to think about Nepal's people, their culture, traditions, or religion. I had been dreaming only about high mountains, scaling peaks, attempting Everest, and maybe just a little, looking into Sherpa and Tibetan culture.

This made me feel like I had been deceiving myself and that my intentions and motivations had seriously lacked integrity before God. As a result of that, I decided to relinquish my sense of wanting to go to Nepal and become willing to serve in other places. I wanted to make sure that I was really following the call of God, not following my own dreams of high-altitude exploits, extreme adventure, and exploration.

Louise responded that she could understand that, but why not reconsider Nepal now. I replied that I had already settled this matter and I didn't think it was appropriate to bring it up again. She pointedly asked if I could at least pray about it. I said I would, and then discuss it with my wife and pray with her. Privately, I was dreading this, as I anticipated that Beth would look me straight in the eyes and say, "This is just another one of your adventures, isn't it? No, we're not going to go off on one of your escapades." With that apprehension in mind, I went back to our apartment, sat down with Beth, explained what happened and said, "Would you be willing to pray together with me about Nepal?" To my surprise, Beth said, "Of course, let's pray about it." We did right then. After we had dinner, we decided to see what was on the National Geographic channel that night. When it came on, what do you think it was about? Nepal.

The following morning we were outside on the sidewalk getting ready to go out when Faithanne, one of our friends and fellow missions student, came by. We noticed that she had an unusually big smile on her face. She began to tell us about her engagement. We congratulated her and asked whom she was engaged to. She told us his name and that he was from Nepal. Beth and I looked at each other and said something along the lines of, "Here we go." Later that day, I was studying at the library in the U.S. Center for World Mission. Several hours later I took a break and went to the periodical area to look at some magazines. You may have already guessed what happened: In that month's Smithsonian, there was an article about Nepal.

These kinds of events happened every day for the next two weeks. In our prayers, we had many strong images about Nepal and God's purposes and plans for Nepal. Prior to that, I had rarely heard about Nepal from any source. Beth and I felt that God's hand was moving visibly in the story of our lives and our experiences. We began to do research on Nepal.

In a time before the internet, such research wasn't that easy. It meant going to libraries, doing some digging in the card catalog, looking through microfiche, and poring over journal articles, some of which were dry and boring. Thankfully, many others were exciting, informative, and insightful. Through contacts, we learned about the America-Nepal Society in the Los Angeles area and went to our first meeting with them. These were the first Nepalese we had ever met. They were warm and inviting, and they welcomed us into their community. Through them, we learned so much more about Nepal.

Later that year, when we were back in New York City visiting people in our parish, my best friend Greg asked me probing questions about what were we going to do in Nepal. I realized I had no idea and I could not answer his question. Later that day, Beth and I discussed this, and it was then that we decided that we needed to go to Nepal for a trip of research and discovery. We began to make plans for the trip.

OUR EXPLORATORY TRIP TO NEPAL

In January 1986, we went to Nepal for four months. Our goal was to learn as much as we could about Nepal and any potential mission work that we might do there. What are the ethno-linguistic groups of Nepal? How many of them are unreached? How do you get a visa to live in Nepal? What kind of work can you do? What is the government like? How do you learn Nepali, the national language? What's the weather like? The economy? Society? What are Hinduism and Buddhism, as practiced by people in the Himalayas, really like? We decided that we could best answer these questions by interviewing people in Nepal and traveling widely through the nation. We broke the goal into categories of interviews: Nepalese Christians, Nepalese generally, expatriate Christian missionaries, and other expatriates.

Having never been to Nepal, we assumed that travel would be simple and straightforward.

Initially, we made our base in Kathmandu with the Sodemba family, relatives of Faithanne's fiancé. While staying with them, we got accustomed to life in Nepal and began traveling around the Kathmandu valley. We attended a Nepalese church in Patan, the twin city of Kathmandu on Saturdays (Sunday is a work day in Nepal) and began to have discussions with church pastors and leaders. We saw the cultural and historical sites, began to meet people and learn what life was like. We used bicycles and local buses (*very* crowded!) for transportation. Our home had no heat and no hot water. We ate rice and lentils every day for lunch and supper, and learned that this is what most people in Nepal eat every day. Even though we were careful about drinking water and the food we ate, we got sick. A lot.

We found the offices of the two main mission agencies in Nepal, the United Mission to Nepal and the International Nepal Fellowship, and began to make appointments to interview agency staff. We went on four "treks" to the remote corners of Nepal. After the conclusion of our trip, we returned to the U.S., compiled our discoveries, and thought about possible ways we might serve in Nepal and how we might return for a long-term mission. Finally, in late 1987, we returned to Nepal. We went through a program of language and culture learning for six months, and we then moved to Baddichaur, a small town in a remote region of western Nepal. There we worked with a team of eight Christian missionaries doing community development work (clean drinking water system, animal husbandry, income generation, and adult literacy). And we engaged in low profile evangelism.

A TREK OF INSIGHT AND REVELATION

Our work among the Tamang people began in 1990 when on a trek into the high mountains near Nepal. During the trek, I had my first encounter with some Tamangs in their region of the Himalayas. There were six of us, three Tamangs, one Nepali, and two Americans. We walked further than you might normally walk, as our starting point was west of Gorkha. We trekked thirty miles in rugged mountains our first day, and even further the second day, arriving in Saleri, Dhading. While in that region, we met many hundreds of Tamangs. Most of the Tamangs we met were Buddhist, which they have been for two millennia, but surprisingly, quite a number of villages had groups of Christians, varying in number from just one or two families, in most cases, to almost a whole village in one case. We learned of a recent outpouring of the Holy Spirit that sounded like the book of *The Acts of the Apostles* in the New Testament—healings, miracles, mass conversions and transformed lives. All to the glory of God!

On the third day of the trek, three of the other five in our group announced that the day's agenda was to go north to another village and then return to Saleri for the night. I told them to go on; I felt I should spend some time in prayer and reflection. They walked off north. Shortly after, I walked north too, but stopped on the east side of a high ridge where I found a very large, flat-topped boulder. I climbed atop and, after warming up in the early morning sun, began to pray and read the Holy Scriptures. In the reading for that Saturday morning in October of 1990, I read Matthew 9:35-38:

> And Jesus went throughout all the cities and villages, teaching in their synagogues and proclaiming the gospel of the kingdom and healing every disease and every affliction. When he saw the crowds, he had compassion for them, because they were harassed and helpless, like sheep

without a shepherd. Then he said to his disciples, "The harvest is plentiful, but the laborers are few; therefore pray earnestly to the Lord of the harvest to send out laborers into his harvest.

As I was reading that passage, I thought of Jesus' description of the human need and potential harvest in John 4:35, "Do you not say, 'There are yet four months, then comes the harvest?' Look, I tell you, lift up your eyes, and see that the fields are white for harvest."

This came to mind because there was a powerful visual parallel all around me. The stepped terraces on the steep side of the mountain, as it descended below me, were filled with the light golden-blond heads of ripe millet. With the bright, high altitude sunlight glinting off the ripe heads of seed, it appeared white. For the first time, "white unto harvest" had a literal meaning for me.

A much more powerful spiritual meaning was emerging in my heart at that very moment, as a harvest time scene unfolded before me. A little old Tamang woman, whose face had a thousand wrinkles from years of mountain weather and high altitude UV rays, came my way with a small girl. They were walking up from terrace to terrace through the millet fields. The older woman had a crescent-shaped cutting tool for the harvest in her hand, and greeted me in their characteristic banter, "Hello son, have you eaten?" I replied, "Hello grandmother, yes I have eaten. And you? Have you eaten? How are you?" Then she asked me what I was doing. I explained that I was praying, which she understood, and that I was reading the story of Isa (this is the Tamang name for Jesus). She did not know who he is or anything about him. I told her about Isa, but she could not understand Nepali very well. As we concluded our conversation, the Holy Spirit touched me. It felt like I had been struck with a pleasant lightning bolt. The Lord spoke these words in my spirit, "These people are the people I want you to work with, and this is the place of "fields white unto harvest" that I want you to labor in. I am sending you to the Tamang people."

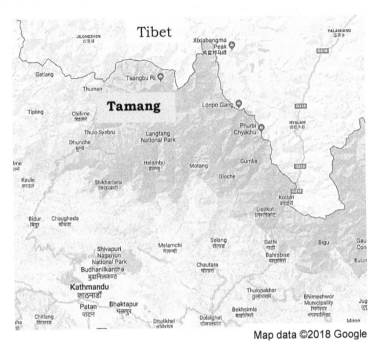

Figure 2
Location of the Tamang People

When our group reunited that evening, we walked to another village and joined a large group of Tamang Christians. We sang and prayed with them. We shared our testimonies with them, and they with us. The following day we went much further north to a small village. We were informed that the people with whom we were to meet hadn't arrived yet. I wandered up the trail a bit and encountered a large group coming our way. After the usual greeting, I asked where they were coming from and where they were headed. They answered that they had arisen before dawn and begun walking from their homes (while the leader pointed with his lower lip as is their custom) to the village on the next ridge above and beyond us, and that they were headed to exactly here. So this was the group we were expecting. We followed their established pattern of worship (or liturgy) of singing and praying; then they asked me to preach. In Nepal, a short sermon is fifteen-to-thirty minutes, but a proper sermon is one-to-two hours. They had come a long way and expected a good full sermon. I think I preached for about two hours, and nobody was mad at me. Instead, I was well received. What a great time we had together!

I devoted the next twelve years to working among the Tamang. I worked to draw other people to Nepal, who would live among the Tamang, Western and Eastern. I encouraged the work of Wycliffe Bible Translators, facilitated the translation of the *Jesus Film* into Tamang, encouraged evangelistic teams to be among them, helped village leaders get young people to write Christian hymns in the Tamang language instead of Nepali, in which virtually all Christian songs in Nepal had been written. I encouraged development projects and was executive director of a project that supported adult literacy classes in thirty remote mountain villages in Dhading and the district east of it. The goal was to teach Tamang people to be literate in their mother tongue so that they could read their Bibles in their mother tongue, and not have to read it in Nepali, which for them is a second language.

Over the next years, many people got involved, and there was a huge turning to faith in Jesus Christ in villages all over Dhading and the surrounding districts. Around 2010, I read that Dhading had become the only district in Nepal that was majority Christian.

FIRST CONTACT WITH REV. TAD DE BORDENAVE

In our first years of mission, we lived in western Nepal. In that region, the Karnali River flows from the snowmelt of the high Himalayas down through the lower mountains and hills, and onward to the plains of India. Just south of one dramatic turn of the river, there lies an area of Nepal called Kunathari. Beth and I lived in this area from 1988 to 1993 during our first two terms of service as missionaries to Nepal. We lived in the small village of Baddichaur during the first term and in the town of Surket during the second term, where we served in a community development project of the United Mission to Nepal.

Our home was on the second and third floors of a stone and dried mud-walled house with a thatched roof and dried mud floors. In those years, Baddichaur had no electricity, running water, telephones, doctors, medical supplies, or paved roads. The homes could not be cooled by fans in the hot season and were not heated except for the kitchen fires in the winter. It could be reached only by foot on a trail that was about eighteen miles to the nearest town from which we could take a bus to other destinations (on many miles of dirt roads), or take a plane. Even so, the flights were once a week, except during the monsoon season, and the airport had a grass landing strip.

At some point in 1989 or so, while we were living in Baddichaur, we received a letter that had been delivered by our mail courier from Kathmandu (considerably more secure, reliable, and speedy than the governmental mail). It came from Rev. Tad de Bordenave, the rector (priest) of St. Matthew's Episcopal Church in Richmond, Virginia. As I sat under the thatch roof of our home, I read with avid curiosity. He had written to Beth and me asking about the work we were doing in Nepal. He wrote that he and his wife Constance had been following our work in Nepal through our newsletters. They were learning about Unreached People Groups (UPGs) through a course that they were taking, and wanted us to share with them more about what we had been observing and learning.

It wasn't every day that we got mail of any kind, but it was even more unusual to get such an inquiry. We were excited and encouraged by their interest in UPGs and our work. We were then living among the Magar tribal group of central and western Nepal and had not yet gotten involved with the Tamang people. As far as we knew, not one of them anywhere in our district had become Christian. Tad was asking what were we doing to reach UPGs and how he and his wife could get involved in some way. They were seeking to become more involved, not just in support of us but in other ways as well. I wasn't sure what he meant, but I added them to our prayer list.

Later, both Tad and Constance came to Nepal, and we went on several treks together, up into the mountains and into some of the Tamang areas. We got to know each other well and were quite happy to learn later that they would be starting Anglican Frontier Missions, which was the major "other way" of involvement that Tad had earlier predicted. We joined in 1994. Through the subsequent friendship we have enjoyed with Tad and Constance, all four of us have benefitted. The de Bordenaves, through visits with us, grew in their knowledge and love for the unreached of Nepal. Beth and I took our experience and passion to the agency Tad founded, Anglican Frontier Missions. Having Tad and Constance as fellow travelers has been a rich joy through many years. It was a great privilege and honor to serve the Lord in Nepal as a member of Anglican Frontier Missions. Even more important, it was great to have a director who really cared about pastoral care and the focus on UPGs. Tad was a wonderful pastor to us and kept our conversations on point. He always kept us up-to-date on the research end of things; he encouraged us to be on the cutting edge with regard to learning the complex and extremely diverse matters involved in becoming strategy coordinators for the reaching of a UPG.

THE INTERSECTION OF THE CONVERSION TO CHRIST OF THE TAMANG PEOPLE AND THE ANGLICAN CHURCH IN NEPAL

This brings us back to the story of the Anglican Church in Nepal (ACN) and how the Tamang people and their mountain churches of Dhading became Anglican as well. This is important to notice: Significant numbers of a UPG became Anglicans.

One of the pastors who had expressed an interest in the Anglican church in 1996, was with me on that eventful first trek up to Dhading. We had become good friends. Indeed, once he saved me from falling over a sheer cliff face when I lost my balance on a narrow mountain trail after dusk.

Over the period from 1996 to 1999, as I traveled throughout Dhading in the higher villages, two groups of Tamang churches emerged that were interested in an Anglican identity. The first group was with the leader from the first trek, and the second group was from another group of churches in villages higher in the mountains. In May 1999, when the Synod of the Diocese of Singapore voted to have us come into the diocese, these two groups were part of the larger group, and in fact were the majority.

At that time, there were approximately forty-five member churches:

- Three in the mountains east of Kathmandu;

- Three in Kathmandu;

- The remainder in the mountains west of Kathmandu *and every one of those was Tamang.*

We began church planting efforts, which resulted in four new churches over the next few years. Other independent churches wanted to join, but we put that on hold to properly evaluate their motivation. We wanted to make sure that their motivation was not about money or other inappropriate purposes. We also wanted to be sure that this new church body did not "overheat" in an expansion that was too rapid to be properly led and administrated, or shallow in the level of individual discipleship. We reached out to other Nepalese churches and denominations in fellowship and goodwill, requesting their prayers and inviting some key leaders to be part of our leadership training program. The ACN leaders continued to work with many Nepalese pastors, and we became well known in the emerging Christian community in Nepal, including the National Church Fellowship–Nepal, the Agape Group, the Nepal Christian Society, the Assemblies of God, and the Baptists. We are thankful that we have had good relationships with these other church groups in Nepal and that their leaders have been encouraging and cordial. We also met with the UK Asia director of the Church Mission Society, seeking to build bridges. Finally, we established a strong relationship with the United Mission to Nepal and its executive director, as well as with the Roman Catholic Jesuit community, among whom are many friends. One of the Jesuits was my close friend, who also worked among the Tamang people.

A state of emergency was declared by His Majesty's Government of Nepal in November 2001 and continued until the Peace Accord of 2006. The emergency was declared because of the Maoist insurgency and its increasing violence, which made public meetings and travel of large groups both illegal and dangerous. Some of the pastors in the ACN were arrested. All were later released, though one mountain village pastor was so badly beaten that he could no longer do his farm work. (He was a bi-vocational pastor/farmer, as are most pastors in the mountains.)

Through the years, I often brought in those who could teach, coach, and train the growing cadre of pastors of these new Anglican churches. Many came through the auspices of

SOMA (Sharing of Ministries Abroad, a ministry of the global Anglican Communion), and traveled from their homes in Australia, New Zealand, the UK and the USA. Now mind you, I wanted to carefully avoid introducing any person, cultural input, tradition, or anything else that would subvert the Christian faith among the Tamangs. The people of other tribal groups (approximately 43% of Nepal) and the caste-based Nepalese people (approx. 57% of Nepal) of the other mountain areas, the lower valleys, and the smaller towns were, for the most part, out of touch with the modern world of the West.

This was in contrast to the experience of the people in larger towns and cities, who had exposure to TV, movies, music, and other outside influences that collided with traditional Nepalese culture; Western practices were familiar to most of the city people, especially the young. The Tamangs, however, had virtually no exposure to these alien cultural forces. I was reluctant to take groups of Westerners among them because unintended consequences of cross cultural miscommunication could cause untold damage to their understanding of the gospel, morals, use of money, and expectations of wealthy foreigners who may give them funds or goods. As a result, I thought and prayed long and hard about introducing the Tamangs to a foreign and outside influence in the form of Anglican worship, liturgy, polity and ethos. Then it hit me: These people love ritual, ceremony, tradition, liturgical forms. Anglicanism is perfect for them!

A specific example of this occurred during my trip to Jameswor. I traveled there in 1997 with Pemba, with whom I first traveled to Dhading in 1990. He wanted me to visit the Tamang community of Jameswor with him, and we arrived about midday. We found a place to stay, had something to eat, and then began to prepare for an afternoon and evening of teaching sessions.

By this time I was fairly fluent in Nepali but had just begun to learn Eastern Tamang. There were significant language differences between eastern Tamang and western Tamang. While there are many cognates for nouns, verbs are very different, and the two groups have difficulty understanding each other. This meant I had to resort to the language we all had in common—Nepali.

I was teaching on the meaning of Holy Eucharist. I had been praying and studying about this for some months and felt like it was an area of Christian practice that was little understood by most Christians in Nepal. After teaching for about an hour and half, a political leader of the community, who was also a church member, stood up and began to speak. He said, "None of us have ever heard of this or seen this. Yet we see that it is from the Holy Bible and that Jesus told us to do this. This thing that you have spoken about we will do now." It was obvious that he was a person accustomed to having people listen to and follow what he said. I responded that it would take some time to gather the elements necessary for the service and to prepare. I asked him if it would be all right to have the service in the morning. He agreed. That evening we gathered the elements. For bread, we used roti (flatbread). However, there was no wine, and the only liquid that we could get was a kind of juice from a local berry. This was a step up, in my opinion; in other circumstances, the only thing anyone could find other than water, tea or liquor—all of which were unacceptable—was Orange Crush, a carbonated soda drink.

The following morning at seven o'clock, we gathered again in the simple church building and began to sing Nepali hymns and pray. I lead the Holy Eucharist from the *Book of Common Prayer*, translating on the fly from English to Nepali. When it came time for the people to come forward to receive the body and blood of Christ, there was a profound sense of reverence and holy quietness. This was the first time any of these people had come forward and received Communion. After they had all finished and returned to their seats— the men on one side, the women on the other—they began to sing. The volume grew, and it was beautiful. The volume became very loud. I thought perhaps the roof might even lift off. People were raising their hands high above their heads and blissful, heavenly expressions were on their faces as the music came to a crescendo and then stopped.

Several asked if they could do this again. I told them they could, and then realized that I had misunderstood. They wanted to do it for a second time, right then and there. I explained that once was good and appropriate, but that they could have Communion every week when they gathered on Saturday. (In Nepal, church is held on Saturday as it is a day of rest; Sunday is a workday.) It struck me: They had never experienced Holy Eucharist or even heard of it, yet when they had their first Communion, using a liturgical form, they loved it. My conclusion was that it is true: Ritual and ceremony are very important to the Tamang people. Over the following years, I wrestled with how all of this could work. Now, many years later, I can look back and summarize.

God put it on our hearts to go to Nepal, seek out a UPG, begin to learn about them, and work among them. The Lord gave us ways to form a strategy to reach the Tamang people, together with a number of other people whose goals were similar. Those Tamangs who already had faith and the ones who joined them in new-found faith needed to be gathered in churches, and this happened. Once the unreached are reached, then a set of very important questions arise: How will the churches be led and governed? How will their leaders be trained and ordained? How will they worship and express themselves regarding the sacraments, baptism and communion, which Jesus taught? How will they evangelize their own people group and beyond? How will they plant new churches in their own people group and beyond?

The answer was right there, hidden in plain sight, right in front of us and among us. We were Anglican then, as now. While we will never claim that the Anglican form of faith and order is the only way, it is certainly a very good way. In this situation of tribal sensibilities and cultural currents, the Tamangs were joined together in Anglican polity, worship forms, and traditions; this did indeed seem to be a custom made solution for these people and a very good answer to all of the above questions. As of this writing in 2017, there are over one hundred churches in the Anglican Church in Nepal, and their vision and growth trajectory is to keep on growing. Thanks be to God!

The Beale Family

5

STRATEGY COORDINATION
A CASE STUDY

by Andrew and Phoebe Johnson

GOD'S CALL

"And I heard the voice of the Lord saying, 'Whom shall I send, and who will go for us?' Then I said, 'Here I am! Send me.'" For years, I (Phoebe) cried out to God with this prayer from Isaiah 6:8. I had served on the support team for a family from our church that went to Africa for four years. I visited them on the field and kept uttering that prayer but clearly felt that I was not called to Africa. I kept praying Isaiah 6:8 for another four years until the call became distinctively clear at a mission conference. The missionary family to Africa had been at the New Wineskins conference in April of that year and came back with a message to share with our church:

Phoebe had thirty years as a business owner prior to becoming a strategy coordinator for an unreached people group in the 10/40 Window. Andrew was snatched by God out of his own thirty-year business career into a whole new adventure serving God on the mission field with Phoebe. While others were retiring, Andrew and Phoebe (their names have been changed for security reasons) testify that God had a better idea. Phoebe moved from managing an art gallery to taking her skill set as a strategy coordinator for a group in Asia. Andrew served on her support team, taking it very seriously by marrying her. Together, they have lived in a city in Asia as the first Christians and planted the city's first church.

"Catch the Wave!" They shared a vision of God's work among the nations and how it was like a wave rolling forth to engage the unreached peoples of the world. I could no longer sit back but had to jump in with both feet!

Little did I know how God would take me, an inexperienced single woman in my early fifties, and use me in ways that I could never have imagined. "Now to him who is able to do immeasurably more that all we ask or imagine, according to his power that is at work within us, to him be the glory in the Church and in Christ Jesus throughout all generations, for ever and ever! Amen" (Ephesians 3:20-21, New International Version). Looking back over twenty years since that call in 1997, God has indeed done more than I could ever have asked or imagined—both in my life, but more importantly, in the lives of the Marloo people, an Unreached People Group (UPG) numbering over one million, living in a remote part of a creative access country.[1]

So what is a single, middle aged lady supposed to do to impact a tribal people who have never had access to the good news of our Lord Jesus Christ? The first step was to join a sending agency and, as an Episcopalian, I reached out to a very young organization, Anglican Frontier Missions. I thank God that Tad de Bordenave, the founding director, had faith in God that he could use an older single lady to go where no one else had gone before. AFM took me on, nurtured and encouraged me, and provided the initial training to get me started. It was there that I learned what it means to be a strategy coordinator: research, advocacy, mobilization, people group profile, mission resources, church planting methodology, and a master plan for reaching my specific

---

[1] A creative access country is one that does not grant visas to foreign missionaries, and where in-country church activities are greatly restricted. https://home.snu.edu/~hculbert/access.htm.

group, the Marloo. It was a stimulating four weeks of training. And then AFM set me loose! Looking back, I can see that they were really trusting God and not what I could do on my own.

So what could I do? I started by researching this UPG and getting people to pray for them, and for me, and for more workers for the harvest. Then I made an exploratory trip to meet the Marloo. Amazingly, in just one week of being around the Marloo people, I fell in love with them and did not want to leave! It was a God thing, right from the start. But, aha! You guessed it: The people there surely wondered what a Caucasian middle aged lady was doing in their midst. Who was I to be among this UPG? Surely not a "missionary" in this country that would not welcome missionaries. So, who was I? Thanks be to God, I had been an entrepreneurial small (very small) business woman in my pre-missionary days. So I put on my business hat and told them that I was interested in bringing tourists to this beautiful place, and they loved it! Yes, and indeed I was planning on bringing tourists there, tourists who would come with me and pray over this people and land—prayer walkers.

The prayer walking tourism business morphed into buying cute little handcrafted products from a local shop and selling them in the U.S. But here was another God thing. The owner of this little shop was married to a Marloo woman and turned out to be God's "person of peace." This couple, Mr. and Mrs. Yoo, became close friends and believers, and became instrumental for so much of what God was calling us to.

Yes, that pronoun "us" is another amazing God thing! As a single woman, I stepped out in faith and God began to bring many people into my path to help bring about his kingdom purposes. The following year, after I had found these cute little crafts, God brought a husband into my life—a man I had known for years in my home church. Andrew was a

leader in our church and very talented, and one year earlier
he had agreed to be a part of my home support team. He
became my best supporter, my best friend, my husband, and
later a full partner in the mission work to the Marloo people.

God has his ways of accomplishing his kingdom
purposes, and marrying Andrew meant that I had to leave
the field in the land of the Marloo and return to the U.S. for
a season. This season turned into five years, during which
time God called Andrew into full time work in the mission
field and allowed us to develop the marketing arm for the
handcrafts. During this time, Andrew's youngest child
graduated from high school, Andrew's mother went to her
heavenly reward, and it became clear that our time to
relocate to the land of the Marloo was upon us. It was an
important season during which God was preparing us and
others for his kingdom purposes.

AS ANDREW DESCRIBES HIS CALL

For me it was a series of sudden, unexpected events and
relationships that, in retrospect, had profound, even eternal
significance. In a life devoid of God, God brought one
Christian after another to witness God's love to me in word
and deed: a coworker in Wichita, a housemate in Louisville,
a couple in Pittsburgh. The ground was being prepared over
years, but the realization of God's existence and love was, for
me, both instantaneous and undeniable. But that God also
had a purpose for my life as well, which took a few more years
to be revealed.

Both Phoebe and I had led full, separate lives before God
brought us together for a whole new season. Phoebe
experienced the call to an unreached people group, the
Marloo people, as a single woman in her fifties. She
researched this group thoroughly and, because of AFM's
relationship with a much larger, well established mission

agency, she was able to receive training in the Strategy Coordination approach to bring Christ to a UPG. Though Phoebe had prepared a detailed master plan, the bottom line was "Do whatever it takes." The question to be asked each step of the way was not, "What can I do?" but instead, "What's it going to take?" Phoebe was ready. She was preparing to move among the Marloo people. But God had a better idea!

My ancestors lived many years in the same country where the Marloo live, ministering Christ's love to a different people group. But I knew very little of this heritage. Phoebe thinks that when my ancestors were forced out by the government, they certainly would have asked God to send a descendant back when the time was ripe. Maybe Phoebe was God's provision for answering this prayer. (Phoebe likes to say she was a pawn in God's hands to get this missionary descendant over to the country of the Marloo!)

For a time, I continued with my professional career, while accompanying Phoebe once or twice a year to the land of the Marloo, registering the business, setting up the business systems, building relationships with the people, doing some language learning, and so forth. Two years later, my employer mysteriously withdrew an employment agreement that allowed foreign travel. My initial anger and confusion quickly turned into excitement as I realized that this was another of those unexpected events in my life through which God speaks to me—if I will listen. He was saying, "It is time. Dive headlong into my lap. I will catch you!" That was when He called me to leave my thirty-year career and the comfort of regular paychecks and move with Phoebe into the land of the Marloo.

GOD'S PROVISION

James Hudson Taylor wrote, "God's work done in God's way will never lack God's supply." This has been our experience, but it is worked out by the sweat of our brow. Right from the beginning, God brought people into our lives who were willing to invest, first in Phoebe, and then in Phoebe and Andrew, with prayer coverage, with financial support, with advice, with godly correction, and with personal connections.

Yet God has been wise enough to keep us on a short leash! Here is an excerpt from our report in March 2005:

> "We are not yet to our last bowl of rice." This was a line in a video we watched about Hudson Taylor. In a scene where he and his first wife are down to their last bowl of rice, in walks someone with some letters that contain some much-needed contributions. Our finances have been very tight and we are in a mode of trusting him who is faithful. We sense that God has us on a very tight leash right now and that He is training us both in trusting him more and in reordering our financial priorities that we might live even more simply. So when times are tough and we are spending only fifty dollars a week at the supermarket rather than one hundred dollars, we remind ourselves that we are not down to our last bowl of rice; we also have a warm home to live in, good health insurance, and more calories available to us than we actually need.

There is something about reading the life of Hudson Taylor, and the approach that the China Inland Mission took, that challenges many of us to move into a place of faith in God's provision. We prayerfully tell God that all we have is his and he can use it however he wants to, and then we wonder if he will want us to use all that we have in savings and retirement funds now. "God's work done in God's way will never lack God's provision" (James Hudson Taylor). It's a big challenge for us, but we keep sensing that God has big stuff for us over the next ten years or so, and he is preparing us to trust in him alone and to hold fast to his faithfulness.

GOD'S STRATEGY

It is always instructive, humbling actually, to review our initial and then updated master plans and compare them with what actually happened. God's strategy is not what we had anticipated and neither is his timetable.

The number one strategy we have witnessed is how God uses *relationships* to advance his work (see the next section, "God's Personnel"). The development of relationships, especially in a culture where relationships are the most important dynamic, has been key and has taken much longer than we anticipated—many years, in fact. It is through relationships that we develop trust, share contacts, reveal weaknesses (on both sides), and unearth needs.

A second, equally important strategy needed in a Creative Access Country is the Business as Mission Approach (BAM). We did not start out with this strategy. As noted earlier, Phoebe, with her entrepreneur background, began the BAM approach, first proposing that she help develop tourism (a *very* big felt need in that country). It was actually a means for bringing in prayer-walking teams. Following that, she began buying local handcrafts for export. When Andrew joined the team with his business background, it was a logical extension, based on available resources and skills, to begin a production model, which has served us well for almost fifteen years.

An exciting, unexpected dynamic we have discovered is that while the *business* is facilitating the mission, the *mission work* is also helping the *business*. As we produce and sell products made by the Marloo people, customers around the world are learning of the Marloo people and praying for them. Our factory became the center for the first translation project, which led to the start up of another BAM. And recently, we had the opportunity to buy another business in our local area, which is now attracting new missionaries to join in the work to reach the Marloo people. The synergy between business and mission is palpable!

A few examples: We had a focus on this UPG and approached it with the attitude of "Do whatever it takes." Later, as we learned from seminary courses and mission conferences, it morphed into the question: "What's it gonna take?" For us, it was to live and work with this UPG as business people. For us, that meant investing in a house and starting a small business that would employ the Marloo people. For us, that meant actually living and working among the Marloo people. As we began this factory, it gave us the opportunity to bring in Fiona, an Asian-American, to work on a Bible storying project that resulted in one of our Marloo employees, Mikki, coming to Christ and translating Bible stories into her native Marloo language. The business was helping the mission.

After a few more years, this translation team decided to start a small business in Mikki's village. Thus the business not only helped the mission goals (to get God's Word into the Marloo language) but it spawned a new business that would further the mission and translation goals. The business helps the mission, and the mission, in turn, helps the business. This concept is somewhat different from a traditional model of just doing business so you can do the mission.

This has been a God thing because we did not plan it this way. We were following the "Whatever it takes" model. The mission and the business have always been intertwined and codependent. Perhaps it is because the long-term focus is on a UPG, and reaching them is what drives whatever else we do. It has taken a lot of sacrifice on our part running a handcrafts business and also on the part of the team running the village business. We keep working day and night on the business *and* the mission, but the sacrifices are worth it because formerly unreached peoples are coming to faith and being discipled with God's Word in their heart language.

We should add that our work among the Marloo was never a smooth process or a foregone conclusion. Thanks to the faithful members of our Barnabas team,[2] our many cries of, "Is it worth it! Should we try another approach? Is it time for us to come home?" have been met with words of encouragement or challenge, prayer and discernment, and sometimes with financial support.

To summarize our BAM strategy: Our experience is that our businesses are vehicles through which our Christian life is lived out. They provide the relationships in which evangelizing, discipling, teaching, training, modeling, and ministering can happen—in a natural, Spirit led manner. There is nothing special about the business. It can really be anything. It is life, though, and it must be authentic. It is also helpful if it addresses a locally "felt need." If it is not an authentic business, any message shared is suspect. If it addresses needs but not "felt needs," it is seen as foreign.

A third strategy we have witnessed, and benefited from, is *Inter-agency Affiliations*. We have so much to learn and there are so many organizations, sending agencies, training groups, churches and other lay people and missionaries who have struggled, failed, picked themselves up, persevered, and overcome. On the field, we work with *Great Commission Christians*, defined as anyone striving to carry out the Great Commission (Matthew 28:16-20). This non-denominational approach helps insulate us from many thorny theological

---

[2] AFM creates a Barnabas Team comprised of eight-to-twelve people from their home church as they prepare to launch to the field. The Barnabas team provides a strong support network that encourages, advises, and serves as accountability partners in missionaries' pre-field, on field, and post-field service with AFM.

conflicts, like those we have witnessed in America, while becoming a powerful witness to the unity (but not uniformity) of the global Body of Christ.

GOD'S PERSONNEL

From the time when God doubled the missionary workforce through our marriage, we have witnessed how God loves to focus on personal relationships to advance his kingdom.

When Phoebe was first training for the field work, she was in a class with many experienced clergy, lay leaders, and missionaries. Though she felt quite out of place, the instructors said: "We find that we are able to work better *with those who are willing* but not able than with those who are able but not willing." She immediately realized that God was looking only for her willingness, for he would supply the skills needed at the right time. And that has been our guideline for addressing personnel needs. Skills are important, but "...the Lord sees not as man sees: man looks on the outward appearance, but the Lord looks on the heart" (1 Samuel 16:7).

God has sent us such a variety of people. First, I think of the couple mentioned earlier, Mr. and Mrs. Yoo; she's Marloo, he's not. They are good examples of *persons of peace*. God sent them into our lives to help us learn the culture, to become established, to help us buy a house, and to introduce us to *persons of goodwill*. They consider us family. We have been through births, weddings, deaths, baptisms and funerals with them. What a joy they are. "Jesus said, 'Truly, I say to you, there is no one who has left house or brothers or sisters or mother or father or children or lands, for my sake and for the gospel, who will not receive a hundredfold now in this time, houses and brothers and sisters and mothers and children and lands, with persecutions, and in the age to come eternal life' " (Mark 10:29-30). This has been our experience.

I think of Wendy, an *overseas partner for a season* with a business degree and a knowledge of the trade language of the Marloo. She helped set up our production processes, negotiate property rental contracts ("I actually only understood about 30% of their local dialect," she later confessed!), and helped oversee the production during those first few crucial months.

I think of Wachu, a *national partner for a season*, who was a native to that country. He took over management of the company when a sudden departure left us without a manager while we were back in America. He oversaw the office move, the accounting, and the transition to a permanent manager.

In 2000, when Phoebe was first praying for "workers for the harvest," God was revealing himself through the *Jesus Film* to a twelve-year-old named Philemon, a village youth who spoke the trade language of the country. Unbeknownst to us or him, Philemon was destined to become a crucial part of our translation work fifteen years later. It took another nine years before God brought Philemon into our town, and he crossed paths with Andrew. Following some teaching, discipling, and sharing of lives and language, Philemon came to Christ and made a ten-year commitment with God to put the *Jesus Film* into a new language—the Marloo language! God had brought us an *unexpected, long-term worker!*

Speaking of *long-term workers*, we cannot forget to again mention Fiona, a woman from another country whom God called out of an urban career to a rural farm life running her own BAM. Her perseverance in the midst of significant spiritual warfare demonstrated to many of the Marloo people the power of our God over the animistic spirits they were worshipping.

Finally, I need to mention Mikki, the *mother tongue translator* who, with her sister, has done most of the Bible translation work so far. Fiona brought Mikki to Christ and trained her in translation. Philemon is working with her on the *Jesus Film* translation. A Marloo *long-term worker*, Mikki is giving her life to reaching her own people. She has been tested to the limit. She has seen God's faithfulness and has stayed the course.

There is not enough space to discuss all the help from *unbelievers*: Greg, the local "friendly spy" who protected us from the police and warned us to "do real business"; Marcus, the local policeman in charge of the foreigners, who has helped us innumerable times while putting up with our attempts to witness to him; Whelan, the government official who assured us "That will never happen!" when we shared that the finance officials threatened to close our business if it did not make money. God is sovereign and can use all of creation for his purposes.

GOD'S ENCOURAGEMENT

"God has opened a door that no one can shut!" This was the message we heard in 2012 at a church in Virginia while visiting with Tad. The pastor was bold, dynamic, and repetitive with this Scripture from Revelation 3:8 as he ministered to his congregation. But at the same time, God was using this Scripture to teach us something about how He was working among the Marloo people. Six years after we had ventured forth to live among the Marloo people, we could now see how the mission among this UPG had taken on a life of its own, driven by God. Over the years, He had called both short-term and long-term workers to reach the Marloo, including those who spoke the trade language and the mother tongue. We started our work among the Marloo praying, "Here am I, Lord. Send me [us]." Now we could step back and see that it all really began with God saying in Isaiah 65:1, "I was ready to be sought by those who did not ask for me; I was ready to be found by those who did not seek me. I said, 'Here I am, here I am,' to a nation that was not called by my name."

God's heart is for the nations. In Matthew 24:14 Jesus proclaims, "And this gospel of the kingdom will be proclaimed throughout the whole world as a testimony to all nations, and then the end will come."

We began to see more clearly that this was, indeed, God's work and God's will. It was God who called us, who called Fiona and Mikki and Philemon, and many others who served with us for weeks, months, or years. What we felt called to initiate (reaching this UPG), God was clearly making sure it was happening and would continue to happen. We were in our fifties when we were called, and now we are in our seventies. Thanks be to God that he is calling a younger generation to reach the Marloo. Much work has been done and there is much work yet to do in order to reach over one million Marloo. But it is happening and, with God's help, it will continue to happen for this nation of the Marloo. We are willing (but less able) to continue our work with this UPG, whether it is in the land of the Marloo or back in America, and we are ready to pass this mission on to a younger generation.

We were willing and we were able to go. God has called and continues to call others to reach this UPG. God's kingdom will come all among the nations. The greatest privilege of our lives has been to be part of his work.

6

SHEPHERDS OF THE SHEPHERDS

by Pete and Shirleen Wait

In the year 2000, Anglican Frontier Missions called Pete and Shirleen Wait to be shepherds to our cross cultural workers, caring for those who went searching for lost sheep. Pete and Shirleen bring a passion for mission, a channel for God's healing, and a desire to serve those who serve the Lord. Their means of transportation range from Pete's Harley motorcycle, to various ocean liners and most of the world's airlines. Along the way they earned enough miles for a month's stay on the International Space Station! What follows is based on excerpts from their newsletters, recounting their travels and reflecting on the lives of the missionaries they love and serve. True to Isaiah, they have walked, flown, and climbed, but renewed by the Spirit, have not grown faint or weary.

The Reverend Canon B. W. Pete Wait III, D. Min. and Shirleen Wait, PhD have served the body of Christ in several capacities. Pete, a cradle Episcopalian, had a dual career in the electric power industry and the church. He served as Canon for Evangelism (local and global) for the Diocese of Florida when he volunteered his services to AFM. He earned a Doctor of Ministry, project entitled, "Developing a World Missions Focus." Shirleen has more than sixty years of experience fixing every non-mechanical thing from boo-boos to broken hearts. She has spent many years in teaching and earned her PhD in reading education. She is the author of two reading textbooks.

THE CALL TO SERVE THOSE WHO GO

"How can two retired people in their mid-sixties spend the balance of their active lives in service for the advancement of the kingdom of God? What's the most important thing we could do with the time, energy, and resources we have left for the rest of our lives to make the largest impact on the world from God's perspective?" These were the questions we asked each other one afternoon after coordinating the course, "Perspectives on the World Christian Movement." We were sitting in Pete's home office and reflecting on the 'World Christians' we so admired and the impact they made on Christ's Great Commission and his charge to his followers. We felt we had to be involved in some way in frontier missions. Pete said, "I know what I'm going to do: Call Tad de Bordenave and see what we might do with AFM!"

We began our role with AFM by attending two intensive conferences on missionaries' mental health and becoming effective pastors to missionaries. We participated regularly thereafter and continued to grow in our understanding of spiritual warfare and healing (spiritual, emotional, and physical).[1]

PRAYER, GOD'S PROVISION, AND THE BEGINNING OF MISSIONARY VISITS

Our initial charge was to visit missionaries in the field every other year, and minister to them in alternating years at scheduled overseas retreats in various locations. As of this writing, we have made some seventeen international pastoral trips—with another one planned in 2018—usually visiting multiple families in multiple locations.

---

[1] Both Pete and Shirleen are trained members of the Order of St. Luke the Physician, and Pete is a Chaplain.

We sent our first prayer and financial support letter in August 2001 to raise funds for travel from September 15 to October 13 to visit AFM missionary families in East Asia. We got our passports in order and arranged for our shots and visas. We returned from our first visit to the travel medicine office, having just paid $1,000 and wondering what we had gotten ourselves into. We thought, "God, help! We have no idea how much more it will cost before we can even begin the trip!" But in the mail delivered that afternoon, there was an envelope with a return address from somewhere in Alabama and a name we did not recognize. Inside was a check for $1,000 and a note pledging prayer support for the trip. We never looked back, knowing God would meet every need.

We embarked for East Asia for a month-long mission trip on September 15, 2001, on the first airplane departing from Jacksonville after the 9/11 attack. As it turned out, many of the Asians we visited interpreted our immediate departure after such a horrible event as an indication of the authentic spiritual burden we bore for them—which we did and still do! After arriving in East Asia, God gave us the privilege to fellowship, minister, and teach for two weeks in many underground church congregations and among unreached people groups.

BUSINESS AS MISSION[2] IN EAST ASIA

After more time on the road (airplanes and terminals) than we want to remember, we arrived at about 8:00 p.m. one night in a new area with a new unreached people group. Here, some of our missionaries ran a factory for the benefit of the people they ministered to. In missiological terminology, it is called a Business as Mission (BAM), and

---

[2] Business as Mission is a strategy missionaries employ to obtain residency in countries that do not issue religious workers visas. Other strategies include English teaching, relief and development, and university studies.

their BAM happens to be located at the top of 104 steps from the street below it. Sometimes, hard physical work is required to visit our AFM missionaries! In fact, most of our missionaries live several stories above ground in buildings without elevators.

At this missionary's house, we observed the marvelous handwork made by indigenous women. Our missionaries had established a business enterprise that employed skilled artisans in the indigenous handwork. Their process is intricate, using local resources and raw materials to create amazingly beautiful handcrafts. In their off hours, the indigenous factory workers act as evangelists, Bible teachers, and role models. Thus, the business provides a beachhead from which the good news of Jesus is spread to these beautiful people, whose animistic beliefs lead to a life of fear and hopelessness.

We worshipped and prayed with our missionaries and factory staff on numerous occasions throughout our visit. One evening we had a "dinner party" with the factory workers, who did much of the preparation and invited a few friends. Two of the friends had come to faith the previous week. This time they brought another friend who wanted to know more about Jesus, too. One factory worker outlined the gospel to her and we all prayed and watched as she placed her life in Jesus' hands.

AFRICA

"If the vehicle stalls out in front of the president's compound, jump out and run for safety!" This was the warning our missionary gave us as we drove along the street on which the president and his family lived. It was heavily guarded and only those vehicles on official business with the president were allowed to stop anywhere near the gate. The guards considered any stopped, unofficial vehicle a potential threat. They were likely to shoot first and ask questions later.

Our missionary took the civil unrest and primitive living conditions in stride, as she lived in a small town of mud-walled buildings and unpaved streets about two-to-three hours southeast of the capital city. In addition, the town had no electricity, running water, sewer, streetlights, or paved roads. During the rainy season, many of the roads were simply impassable for motorized vehicles. We visited our missionary during the most hospitable season, and most of the roads were dried out—in horrible shape but dry! She had a guard, who spent the nights in her compound in a separate mud building. During the daytime, the guard worked as a building contractor, and he also had a family living in a different compound from that of our missionary. We slept on the porch under mosquito netting. At bedtime, we could feel the perspiration rolling down our sides and arms; however, from 3:00 to 6:00 a.m., a sheet or light blanket was necessary.

THE MIDDLE EAST

This Travel Warning is being issued to inform American citizens that the Department of State has lifted the ordered departure status of non-emergency American employees and adult family members of all employees at the U.S. Embassy in this Middle Eastern Country. The Department recommends that American citizens defer non-essential travel to this country. American citizens remaining in this country despite this warning should monitor the U.S Embassy website and should make contingency emergency plans if necessary. This supersedes the Travel Warning issued April 7, 2008.

This may not sound much like good news, but any easing of travel warnings was good news to us, especially in light of a recent bombing of the U.S. Embassy there. Our missionary was safe, but we were sure the travel warnings soon would be heightened again.

Our missionary met us at the airport around midnight and escorted us to a marvelous hotel in the old city near his home. The hotel, converted from a private residence some years earlier, was a four-or-five-story building with a 30' x 30' cross section. We occupied a three-room suite on the third floor and were not allowed to go higher due to a "THE ROOF CLOSED FOR FIX WORKS" sign posted in the stairwell. The stairwell was in the center of the building and very challenging to climb due to irregularities, especially stair height (many risers being 18-20") and low ceiling clearances. Moreover, many of the doors were no more than about five feet high with a threshold 6-8" high—real noggin bonkers!

Our suite had one of those all-purpose bath/ laundry/washbasin/toilet (western & squat) rooms and a window (with no curtain)! The middle room had a sofa at floor level, and the bedroom had twin beds and four windows. Our missionary introduced us to many of his friends, and we celebrated Communion[3] with him on Sunday morning before he left for his language class. (Sunday is a working day in Islamic countries.)

In addition to pastoral ministry, we always sought ways to help our people with their ministry, as we were able. To that end, we visited a special family who had invited us to dinner (beans and bread plus the soda we brought). The three of us, the host, and several of his male kin sat on blankets in one room while the host's wife (who never entered the room) made dinner. Shirleen was invited to visit the

---

[3] We always incorporate the culture-specific oppressions into the more generic list in the Eucharistic Liturgy for the Healing of Nations. See Benjamin W. Wait III, "Developing A World Missions Focus" (Doctor of Ministry, School of Theology, University of the South, 2006), 125-173.

kitchen where she laid hands on the wife and prayed that she would conceive and bear a son.

While in the kitchen, the host inadvertently drank from Shirleen's cup. Later in the living/dining room, he explained that no Arab would ever share a cup with anyone except perhaps his child or most intimate friend. That gave Pete an opportunity to share how Isa (Jesus) on the night before he died, took a cup, blessed it and all of his friends at the banquet; they all drank from the cup to show their undying love for each other and their eternal relationship. Pete told the host that this was the fellowship offered to all believers. Later, our missionary reported that the host, his friend, was more and more coming to see that the God of Love was calling to him as we prayed for a powerful conversion!

MISSIONARY CHILDREN

Some of the missionaries we visited had children, which gave us a special ministry opportunity. This could mean babysitting to give the parents time away from responsibility, washing dishes and clothes, helping with home and school projects, i.e., doing whatever we could to help both parents and children. We were always careful to come alongside our missionaries, thereby helping to facilitate Christ coming alongside them, especially in times of trial. Many occasions occurred when we accompanied missionaries on field trips for recreation, ministry, or both. Lots of issues could be discussed collectively in those relaxed settings.

The perils of reentry to the U.S. for such families are almost staggering. This is as true for the adults as for the children who are confused about where their home is. One summer, we got close to a family who had spent many years in foreign countries, and their daughter, a teenager, had never lived in her home country. We prayed and raised funding for the daughter to attend a conference for returning missionary children. God provided the funds from our supporters for both the daughter and one parent to attend.

Afterwards, her mother wrote, "There were about 30 missionary kids from all over the world at the reentry camp. My daughter reported, 'I felt less alone ... there were other kids going through the same stuff as me ... some worse!' Camp was fun. She had seminars, played games, did small group work, attended Bible studies, and went on field trips in the Colorado Springs area. She says she is now more confident that she can survive in the U.S. She shared, 'During my time in Colorado, I was transformed from a person who had not a heck of a lot of confidence about the future into an individual who feels that she can step out into the world and do just fine'—with lots of continued effort and your prayers."

Over time, our house became kind of an off-site home office for all kinds of AFM (and indirectly related) activities including storing and selling products some of our missionaries produced through their BAM. We also scheduled and hosted speaking engagements, hosted workers and their families, and provided transportation as needed. We hosted staff and AFM board members while they attended local meetings. Shirleen even taught one worker to swim in our pool!

MISSIONARY RETREATS

Approximately every two years, all the AFM missionaries in the field would gather together for a one-week retreat. The time was for fun, talks, relaxation, and study. Pete's particular contribution was what the AFM's director called *risotherapy*. That's a fancy word for laughter. Pete, a master at telling jokes, was charged with beginning each session with risotherapy. It was a hit! The challenge lay with the speakers who came after him.

Our most memorable retreat occurred in Malaysia, where twenty-three AFM family members, badly in need of ministry, gathered together with six AFM staff and two more children's ministry helpers (one from Singapore and one from the U.S.) for a week of prayer, praise, tears, consolation, healing, assurance, edification, good (but strange) food, corny jokes, goofy CD movies, games, and lots of fellowship. Each couple got to share their heart issues with the group and receive deep ministry according to their needs.

We were also available in the afternoons and evenings for special times of prayer and companionship. It was a wonderful time to renew friendships we had established the prior year and replace emails with personal conversation. All agreed the retreat was highly successful and a much needed event to bind up the wounded who serve on the cutting edge of the gospel's reach.

ON THE AIRPLANE

We had just taken our seats and buckled in for the morning flight to Newark where we would catch a flight to Hong Kong, when the flight attendant came down the aisle wanting to know our choice of beverage. Pete said, "Two diet colas, please," and asked, "How is your day going?" She responded, "I just wish it was over." Then Pete said, "Oh my, I thought you would start by telling me how great it was to be alive and working for an airline that provided magnificent opportunities to meet wonderful and interesting people and how excited you were to have the opportunity to..." She interrupted him by saying, "Wow! I don't know what you are on, but I want some of it!" Pete just smiled and said, "Jesus, just Jesus." We never got to finish the conversation, but seeds were planted. We trust God for growth.

One year, we returned from a trip eastward, with just enough time before a subsequent trip westward for Pete to develop shingles. He decided he might as well be miserable on an airplane as at home, so we went ahead with the trip. At the airport before our departure, we discovered the joy of being escorted through customs and security by wonderful people pushing wheel chairs and providing preferential treatment for both of us! Our God is able! Wheelchairs are now standard airport strategy! Even TSA becomes your friend—kind of.

CONCLUSION

Michael Nazir-Ali recently wrote, "Once again, it is very likely that the renewal of Anglicanism will come about not through the reform of structures (necessary as that is) or through institutional means, but through movements raised up by God. These can be mission movements for planting churches among the unreached."[4] To be sure, AFM is such a movement. Its task is formidable, but God's resources are inexhaustible, and his direction is clear.

We are now in our early eighties and nearing twenty years of AFM ministry. Thus far our age has been a distinct asset in our AFM ministry to the peoples at the ends of the earth. All such peoples we visited hold great respect for the aged, so we kept getting better and better. And it's not too bad having the most comfortable chair or a front row seat. We can't make the forty-eight-hour all-nighters and sleep on chairs and floors in cold airports anymore. We can continue to make more relaxed trips around the States, and we may have one or two more comfortable foreign trips left in our

---

[4] Michael Nazir-Ali, "How the Anglican Communion Began and Where It Is Going," *Reformation Anglicanism: A Vision for Today's Global Communion,* 1 (2017): 43.

bones—His grace will tell. We can continue to host AFM families in our new home in the full lifecare facility just two miles from the place where we started our AFM ministry. We can continue to advocate for AFM and provide the spiritual and physical help that our creative God inspires. We have been through major surgery, sickness, and lifestyle changes in recent years, but we look to the future and press on to the finish line by the grace of God, propelled by the wonderful financial and prayer supporters who have been so faithful. We will go on until he comes and work until he stops us.

We don't worry much about the future. It's so much fun living in the present with Jesus and all his followers—and those who are about to become believers whether they be at the end of the block or the end of the earth. Our God Reigns!

PART THREE

CHALLENGES OF THE
TWENTY-FIRST CENTURY

7

SOUTHEAST ASIA AND FRONTIER MISSIONS

by Kuan Kim Seng

Anglican Frontier Missions and the Diocese of Singapore share a unique spiritual *adelphoi* relationship. Some twenty-five years ago, though thousands of miles apart, Anglican Frontier Missions was born, and the Diocese of Singapore went into missions mode. Both Anglican entities were concerned about reaching unreached peoples beyond their own comfortable settings.

The Spirit of God, who inspired Rev. Tad de Bordenave to found AFM, also challenged a small diocese in a small city-state to plant churches beyond their small island. Interestingly, as AFM celebrates her twenty-fifth anniversary in 2018, the Diocese of Singapore does so likewise for our church planting work in Cambodia, Indonesia, and Vietnam. We celebrated the twenty-fifth anniversary of our work in Thailand in 2016 and Laos in 2017.

In this chapter of AFM's twenty-fifth anniversary publication, I seek to share some stories of God at work in

The Rt. Rev. Kuan Kim Seng is the assistant bishop for the Diocese of Singapore. Before his appointment as bishop, he served St. Andrew's Cathedral, Singapore, and was the diocesan mission director. Bishop Kuan has been instrumental in expanding the mission vision and ministry of the diocese.

Southeast Asia and to highlight the occasions when the ministries of AFM and the Diocese of Singapore intersected. The resulting collaborations have advanced the gospel of the kingdom, to the praise and glory of God Almighty.

BRIEF INTRODUCTION TO SOUTHEAST ASIA

It is helpful to begin by explaining the locus of Southeast Asia. It was not uncommon, especially twenty-five years ago, to hear people asking in all innocence, "Oh, by the way, in which part of China is Singapore situated?" The question was as innocuous as, "Where in Africa is Timbuktu?" (Answer: in Mali, twenty kilometers north of the River Niger.) Then, the recipient of the Singapore question had to patiently explain that although many Singaporeans are Chinese, Singapore is not part of China!

Southeast Asia is defined and shaped by two billion-sized Asian giants, China and India. Our region is broadly located south of China and east of India. In short, the land mass and the thousands of islands that lie south of China and east of India make up Southeast Asia. Historically, these two giants have deeply influenced and shaped the history and culture of Southeast Asia.

Until the advent of Islam, many Southeast Asian countries and societies were shaped by Indian culture and Hinduism. The influence of Hinduism remains. As an example, the national airline of Indonesia, now a largely Muslim country, is named Garuda—the name of a birdlike Hindu deity, although most people are ignorant of that connection today. Another example of the lasting influence of Hinduism in Southeast Asia is the Indonesian island of Bali: 83.5% of the population is Hindu. Thailand and Cambodia are also full of vestiges of Hinduism, although both countries today are predominantly Buddhist. Angkor Wat, the most famous landscape of Cambodia and the image that dominates the Cambodian national flag, is a Hindu temple.

China, too, influenced many parts of Southeast Asia. Vietnam was influenced significantly by China regarding Confucian social and moral ethics. In fact, until the coming of the Jesuits, who introduced and popularized the current Romanized Vietnamese writing script, the Vietnamese used Chinese characters, supplemented with characters developed in Vietnam. Even today, we can still see such Chinese characters in some old Vietnamese buildings, such as temples. Many Vietnamese can still write their surnames in Chinese characters.

Virtually all the countries in Southeast Asia have citizens who are of Indian and Chinese descent. The Chinese tend to live in the cities, and they dominate the business and commercial landscapes of the host countries, even though they form the minority in these nations, with percentages ranging from 31% in Malaysia to 10.6% in Thailand and 3.9% in Indonesia. The only exception is Singapore, where the Chinese form 74.2% of the overall population.[1]

Regarding political entities, Southeast Asia is a region of eleven countries—Brunei, Cambodia, East Timor, Indonesia, Laos, Malaysia, Myanmar, Philippines, Singapore, Thailand, and Vietnam. All the countries, with the exception of East Timor, are members of the Association of Southeast Asian Nations (ASEAN). ASEAN has a combined population of 625 million.

Southeast Asia is the confluence of three major world religions—Hinduism, Buddhism and Islam, as well as Confucianism. Though Confucianism is not exactly a religion, it has given clear social and moral teaching and has

---

[1] Jason Mandryk, *Operation World: The Definitive Prayer Guide to Every Nation*, (Westmont, IL: Intervarsity Press, 2010). Source of the statistics in this paragraph.

brought about religious-like adherence. It was into such a setting of well organized faiths and belief systems that the Protestant missionary movement began in earnest in the nineteenth century. The Roman Catholics were in this region much earlier. In this article, I will focus only on the Protestant missions and especially Anglicanism.

EARLY WESTERN INTEREST IN SOUTHEAST ASIA VIS-À-VIS CHINA

It needs to be highlighted that for the Western missionary enterprise of the nineteenth and even the twentieth century, Southeast Asia was accorded only secondary effort and focus. The main missionary focus, the "big fish," was India and China. Anglican ministry in India was already well established since the early days of the British in India, with the appointment of the first Chaplain in India and the East in January 1657. The Diocese of Calcutta was established in May 1814.

China in the nineteenth century had chosen to close itself to the outside world. But the Western world was interested in the silk, porcelain, and tea that China produced. The British had produced opium in India, which they sold to the Chinese for huge profits; then they used the profits to pay for the silk, porcelain and tea. The tragic result of the opium trade was the ever increasing number of opium addicts.

When the Chinese government decided to restrict the importation of opium into China, it led to the two "Opium Wars" of 1839-42 and 1856-60. China lost both wars and was forced to accept open trading with the Western world, including the importation of opium and the ceding of Chinese territory to Western powers—seen as a national humiliation by (Mainland) Chinese even to this day! The problem of opium addiction amongst the Chinese was finally eradicated by the Chinese communist government after they came to power in 1949.

When China was forced open by the Western powers in 1842, virtually all the missionaries working in then Malaya and Singapore left for China. (They must have seen the opening of China, albeit by military force, as an answer to their prayer!) It was an understandable response as those missionaries were working with the diaspora Chinese in Southeast Asia simply because they were not allowed to function and serve within China itself, their ultimate goal. For those missionaries, the opening of China was a very long wait if we recall that the first Protestant missionary to the Chinese, Robert Morrison, landed in Macau in 1807, some thirty-five years earlier than China's official opening in 1842!

THE GENESIS OF ANGLICANISM IN SOUTHEAST ASIA

Although Southeast Asia was accorded only secondary focus and effort by the early missionaries, there were reasonable results regarding locals coming to faith in God. At the human level, we can attribute the success stories to the fact that both the Anglican ecclesial and missional structures had played their respective roles and responsibilities admirably. Interestingly, in many instances, it was the ecclesial rather than the missional structures that started the ball rolling.

Of course, at the divine level, it was God at work, bringing people to salvation through human effort, although in many instances these efforts were less than fully adequate. In fact, we may even say that the divine spread of the gospel happened despite human hindrances, especially in the early years of the emerging missions movement in the nineteenth century.

It is a well known fact that the British East India Company, the trading arm of the British Empire, which controlled much of the sea routes from Britain to Asia, originally refused to allow missionaries on board their ships! They had no problems carrying Anglican chaplains as these clergies served an important spiritual need for their own people, but transporting missionaries to preach the gospel to the locals? That was quite another matter.

A case in point is the first Anglican church in Southeast Asia—St. George's, Penang. The British arrived in Penang in 1786, and for a long time there was no formal Anglican church building, although there were worship services carried out by Anglican clergy chaplains attached to the British East India Company. It was a good twenty-four years later, in 1810, that the idea of an Anglican church building was mooted. It took another eight years before the building was completed in 1818 and consecrated by the bishop of Calcutta, Thomas Fanshawe Middleton, on May 11, 1819, thirty-three years after the British first landed in Penang. We can safely say that establishing a church was secondary to the commercial and trading interests that brought those Westerners to Southeast Asia.

It should also be noted that the church thus built was essentially a white man's domain, a chaplaincy church serving the spiritual needs of British people who had come to Penang as part of the British establishment, whether employed by the British East India Company or simply part of the ruling colonial structure. The church was not built for the purpose of reaching the locals with the gospel.

It was another eight years later that the missional response appeared in the form of a missionary couple, Samuel and Maria Dyer, of London Missionary Society (LMS). They were recruited by Robert Morrison and arrived in Penang in 1827. The Dyers also served in Malacca, where there were a substantial number of Chinese residents. Like many of their contemporaries, they left for China as soon as she was forced open in 1842.

(In comparison to the London Missionary Society (LMS), the Church Missionary Society (CMS) was a latecomer by seventeen years, using the Dyers' arrival in Penang as the reference point, and thirty-seven years if we use Robert Morrison's arrival in Macau in 1807 as the reference point. CMS sent their first missionary to China in 1844, bypassing South East Asia completely!)

The second Anglican chaplaincy church in Southeast Asia was established in Jakarta in 1819. All Saints Church, Jakarta, originally started off as a base for the LMS's mission to China. When the need for such a base ceased with the opening of China, the church then functioned as a colonial chaplaincy. In the last fifty years, All Saints, Jakarta, has been functioning as a church catering to internationals.

Singapore was established as a British colony in 1819 on the back of the Anglo-Dutch trading rivalry. The Dutch had control of Malacca, and the British were looking for a port to fit and fuel their ships on their way to China. Penang, although under British control, was too far away. The almost uninhabited island off the tip of the Malay Peninsula, Singapore, was deemed ideal.

With the founding of Singapore as a colony, the British establishment immediately gave land for the building of an Anglican church. Naturally, St. Andrew's Church (thus named because it was the Scots who contributed the bulk of the funds for the church building!) was originally built to serve the needs of the British. The first building was completed in 1837. But it was a phenomenal event beyond the church building that changed everything.

On Pentecost Sunday 1856, Rev. William Humphrey, the residency chaplain at St. Andrew's Church and a CMS missionary, preached a Spirit inspired sermon calling for the church to become a *missionary congregation* and raise funds to hire Indian and Chinese catechists to take the gospel to the many Indians and Chinese who were flocking to

Singapore to seek their fortunes. He called on church members to pledge "a dollar a month" to fund this initiative. This call resulted in the setting up of St. Andrew's Church Mission (SACM), which funded much of the early work among the locals.

It is interesting to note that what happened on Pentecost Sunday 1856 was simply an establishment chaplaincy church, fired by Holy Spirit zeal, deciding to go into missions mode. That changed everything for the Anglican Church in Singapore, as SACM began to establish indigenous congregations and even a school. That was the beginning of the growth of the Anglican Church in Singapore and Malaya (subsequently "Malaysia").

During the same period, Anglican work in what is now East Malaysia began under the Borneo Church Mission, established in England in 1846. The Diocese of Singapore, Labuan and Sarawak was created in 1881, which continued until 1909, when it became two dioceses. The Diocese of Borneo subsequently became two dioceses (Diocese of Kuching and Diocese of Sabah), and the Diocese of Singapore, renamed as Diocese of Singapore and Malaya in 1960, also became two dioceses in 1970 (Diocese of West Malaysia and Diocese of Singapore). All four dioceses subsequently formed the Province of the church in Southeast Asia in 1996.

INDIGENIZATION OF DIOCESAN LEADERSHIP

To understand the spread of the gospel in Southeast Asia in the second half of the twentieth century, we need to appreciate the process that led to the indigenization of church leadership there. It was the indigenous church leadership that was subsequently responsible for the spread of the gospel beyond what was accomplished by the missionaries and expatriate clergy. We will view the matter only through the "Anglican lens," although it is largely the same for the other denominations.

Strangely, the indigenization of church leadership in Southeast Asia in the twentieth century may be traced to the Japanese invasion and conquest that began with the bombing of Pearl Harbor in December 1941 and the subsequent occupation of much of Southeast Asia, Singapore included. Prior to the Japanese invasion, virtually all of the key church leadership, like much of the colonial political and even social leadership, was in the domain of the British.

While it is true that Henry Venn and other missionary statesmen of his era had advocated the concept and importance of establishing self-supporting, self-governing and self-propagating indigenous churches since the latter half of the nineteenth century, the reality on the ground was quite different.

It was not without reason that Roland Allen wrote his now famous classic, *Missionary Methods, St. Paul's or Ours,* first published in 1912.[2] His warning about the danger of Western missionaries holding onto church leadership for far too long, and thereby hindering the development of indigenous leadership and the rapid spread of the faith, went largely unheeded.

Part III of his book gives us a good insight into what Allen saw as one of the problems of the missionary enterprise of his day—the general reluctance by missionaries to develop and empower indigenous leadership. Allen wrote, "Our converts often display great virtues, but they remain, too often for generations, dependent upon us." In fact, Allen was reported to have said that it would take another fifty years before his views, including the importance of the

---

[2] Allen Roland London, *Missionary Methods, St. Paul's or Ours* (Forgotten Books, FB &c Ltd, 2017).

indigenization of church leadership, would gain widespread acceptance in the Western church. But fifty years was just far too long a wait!

It is not without merit to claim that God became impatient with the church situation in Southeast Asia, and he, therefore, let in the Japanese army to accomplish his will! The same perspective can also be said about the situation then in China. At the human level, the man most responsible for the spectacular growth of the church in China was Mao Tse Tung! He accomplished much more than what he had expected when he ushered all the Western missionaries out of China after the communist victory in 1949. The local Chinese church leadership was forcibly and rapidly indigenized, and that has been one main factor in the explosive growth of the church since then. Mao accomplished more in fifteen years than all the missionaries did in a hundred and fifty years!

When the Japanese occupied Singapore, our bishop and all the Western clergy, including that of other denominations, were imprisoned along with non-missionary Westerners. But before his imprisonment, Bishop Leonard Wilson, in good Anglican order, appointed several local clergies to take full charge of ministry and worship in the Anglican churches. This emergency-induced responsibility, replacing previously assigned minor roles, was handled admirably well by the local clergies during the period of the Japanese occupation.

But what happened inside the prison was even more remarkable. The Anglican, Methodist and Presbyterian church leaders, all Westerners, met during their time of imprisonment and decided that when the war was over, they would quickly set up a theological institution to focus on the training of locals for church ministry and leadership. Thus, Trinity Theological College was set up in 1948, three years after the Japanese surrender in 1945.

It was not beyond God to use something as drastic as the Japanese invasion of Southeast Asia, with all its tragedy, mayhem and pain, to kick into action the process that subsequently led to the accelerated proclamation of the gospel in Southeast Asia.

After the return of the British, we had two more English diocesan bishops until 1966, when Joshua Chiu Ban was consecrated as the first Asian bishop of the diocese. With this development, the process of indigenization of church leadership in the diocese had come to full completion. Bishop Chiu served as diocesan bishop, initially covering both Singapore and West Malaysia, until 1981, when he was succeeded by Bishop Moses Tay, who served as diocesan bishop from 1982 to 1999. A new Diocese of West Malaysia was formed in 1970 to look after all the Anglican churches in Peninsula Malaysia.

GROWTH OF THE DIOCESE OF SINGAPORE BETWEEN 1970 AND 1990

When the Diocese of Singapore was divested of all the parishes in West Malaysia in April 1970, there were just thirteen parishes in Singapore that remained, plus a couple of expatriate chaplaincy churches outside of Singapore. The 1970 Synod Report indicated a total confirmed membership of 4,726, not counting those outside the island of Singapore.

The 1970s and 1980s were periods of significant church growth in Singapore. This was a period when many youths in Singapore were coming to faith in the Lord Jesus Christ, across all denominational lines. At a human level, we may attribute this phenomenon largely to youth outreach ministries like Youth for Christ and Campus Crusade for Christ. This development, of course, benefitted the churches, Anglicans included, because these youths who had come to faith needed to be churched. By the year 1990, from the preceding twenty-year period, the Diocese of Singapore had slightly more than doubled its membership to 10,370, as indicated in the 1990 electoral roll.

During the late 1980s and 1990s many of the young people who had come to faith in their teenage years in the earlier decades were going into full time ministry, serving as clergy and non-ordained pastors; they also served in the many parachurch organizations that were sprouting in Singapore. This period was the latter half of the tenure of Bishop Moses Tay, and the season when the Diocese of Singapore went into missions mode.

DIOCESE OF SINGAPORE IN MISSIONS MODE

It is useful to sketch a big picture summary of what the Diocese of Singapore looked like at this juncture. In 1990, there were 10,370 electoral roll Anglicans distributed in twenty parishes within the island of Singapore. These twenty parishes would often have multiple congregations. In addition, the Bishop of Singapore licensed the clergy for chaplaincy churches in the capital cities of Indonesia, Thailand, and Laos. As for ecclesiastical boundaries, the Diocese of Singapore also included five other Southeast Asian countries—Cambodia, Indonesia, Laos, Thailand and Vietnam. However, no Anglican ministries took place in these five countries, except for the chaplaincy churches that catered to the spiritual needs of English speaking expatriates. This was soon to change.

The late 1980s and 1990s comprised a fervent season in Singapore for ministry outside of the small island. It was not just the Anglicans; many other churches in Singapore were also into missions mode. Why this happened is kind of difficult to explain comprehensively in a brief article, except to say that this was the grace of God poured out upon the church in Singapore. I will just highlight four reasons for this development without going into too many details.

One possible reason for this happy development is that the clergy and other church leaders during this period were mainly first generation Christians, converts from pagan backgrounds. Consequently, they tended to be focused on the Great Commission and, therefore, on missions. Second, the smallness of Singapore was another factor. Going to the nations around us was a natural development, akin to the business and commercial enterprises that were looking overseas, beyond the small internal market, for expansion. Another reason was the charismatic renewal that took place in Singapore during this same period. A fourth reason is the spiritual maturity that was dawning upon these newly established churches. Between 1970 and 1990, within the Diocese of Singapore, seven new parishes were planted. Also, many new congregations were added to the earlier established parishes, making virtually all parishes multi-congregational.

By the beginning of the 1990s, Bishop Moses Tay began encouraging the clergy and the parishes to plant churches outside the island of Singapore. Several of the more experienced vicars were given additional responsibilities as deans of Cambodia, Indonesia, Laos, Thailand and Vietnam, with the goal of planting indigenous Anglican churches in these countries. Practical initiatives, like quota exemption to the diocese for missions-related expenses, were also introduced.

In 1991, Rev. Gerald Khoo, then a young vicar of a newly minted parish, and his wife Dorothy felt called by God to serve him in Thailand. They were facilitated by the diocese to plant a Thai-speaking Anglican congregation. This initiative was backed by his parish as well as other Anglican churches in Singapore. The happy consequence of this effort was the first Thai language worship service held in Christ Church

Bangkok on October 7, 1991, with a grand attendance of seven!

By 1993, all five countries where the Diocese of Singapore had ecclesiastical responsibility—Cambodia, Indonesia, Laos, Thailand and Vietnam—had deans who were all vicars of local parishes. They were given, so to speak, two jobs each! (The only exception was Rev Gerald Khoo, serving fulltime as a missionary and as the dean of Thailand.) These additional responsibilities became the practical norm in the deaneries for quite a while.

Ministries in the five countries went according to the pace and speed at the ground level. In countries where the local laws forbade the planting of churches by non-locals, we went into social concerns or community development mode, often in cooperation with local churches or Christian groups. This was the case in Laos, where we started the Anglican Relief and Development Agency (ARDA) in 1996. ARDA is now the premier English language center in Laos.

The same methodology of working alongside local churches, often in terms of medical outreach and other community services, was also adopted in Vietnam. This went on for more than a decade until the political climate in Vietnam changed to the point that it became possible for us to plant Anglican churches.

In countries where the planting of new churches was possible, we went into full swing as soon as it was feasible. Apart from Thailand, we now have indigenous Anglican churches in Cambodia, Indonesia and Vietnam, with local clergies often complemented by ministry workers from outside the countries.

BUT NEPAL IS NOT IN SOUTHEAST ASIA!

A word of explanation is in order when it comes to Nepal, where the Diocese of Singapore is anchoring Anglican church planting. The history goes back to the 1990s when Rev. Norman Beale of Anglican Frontier Missions was serving in Nepal. A group of Nepali pastors of newly established independent churches was keen to affiliate themselves with some global church structures. Norman and his diocesan bishop felt that it was wise to consider the Diocese of Singapore to anchor this matter, and the issue was deliberated at Lambeth 1998 between Bishop Keith Ackerman and Bishop Moses Tay.

Following a ground visit to assess the matter for himself, Bishop Moses Tay brought the matter to the Diocesan Synod in 1999. That body accepted his recommendation; they voted to receive these churches and help them develop the capacity to become an Anglican diocese that would take the gospel of the kingdom into the Himalayan region and even beyond. Rev. Norman Beale was appointed the first dean of Nepal, a responsibility he held commendably for a ten-year period until November 2009.

By the grace of God, this work has grown tremendously. The total membership of the Anglican Church in Nepal (ACN) is now 12,500, with nine ordained clergy and nearly a hundred other pastors. As the ACN is poised to become a diocese, it may become the first diocese formed from the Singapore deaneries!

SECOND WIND

Bishop Moses Tay was succeeded by Bishop John Chew in 2000, who continued the missions focus of his predecessor. Bishop John Chew took the diocesan missions drive even further. He called one of his first missions initiatives, in fact, on the day after his installation as diocesan bishop; he held a quick meeting with bishops and other church leaders to see if they were willing and able to answer a Macedonian call to help the Diocese of Singapore with church planting ministries in the six deanery countries.

The answer was a resounding yes, and thus was born the Missions Consultation Roundtables, the first of which was held in 2001. Since then, five other roundtables have been held and this has resulted in many like-minded fellow Anglicans from around the globe coming on board to assist in the vast scope of ministries in the six countries, a job beyond the capacity of a single small diocese, or even the Church of the Province of Southeast Asia, to accomplish.

One further contribution of Bishop John Chew was his perspective that we need to think in terms of establishing dioceses, rather than just planting as many Anglican churches as we can in the six deanery countries. This perspective requires us to think strategically and long-term, with special consideration for the raising up of indigenous clergy leadership.

In 2012 Bishop John Chew was succeeded by Bishop Rennis Ponniah, the current bishop of the Diocese of Singapore. Again, the missions focus was maintained. Bishop Rennis' chief contribution to the missions thrust in the deanery countries may be summarized by the tagline, "Mainstreaming the Deaneries." This call is one that seeks to place the interests and needs of the deaneries on par with the parishes and other Anglican ministries within the island of Singapore.

LESSONS THAT WE ARE LEARNING

The Diocese of Singapore has been church planting in our six deanery countries over the past twenty-five years. We see the proclamation of the gospel in these six countries as our diocese's primary missions responsibility. However, this does not preclude us from facilitating our church members into serving outside of these six countries if they believe that God has called them to serve in other areas of the world. For example, we do have missionaries sent to places like Egypt, and even in lands as distant as Bolivia. But our main God-given ecclesial responsibility is within these six countries.

We are planting churches with the aim of raising up enough mature parishes in each and every country to establish new dioceses. Of course, this is a job that is beyond the capacity of any single diocese. We are learning that God has his people from around the globe who are willing to come alongside us and the local believers to advance the kingdom of God. This working together by like-minded Anglicans is a precious expression of the unity and oneness which the Lord Jesus Christ has endowed on his Church.

Our church planting experience in Vietnam is most interesting. After more than a decade of simply coming alongside local churches and Christian community service organizations, we felt it was time to go into church planting mode. In our usual Anglican way of doing things, we met with government officials and negotiated for permission to plant churches. We were politely told about the parameters within which we could function, and also to send in formal letters of application, which we promptly did. But these letters were never answered! After several attempts, we finally got it—that we should just go ahead and do what we had requested, so long as we did not rock the political status quo! Thus, we gingerly started our work in Vietnam.

There is another lesson from our work in Vietnam, which we had known for quite a while. Our church planting in Hanoi was birthed out of an English language center. In 2009, we started an English language teaching center in Hanoi with five Singaporean young adult volunteers. The English language center put us in contact with multitudes who wanted to learn the language, mainly for commerce and related reasons, but God had a larger agenda for them.

The same happened in Thailand when we wanted to start a new church plant in Bangkok. After a careful choice of the locality, Lat Krabang, an outskirt district of Bangkok close to the Suvarnabhumi Airport, we established an English language center within a university hostel district there. This ministry has spearheaded the new church plant in Lat Krabang, which now has a thriving congregation.

I would venture to add that the English language (regardless of whether it is the Queen's English or Microsoft English!) in the twenty-first century has the same kingdom of God importance as *Koiné* Greek did in the first century. Here is a ministry platform that we in the Anglican world should not miss, given the fact that we were birthed out of the English spectrum of the Reformation!

Another lesson that I would add is that God was already at work, long before we were even ready! In our church planting work in Hanoi, the person whom we finally ordained as clergy for the church planting ministry was already well prepared by God long before we began our work. Jacob Hong Thai Vu had come to faith in the Lord Jesus Christ in Hong Kong, as a Vietnamese refugee fleeing the country years earlier.

Upon his conversion, he was led by God to return to his homeland so as to share the gospel with his own people. He was busy bringing people to faith and discipling them when we approached him to serve as the business manager of our English language center, while continuing with his ministry. After several years of working together, Jacob felt comfortable enough to serve beyond the business manager role and entered into a church planting working relationship with us. God had prepared him for the role long before we began our ministry in Hanoi.

This same lesson of God already at work, and we simply catching up with him, is seen most vividly in the ministry in Nepal, a Hindu-Buddhist nation (75% and 16% of the population, respectively). Until 2008, the country was ruled as the world's only Hindu kingdom. It may surprise many that Nepal is the motherland of Buddhism; Lumbini in Nepal is the birth place of Gautama Buddha.

Using the years 2000 and 2017 as reference points, we are amazed at the spectacular growth of the Anglican Church in Nepal (ACN). In 2000, we had seventeen churches comprising 1,700 members, cared for by twelve pastors. By 2017, the number had risen to eighty-two churches, 12,500 members, ninety-five pastors and nine clergy. We may attribute this spectacular growth to the evangelistic zeal of the pastors and church members ministering in the context of a people shaped by God and therefore open to the gospel.

The social unrest and pain caused by the Maoist insurgency previous to 2008 and the tragic 2015 earthquake became focal points when Nepali Christians, living out the God-given mandate to love our neighbors as ourselves, pointed the person of the Lord Jesus Christ to many Nepalis. In the case of the Anglican Church in Nepal alone, our church attendance rose by 2,500 in the year following the 2015 earthquake, with many coming to faith as a result of our crisis relief response to the tragedy. God was indeed already at work long before us.

The tragic earthquake in Nepal in 2015 reinforced for us a lesson that we had learned over the prior decades: that crisis relief, particularly in the face of a natural disaster, is an important means of fulfilling the Great Commission as we the live out the Great Commandment. In fact, we may add that it is the Great Commandment that becomes the platform to fulfill the Great Commission. Consequently, we developed a crisis relief arm in the Diocese of Singapore, staffed mainly by volunteers, with minimum full time staff. That way, it enabled us to inspire church members to put feet to faith.

CONCLUSION: RUNNING TOGETHER

We are living in an era of phenomenal opportunities, albeit with challenges as well. When we look at the progress of the Great Commission since its inception two thousand years ago, the last two hundred years of church history is just plain amazing. Christianity was transformed from a religion locked within Europe for a thousand years into a global faith. The last fifty years—and more so, the last twenty-five years—are even more amazing as the people who had received the gospel of the kingdom of God are now themselves sharing this gospel beyond themselves, to fellow Asians, Africans, Latinos, and even far beyond.

Anglican Frontier Missions and the Diocese of Singapore, like all authentic followers of the Lord Jesus Christ, are on the same trajectory with regard to the Great Commission— that we need to fully give of ourselves to obey the words of the Lord Jesus, "As the Father has sent Me, even so, I am sending you" (John 20:21). What we refer to in missiological jargon as the "10/40 Window" is where we need to focus our attention.

AFM is committed to going where the need is greatest, planting indigenous churches among the largest and least evangelized peoples in the world within the 10/40 Window. The Diocese of Singapore lies within the Asian region of the 10/40 Window (although geographically slightly off, but in terms of unreached people groups, right within the Window!), and in fact, our church planting effort covers many people groups that are categorized as unreached. In this regard, we and AFM are on the same end of the missiological spectrum.

It is, therefore, no coincidence that AFM and the Diocese of Singapore have this unique spiritual *adelphoi* relationship. We are linked together by the common purpose of seeing the ultimate fulfillment of the Great Commission given by the Lord Jesus Christ to his Church two thousand years ago, or, if we look further back to four thousand years ago, God's solemn promise to Abraham that "all nations of the earth will be blessed" (Genesis 26:4).

As we each celebrate in 2018, the twenty-fifth anniversary of the founding of AFM, and interestingly, also the twenty-fifth anniversary of the Diocese of Singapore's church planting work in Cambodia, Indonesia and Vietnam, we have much for which to thank God. And we must encourage each other in doing the will of God to the point of completion. Perhaps the words of Paul, the great missionary pioneer of the Church, says it all in Romans 1:12, "... that we may be mutually encouraged by each other's faith, both yours and mine." It is a great joy to run together, collectively doing the will of God.

8

CHINA TODAY AND TOMORROW

by Julian Linnell

"We owe a gospel debt to the world. Only when our missions sending surpasses what we have received can China be considered a truly missions-sending country." With these words, a Christian leader in China recently defined the goal of mobilizing twenty thousand Chinese missionaries by 2030 as a way of giving back to God for the approximately twenty thousand non-Chinese missionaries who have served in China over the last two hundred years. This is the voice of an insider from the Chinese church today. In this chapter, I will expand on what the voices of the Chinese leaders are saying about their mission.

Many voices from the outside emphasize political issues, such as church-state relations, human rights, or religious freedom. Still others continue with a single persecution narrative to describe the church in China today. What are non-Chinese Christians to make of the church in China

Julian Linnell taught English in China where he met his wife, Kim. In 2007, he became the second director of AFM. Seven years later, he and his family moved to Boston where he leads the global mission department at historic Park Street Church. With their four daughters the Linnells are all immersed in international outreach.

today, and how are we to think about her future? More importantly, what are the Chinese leaders saying?

In addressing these questions, my approach is missiological, theological, and pastoral. I write as a Westerner (British), a non-Chinese, an amateur China watcher, and not as an insider to the church in China nor as a specialist trained in East Asian studies. My observations as an outsider are limited to house churches and some government-sanctioned official churches from the Protestant tradition. I will not focus on Catholic churches, though these are important to a fuller understanding of Christianity in China today.

Over thirty years ago, as an undergraduate member of the Chinese Christian Fellowship at Cambridge University in England, I had the immense privilege of receiving prayer, encouragement, and kindness from several Chinese international students. Just prior to graduation, I remember receiving a handwritten copy of the first few chapters of John's Gospel in Chinese from a member of the fellowship. It was a gift to encourage me to read the Bible in Chinese. I still have that cherished gift tucked away on a bookshelf. This was a joyful and energetic group, who shared the gospel with non-Christians and patiently helped an outsider like me appreciate some of the riches of Chinese faith.

In writing this chapter, I hope readers may be open to perspectives from our Chinese brothers and sisters. Hopefully, you might begin to understand the perspective the Chinese themselves have in looking at the church in China. Is it purely a socio-political framework? Is it mainly demographic? Is it an outlook that sounds foreign to non-Chinese ears? Perhaps you have Chinese colleagues at work or know of Chinese international students at a nearby university that you could befriend. Or maybe you could visit a local Chinese church in the U.S.—all with the goal of learning something new about God.

As a disclaimer, I make no claims to originality in this chapter as I borrow heavily from the work of Brent Fulton,[1] whose scholarship and strategic vision for China has shaped my own understanding for the past twenty years.

1. FROM TRAINING TO MENTORING

After China opened up in the late 1970s, many so-called foreign experts arrived in China to teach English, study Chinese, and assist in training in agriculture, industry, national defense, and science and technology. By the 1990s and early 2000s, non-Chinese Christians had become active in training programs in both house churches and government-run seminaries and in areas such as counseling, business as mission, and church planting among unreached people groups. By the 2010s, opportunities for online training, indigenous Chinese programs, and overseas study greatly increased the options for the formal education of Chinese leaders.

Though training is important, often it is not structured to address effectively the practical realities of interpersonal conflict, marriage counseling, work-life balance, Sabbath keeping, inner spiritual growth, and family dynamics. The following graph[2] (Figure 3) highlights the transition from the types of support received by Chinese churches in the recent past (2005-2015) to anticipated support in the future (2015-2020). The data is based on 1,200 surveys and 432 interviews with church leaders inside China and more than 200 overseas mission organizations.

---

[1] Brent Fulton, *China's Urban Christians: A Light That Cannot Be Hidden* (Eugene, OR: Pickwick , 2015).

"Seven Transitions Facing China" webinar April 27, 2017 (www.chinasource.org).

[2] Chinese Gospel Research Alliance (2015), unpublished. http://www.chinasource.org/resource-library/articles/perceptions-and-priorities-leaders-in-china, Accessed 6/2/2017.

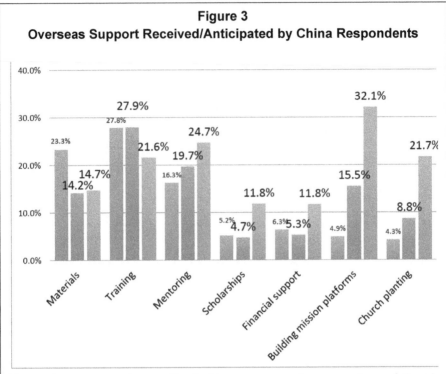

Figure 3
Overseas Support Received/Anticipated by China Respondents

For each resource category, the first bar measures the percentage of church resources received in the past ten years. The second bar measures the percentage now received. The third bar measures the percentage expected in the next three-to-five years.

Clearly, leaders anticipate that overseas materials and training will decrease in the future, while mentoring, building mission platforms, and church planting will increase. If we focus on mentoring, we can do no better than to listen to the apostle Paul in 2 Timothy 3:10-11:

> You, however, have followed my teaching, my conduct, my aim in life, my faith, my patience, my love, my steadfastness, [11] my persecutions and sufferings that happened to me at Antioch, at Iconium, and at Lystra—which persecutions I endured; yet from them all the Lord rescued me.

Paul shared his way of life, purpose, and persecutions with Timothy. This holistic engagement points to a key for the spiritual and mental health of Chinese Christian leaders today—mentoring.

Though there may be non-Chinese Christians who are sufficiently qualified for mentoring leaders, it is my belief that the Chinese church herself has ample resources to revitalize her own leaders both for today and tomorrow. This will require long-term relationships that go beyond a one-off weekend seminar or online class. It will reflect Paul's example of sharing a way of life, purpose, and faith in adversity and in prosperity. Building mission platforms and church planting in the future requires missions not just "with Chinese characteristics" but with Chinese roots and supports developed and enriched over time.

2. FROM LEADING TO MODELING

The issue for today and tomorrow is how Chinese leaders themselves will lead these ministries. Non-Chinese Christian organizations have increasingly hired Chinese nationals to serve in a variety of ministries. Although someone who is not Chinese can model aspects of leadership, the long-term health and vitality of the church depend on Chinese leadership.

A recent law was passed that makes Chinese leadership in the church an even greater necessity. As of January 1, 2017, all non-government organizations (non-profits or charities) fall under the security apparatus of the country rather than under the Civil Affairs department. In the U.S., this would be similar to requiring all non-profit organizations to register with the FBI or CIA rather than the IRS.

As non-Chinese step aside and transition responsibility to their Chinese colleagues for various ministries across China, there will be new opportunities for modeling a biblical lifestyle and ever maturing spiritual life at work, in the home, in neighborhoods, and among relatives. Jesus taught his disciples, "Remember what I told you: 'A servant is not greater than his master'. If they persecuted me, they will persecute you also. If they obeyed my teaching, they will obey yours also" (John 15:20, New International Version). Jesus modeled how to endure suffering, humiliation, injustice, and conflict. He also modeled how to live in a family: "When Jesus saw his mother and the disciple whom he loved standing nearby, he said to his mother, 'Woman, behold, your son!' Then he said to the disciple, 'Behold, your mother.' From that hour, the disciple took her to his own home" (John 19:26-27). Though personal and private, this type of modeling can provide a powerful incentive and encouragement for Chinese leaders.

3. FROM PIETISM TO SOCIAL CONSCIENCE

When an earthquake hit Sichuan Province in 2008, nearly seventy thousand people were killed, over 374 thousand injured, and about five million people left homeless. The ripple effects were felt not only geologically and socially, but also spiritually. It was a wake up call to the Chinese Christians. For perhaps the first time, Chinese Christians organized themselves publicly in response to a national tragedy. Another large-scale tragedy, the explosion in Tianjin in August 2015, when 173 people were killed and 700 injured, provoked Christians to reflect on issues of human frailty, government culpability, and family reconciliation.

As China today transitions from a rural to an urban society, there will be an increasing need for social sector organizations to address the threats and opportunities such changes generate. Some organizations are rooted in a secular or Buddhist worldview; others are founded on biblical principles. The rural-urban shift provides an opportunity to develop an infrastructure within these organizations through strategic planning, fundraising, program management, policies and procedures, financial transparency, and so forth. Those who have begun to provide these types of support are finding that the biblical principles taught for organizational development are attractive to secular organizations. The emphasis on the common good is found in the history of the early Church, such as in Acts 2:44, where, "And all who believed were together and had all things in common." During the first few centuries of the Church, it was Christians who remained behind in plague-ridden cities to help the sick, while urban elites escaped to their rural estates. Non-Chinese who are sensitive to the Chinese context today and tomorrow can, therefore, promote the type of biblical values that will enable social organizations to grow in sustainability, scale, and long-term effectiveness.

4. FROM SOLUTIONS TO SHARED INNOVATIONS

One unfortunate result of the foreign expert syndrome was the expectation that non-Chinese people had solutions to complex Chinese issues. When China first opened up in the late 1970s, there was a tendency for foreign mission organizations to translate Western materials and import them into the country. The dubious underlying assumption was that if a resource had been effective in the West, then it would work inside China. Such solutions birthed outside of China probably deserve a premature death.

In contrast, a collective approach to issues faced by the church is more consistent with Chinese culture. An ancient Chinese proverb states, "The small streams rise when the main stream is high; when the main stream is low, the small streams run dry." Today, Chinese leaders within the church may not have been raised during the persecutions of the Cultural Revolution in the 1960s or in rural fellowships facing police harassment. They may have received advanced university degrees in technology, traveled overseas, started internet companies, and read widely from Augustine, Anselm, Aquinas, Calvin, Luther, Cranmer, C. S. Lewis, Carl Henry, and Rick Warren. They may be the first Christians in their families. Their solutions will be uniquely Chinese and probably quite different from previous generations of Chinese Christian leaders.

However, the non-Chinese believer can still have a role. The apostle Paul sees the whole body of Christ joined to Christ "...and held together by every joint with which it is equipped, when each part is working properly, makes the body grow so that it builds itself up in love" (Ephesians 4:16). This is a portrait of mutual, dynamic growth for the body of Christ as a whole. If conducted in love, each doing its part, then the whole body benefits. If the non-Chinese themselves are transformed in the process, then such shared innovations can truly be two way affairs.

5. FROM RECEIVING TO SENDING

Today, the church in China is sending her own missionaries—both across the country and outside its borders. This is a biblical development of a church that has suffered greatly, but now is changing from a marginal institution to one that is established within society. However, such changes bring their own challenges. I recall hearing from a Chinese sister who, having been sent out as a missionary to Tibet, received an unexpected text from her sending church in eastern China. The church would no longer support her financially. There was no further discussion, no explanation. She was dumbfounded. She felt betrayed. Another told me how missionaries who had not been "successful" felt a loss of face and shame to the extent that they would not return to their sending church. As we noted in the graph shown earlier, Chinese leaders recognize their need to build mission platforms that provide not just finance, but member care, family counseling, career development, and transition care.

The apostle Paul wrote of the Jews that they had "...zeal for God, but not according to knowledge" (Romans 10:2). It would be grossly unfair to use this characterization of the new missionary movement in China today. Many leaders are learning a lot about what it takes to send missionaries. There is a role here for non-Chinese to assist in terms of strengthening the long-term capacity of churches to recruit, train, deploy, support, and care for cross cultural missionaries. However, this has to be done with an attitude of "Don't make the mistakes we made when we sent missionaries out," rather than, "We're the experts and you should copy us."

One cultural issue that Han Chinese missionaries may face in cross cultural mission is rooted in their own history. From the fourth to the eighth century AD., the central states (known as 'Zhong Guo') were surrounded by tribal peoples (known as 'Yidi'). The assumption was that the Zhong Guo were civilized, cultured, and moral, whereas the Yidi were uncivilized, unprincipled, and immoral. One scholar (Ye Shi 1150-1223 AD) noted that the Yidi were not equal to the Zhong Guo and so, therefore, they ought to embrace the superior values of Zhong Guo. The two were different, but also threatening to each other. When the Peoples' Republic of China adopted the Soviet model of identifying national minorities in 1952, fifty-six ethnic groups were identified. Inherent in this classification is an ambivalence toward ethnic groups different from one's own, especially non-Han groups. Under the present constitution, different ethnicities are combined as citizens of the Peoples' Republic of China. This is part of China's political agenda to build a nation state around Han values.

Attitudes toward ethnic groups in cross cultural mission are deeply rooted, and some of these attitudes can be patronizing and disparaging. However, the gospel itself relativizes ethnic distinctions to the extent that no single ethnic group is privileged above or below another: "There is neither Jew nor Greek, there is neither slave nor free, there is no male and female, for you are all one in Christ Jesus. And if you are Christ's, then you are Abraham's offspring, heirs according to promise" (Galatians 3:28-29).

The challenge for Chinese evangelists and church planters, and their non-Chinese and non-Han brothers and sisters, will be to live out this truth cross-culturally without succumbing to a sense of superiority or inferiority. At root, the challenge is to live by gospel values rather than the cultural, political, or historical values of the Han state.

6. FROM ENTREPRENEURS TO FELLOW TRAVELERS

After Chairman Mao's death, many intrepid non-Chinese Christians went to China just as after the fall of the U.S.S.R, missionaries flocked into that country. Today, of course, the context has changed significantly. Many of the Chinese church's leaders have a business or academic background and see new ways to engage society based on technology, the internet, and social concern. Previous generations of leaders in the house churches, especially in rural areas, emerged during a period of deprivation, alienation, and opposition from society and the government.

Now, with the rural-urban population shift as well as changes in the social, cultural, economic and political climate, non-Chinese Christians in China need a genuine humility to learn what the core issues are for churches today. Figure 4 shows attitudinal differences about engagement with overseas Christians between those inside China and those who are outside.

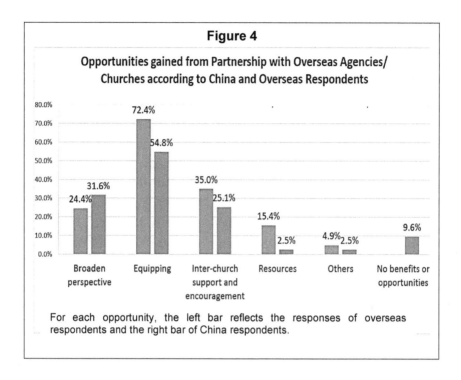

Figure 4

Opportunities gained from Partnership with Overseas Agencies/ Churches according to China and Overseas Respondents

For each opportunity, the left bar reflects the responses of overseas respondents and the right bar of China respondents.

One insight from the above graph[3] is that Chinese believers regard the broadening of their perspective to be an important aspect of their engagement with non-Chinese Christians. This seems to be a catchall phrase to include any way that their view of themselves, their church, their mission, and their culture could be enlarged or redefined as a result of interacting with overseas, non-Chinese Christians.

Non-Chinese can connect Chinese leaders to mentors or coaches who can share best practices or perspectives that will strengthen the next generation of Chinese leadership. Issues such as fund raising, church polity, marriage

---

[3] Chinese Gospel Research Alliance (2015), unpublished.
http://www.chinasource.org/resource-library/articles/perceptions-and-priorities-leaders-in-china, Accessed 6/2/2017.

counseling, witness in the public square, developing mission platforms, and infrastructure, are unique inside China. By walking alongside Chinese leaders, non-Chinese can provide friendship, counsel, and encouragement as they address complex issues. Perhaps one of the deepest issues revolves around identity. Andrew Walls observes: "It is our past which tells us who we are; without our past we are lost. The man with amnesia is lost, unsure of relationships, incapable of crucial decisions, precisely because all the time he has amnesia he is without his past."[4] How does the Chinese church today understand herself in regard to Chinese history, overseas missions history, and biblical history?

CONCLUSION

The present and future of the church in China belongs to Jesus Christ. He is the head of the Church, not any Chinese or non-Chinese leader. The apostle Paul urged the Gentile church at Ephesus to grow up in Christ:

> So that we may no longer be children, tossed to and fro by the waves and carried about by every wind of doctrine, by human cunning, by craftiness in deceitful schemes. Rather, speaking the truth in love, we are to grow up in every way into him who is the head, into Christ, from whom the whole body, joined and held together by every joint with which it is equipped, when each part is working properly, makes the body grow so that it builds itself up in love. (Ephesians 4:14-16)

What does this mean for Christians across the globe who serve in China today and will serve tomorrow? For those in Anglican mission circles, our Chinese brothers and sisters will welcome humble, mission-minded, Spirit-anointed servants of Christ who wish to establish deep relationships

---

[4] Andrew Walls, *The Missionary Movement in Christian History: Studies in the Transmission of Faith (Maryknoll, NY: Orbis Books, 2009),* 13.

anchored in gospel ministry. For all those within the broader overseas missions community, the changing context of China requires changes in how non-Chinese engage with the church. If overseas Christians align themselves with their Chinese counterparts in collaboration with the Holy Spirit's building up of the body in love, then Chinese leaders themselves will surely reach their goal of sending twenty thousand missionaries by 2030.

9

THE WORLD OF ISLAM

by Duane Miller

My family and I have had the privilege of working alongside AFM in various capacities since 2004, and I am pleased to contribute to the book commemorating the twenty-fifth anniversary of AFM. I have studied the history of the Church's mission to and among Muslims and the present state of that mission. In this chapter, I will try to look down the road two or three or five decades in order to offer some informed projections (or smart guesses, if you prefer) about the future of that mission and witness.

This chapter is divided into four parts. First, I will outline some of the main currents within Islam itself. Second, I will explore some of the key issues for the Church in the West to address. Third, I will address some key issues for the Church in the Muslim majority world. Finally, I will conclude with some brief observations relative particularly to Anglican Christianity.

Rev. Dr. Duane Alexander Miller serves on the pastoral staff at the Anglican Cathedral in Madrid, where he lives with Sharon and their three children. He is adjunct professor at the Protestant Faculty of Theology at Madrid (Alcobendas) and lecturer at the Christian Institute of Islamics of San Antonio, Texas. He has authored several articles and books on understanding Islam.

1. CURRENTS WITHIN ISLAM

From time to time, when teaching in churches and colleges, someone will hopefully suggest that what Islam needs is a reformation, just like European Christians had in the sixteenth century. Maybe then Muslims would be happy to live with separation of mosque and state. But this misrepresents both the motive of the European reformers of the sixteenth century—whether Protestant or Catholic—and what reformed Islam signifies. At the heart of this error is the assumption that reformation somehow means liberalization. Not so. Reform movements actually are trying to return to the sources, to the earliest generation of the community, to rid the collective mind of later accretions that obscure the pure vision of the founder. It is as if there were a window caked and smeared with mud, and the role of the reformer is to clean that window—not create a whole new vision. This is certainly the way that Luther and friends envisioned their own task. They had to get rid of superstitions, indulgences and popery (a favorite word) precisely in order to return to what they perceived as apostolic faith.

The twentieth century has witnessed multiple such attempts in the Muslim world. A precursor was the reform of Muhammad ibn Abd al Wahhab (d. 1792), the founder of the Wahabi School of Islam. But a veritable flourishing would come later: the Muslim Brotherhood (founded in 1928), Hizb ut-Tahriir (founded in 1953), Hezbollah (officially established in 1985), Hamas (founded in 1987), Al Qaeda (founded c. 1988), and lately the Islamic State (officially declared in 2013). These Muslims are seeking to return to the pure Islam of Muhammad and his companions. The Arabic word for "companions" is *sulafa,'* hence the English Salafi Islam or Salafists. To speak of the companions of Muhammad stirs up the same emotions in Muslims as speaking of the apostles does in Christians.

The coming decades will continue to witness the interior struggle of the Umma (the worldwide community of Muslims) to discern what precisely Islam is. Can Islam not transform itself into a secular form of personalized piety, as much of Protestantism has (with several unfortunate repercussions, one must admit)? I personally know many Muslims that don't want to force shari'a on the world and who would never think of engaging in acts of terror. Why can't they be the normative ones?

The problem is that the reformed Muslims have a much stronger claim to authentic Islam than do so called moderate or secular Muslims. Their form of life more closely imitates the life and ethic of their founder. The founders of Islam and Christianity both imparted a spiritual DNA to their communities. When either tradition strays too far from that DNA for too long, it loses vitality and dies out unless it is reformed. It is not hard to look at many of the once great mainline churches of the USA and the state churches of Europe and see that taking place right now. Here is an example from the middle ages: We Christians saw Muslims deploying, with great success, a sort of sanctified violence called *jihad*. We wondered if we could do something similar: Could we connect the grace of an indulgence with armed pilgrimage to liberate the Holy Land? These, today, we call the *Crusades*. At the time the word did not exist—it was just a pilgrimage.

The motive for the initial crusades was certainly blameless: to assist our fellow Christians in the East in recovering lands that were taken from them by Muslims in a wanton, unprovoked war of aggression. (The reasoning is essentially the same as that of the USA joining World War I.) And so, we tried crusading for a few centuries. But we discerned, after only a few centuries, that the sacramental violence of armed pilgrimage was not in line with the DNA our founder had imparted to us. And so we stopped.

Incidentally, this is also why anyone who draws a parallel between the crusades and jihad obviously knows nothing of either topic.

And then we have Muhammad. What DNA did he impart? He was not always violent, but at times he certainly was. Late in his life, reflecting on his successful career as prophet and statesman, he noted that, "I have been sent with the shortest expressions bearing the widest meanings, and I have been made victorious with terror (cast in the hearts of the enemy), and while I was sleeping, the keys of the treasures of the world were brought to me and put in my hand."[1] In Islam, Muhammad is the ideal human being, the template for every other person, the pathway to happiness. Now if Muhammad himself was "made victorious through terror," how realistic is it to say that terrorism—using fear to effect political change—is somehow wrong? A Muslim might argue that this or that particular act of terror is not in keeping with the pattern of life (sunna) of Muhammad, but the outright claim that terrorism represents a misreading of Islam is obviously untenable. In the long run, Islam can never be better than Muhammad, just as Christianity can never be better than Jesus.

All of this is to say that Muslims today are often conflicted about Islam and their place in the world. Muslims are questioning Islam like never before. A lot of Muslims value their own heritage and it is difficult for them to envision leaving Islam while remaining a member of their community. Today, a Christian can be a Baptist in Rome or a Pentecostal in London, but those are relatively new developments in the Christian world. What does it mean to be a Christian Turk? A Christian Saudi? Helping indigenous believers think through and present intelligent and livable answers to such

---

[1] *Sahih al Bukhari*, Book 4, Volume 52, Hadith 220

questions must be part of the Church's mission to and among Muslims in the coming decades.

To conclude this section, let me say a word about interreligious dialogue. Not a few leaders in the Anglican world will take the position that interreligious dialogue has replaced the venerable *missio ad gentes,* which explicitly focuses on sharing the gospel with the goal of religious conversion and, ultimately, the establishment of an indigenous, local church. That certainly has always been the heart of what Anglican Frontier Missions is about. The question is hardly a novel one. All the way back in the 1980s, our friends in the Roman Catholic Church were asking the same question, and this occasioned the writing of John Paul II's encyclical *Redemptoris Missio* in 1990. In a nutshell, he concludes that religious dialogue is of some value, but that it never can and never will replace the Church's mission to make disciples of all the peoples of the world.

This is clearly the correct answer, but if anything, I am much less optimistic about the value of interreligious dialogue (IRD) than was that fine Polish *episcopus romanus,* Pope John Paul II. Here is why I conclude that interreligious dialogue is not nearly as worthwhile as people suppose. First of all, the telos[2] of IRD is debatable. What exactly is the goal of IRD? Not to make disciples of all nations, in most cases not to preach the gospel. Preaching and dialogue are different animals. A common answer is that by building mutual understanding between Muslims and Christians they will be able to live together peacefully. This presupposes that there exists a will to live together peacefully. What if there isn't? In the Muslim majority world, IRD can be downright destructive and oppressive. It creates a public venue that attracts the attention of naïve Western scholars and clergy and gives the (often false) impression that Christian minorities are valued

---

[2] The reason why a thing exists, its final cause, its *raison d'être.*

and respected. Once the reporters and folks in purple shirts are gone, the quotidian abuse and oppression of Christians return. If that is not clear enough, IRD is often little more than a dog and pony show or a Potemkin Village.

And what about interreligious dialogue in the West? The divine vision of a Muslim society is not one with liberty and justice for all. The divine will of Allah for society is that Muslims be at the top of the pyramid in terms of power and wealth. Beneath them are the "People of the Book" (which is not a term of endearment, as so many ignorant Westerners suppose), who pay extra taxes and have severely circumscribed rights and security. Last of all are the pagans and atheists, who must either convert to Islam, leave *dar al Islam*, or be killed.[3] IRD is of great importance to Muslims in the West because it creates the impression that Muslims are in fact committed to the Western vision of justice, which supposedly is blind, treating all alike, whether rich, poor, male, female, white, black or whatever. It is certainly in the best interest of Muslims to live under that vision of justice until such a point that genuine justice, with Muslims at the top of the pyramid, can be instantiated to the glory of Allah and for the good of the Umma.

IRD in the West has the tendency to overemphasize the similarities between Islam and Christianity. The motive for this must be therapeutic, I think, for it cannot be based on any real spiritual commonality. Islam intentionally and clearly refutes the incarnation, the Trinity, the atonement, and the inspiration of the Bible. Once you take those out of Christianity, you have nothing left at all.

Finally, IRD often does not disclose the truth about Islam. Many Muslim leaders intentionally quote irenic verses that

---

[3] *Dar al Islam* is Arabic for 'abode of Islam'. It refers to all parts of the world that are (or were) under the control of Muslims regardless of whether or not they are in fact a majority of the population.

are taken out of context, or which they know to be abrogated. Consider this verse which is always quoted in order to explain that Islam and terrorism have nothing to do with each other: "...if any one slew a person...it would be as if he slew the whole people: and if any one saved a life, it would be as if he saved the life of the whole people" (Qur'an 5:32). But look at the whole verse: "On that account: We ordained for the Children of Israel that if any one slew a person— unless it be for murder or for spreading mischief in the land—it would be as if he slew the whole people: and if any one saved a life, it would be as if he saved the life of the whole people." So once we look at the actual verse, we find two curious things: one, that the actual rule was for the Children of Israel, not for Muslims. And two, that killing was permitted if someone was spreading mischief, or as in other translations, corruption.

2. IN THE WEST

In the previous section I outlined how the DNA of Muhammad was open to the strategic threat of fear in order to effectuate political change. Indeed, he claimed that this terror was from none other than Allah himself. Most people would call that terrorism. Any time you have a Muslim population, you will have some Muslims who take this seriously and do what Muslims are called to do, which is to emulate the prophet.

To put it bluntly to the Church in the West: Get used to terrorism. There is no way to avoid it. Even the concept of 'extreme vetting' is powerless in the face of it, for it is often not the first generation (the ones who are vetted) but the second generation born in the West, who take up the call to struggle (that is, wage jihad) in the way of Allah.

Here is a parable: There once was a great snake, it devoured everything in its sight and with time and patience digested everything it ate. One day it came across an animal and devoured it. But with time it could not digest it. So the snake died and decomposed, and from it emerged the strange animal, vigorous and healthy, and devoured the remains of the snake.

The snake is the West, which indeed has shown itself resilient in incorporating people from all around the world from different faiths. The strange animal is Islam. The West, in its foolishness and pride, does not understand that Islam cannot be digested by it, but that on the contrary, will overcome it. The West, with cultural habits unique to it—rule of law, meritocracy, human rights—will die.

The principal reason why the West will succumb to Islam is a confusion of categories. Future generations of Christians will be absolutely dumbfounded to hear that Islam was given all the protections of a religion while the fact that Islam is primarily an entire political-legal system will be ignored. Your great grandchildren in the late twenty-first century will be incredulous when they are told that once upon a time people in the USA could openly speak critically of Muhammad, or that once upon a time Muslims did not have superior rights to Christians in the courts of law, or that the once upon a time Christians and Jews did not have to pay the jizya.[4] They will marvel that Islam was protected even while it was common knowledge (or should have been common knowledge) that it must replace that secular constitution with one based on the immutable, benevolent, divinely revealed legal system regulating all human conduct: the shari'a.[5]

---

[4] The jizya is a yearly tax that Christians and Jews under Islamic rule must pay according to the Qur'an. It is to be accompanied by a public humiliation ritual of the one paying the tax. For more in this see *The Third Choice: Islam, Dhimmitude, and Freedom* (Deror, 2010) by Mark Durie.

[5] For data showing that in most areas of the world a substantial majority of Muslims favor shari'a law, see "The World's Muslims: Religion, Politics, and

Some people will say this is a rather pessimistic picture of the future. Not so. The Church and the West are not coterminous. The West has lost its will to live, as is clearly proven by the fact that each generation fails to produce a generation of the same or larger size. Others will object that many Muslims in the West don't advocate for the shari'a, but I tell you that when they can democratically put it into effect, they will. Most Christians won't go out to protest at abortion clinics, but many will prefer a prolife candidate at the voting booth.

Islam creates societies that most people—including Muslims—don't want to live in. They are characterized by shoddy economies, lousy educational systems, corruption, and nepotism. So people from those countries (mostly Muslims) are constantly looking for a way to leave. Christendom, despite all of its warts, has left a heritage that is attractive to humans around the world. The West has become committed to an ideology that is not based on reality or any sort of empirical or logical reflection— that all cultures are equal. Because of this, the West is unable to tell people that they must abandon certain cultural habits in order to live in the West: anti-Semitism, child marriage, female genital mutilation—all of which have the approval of Muhammad, the "ideal" human being. Any person suggesting that this should happen will be accused of racism. Furthermore, since these practices all have their origins in the divine revelation of Allah's will through his servant Muhammad, they can claim the protection afforded to *religion.*

In Islam, the West has encountered an irresolvable conundrum. Is there a way to safeguard the constitutional

---

Society" by Pew Research Forum (April 2013).
http://www.pewforum.org/2013/04/30/the-worlds-muslims-religion-politics-society-overview/, Accessed February 23, 2017.

orders of countries in the West while also acknowledging the dignity of Muslims? Is it possible to allow Muslims to practice the spiritual part of Islam while forcing them to abandon the prophet's mandate for the entire world to live under his shari'a? The problem is that to parse Islam into the private and the public, the religious and the political, is to violate its integrity. And the whole secular order of the West is founded on this conviction—that in some way, to a significant degree, one can render unto Caesar what is Caesar's and unto God what is God's. And Islam comes and says, "That division is inauthentic and unacceptable." Moreover, since Islam is consistently misconstrued as a religion (rather than an anti-Constitutional legal-political order), there is no possibility of discriminating against Muslims in relation to immigration.

But isn't it true that unprecedented numbers of Muslims are converting to Christ? It certainly is, as Patrick Johnstone and I have documented in, "Believers in Christ from a Muslim Background: A Global Census."[6] But ultimately, the future belongs to those who procreate. This is why a recent study by the Pew Forum estimated that by 2050, "The number of Muslims will nearly equal the number of Christians around the world."[7] The same report estimates that the global Islamic Umma will have increased in population by 73% from 2010 to 2050, mainly by birth and not by conversion. The figure for Christianity is 35%, the same as the estimated population growth for the world. So while conversions are increasing substantially, they are not even close to keeping pace with natural population growth.

---

[6] Duane Miller and Patrick Johnstone, "Believers in Christ from a Muslim Background: A Global Census," *Interdisciplinary Journal for Research on Religion,* 11 (2015): Article 10.

[7] "The Future of World Religions: Population Growth Projections, 2010-2050," by Pew Research Center (April 2015).
http://www.pewforum.org/2015/04/02/religious-projections-2010-2050/.
Accessed 23 February 2017. Available at http://tinyurl.com/gw5k4km.

Another recent study indicated that beginning around 2035 more children would be born to Muslim women than Christian women.[8]

The dysfunction of Islamic societies around the world, coupled with robust population growth and our misclassification of Islam as a "religion," guarantees consistent large-scale Muslim migration to the West for the rest of the century. Indeed, every factor that occasions emigration can be attributed to adverse developments in the Muslim world: civil wars, environmental degradation, lack of water and arable land to support a quickly growing population, corrupt governments, lack of economic opportunity, inferior educational institutions, and so on. The West naively and incorrectly assumes that just because Muslims are allowed to immigrate, they will all be thankful or respectful.

3. IN DAR AL ISLAM

In the course of preparing research and background for this article, I contacted about twenty respected colleagues from various denominations with experience in the Muslim world. I asked for their input on the research questions of this paper. One colleague with experience in Egypt made the following comment:

> As much as the juggernaut of Islam appears to be on the ascendancy, it is trying by all means to hide the fissures that are in its subterranean foundations. Islam is thoroughly unprepared to deal with the democratization of its societies where it is dominant due to the effects of social media, the Internet and the sharing of ideas. No longer can the mantra of control—"Do not ask questions,

---

[8] "The Changing Global Religious Landscape," Pew Research Center (April 2017) .www.pewforum.org/2017/04/05/the-changing-global-religious-landscape/, Accessed April 7, 2017.

thereby some have lost the faith"—function where youth are able and willing to ask hard questions.[9]

On one level, this is true. Muslims are asking questions that before they had not been asking. This is part of the dynamic that is leading some to become disappointed with Islam and seek alternatives—secular humanism and evangelical Christianity being the main two destinations. On the other hand, I have little confidence in those who are the questioners to actually assume power in the Muslim world. Remember the so called Arab Spring in Egypt? The liberal, freedom loving youth filled Tahriir Square in Cairo. Hope was in the air. And what was the result? The election of Muhammad Morsi, representing the Muslim Brotherhood, one of those movements you used to call "Islamist" but now know to simply call it "reformed."

This tells us something about the future of politics in the Muslim world. While many people are questioning Islam and are even disappointed with Islam, they do not have the discipline to actually take power anywhere. And, I predict, they never will. The DNA of the founder is not with them.

It is in this context that we must reflect on the future of mission in the Muslim world. The Muslim world is not growing more secular and more free—quite the contrary. Nonetheless, there are fledgling churches throughout the Muslim world in which most believers come from Islam. (A few of them are even Anglican.) Christians who belong to these churches and participate in their lives face a number of specific challenges:

---

[9] Correspondence with author, February 2017. The quote referenced is a paraphrase of Qur'an 5:101.

Marriage for Converts

The complexities related to marriage and then the raising of children are different from country to country. In many Muslim majority countries, it is impossible for a Muslim to legally convert to Christianity, which means their legal identity will forever be Muslim. Furthermore, a Christian man (that is, from a family legally recognized as Christian) cannot marry a convert from Islam because of the shari'a. A male convert might marry a woman who is Christian from birth, but then all their children will legally be Muslim. The situation is inhumane and immoral, but it is the reality in much of the Muslim majority world. How can the local church help? What wisdom can we bring from Scripture to this complex situation?

The Children of Converts

We have seen the initial harvest in many places—Algeria, Iran, Turkey, Indonesia, Bangladesh.[10] We must start asking how to deal with the children. Adults are accustomed to operating in different ways in different contexts. We are used to having layers of identity. Children are not. What can we say to the child who is, by law, a Muslim, yet is raised in his home as a Christian? If he attends a public school (and unless his parents are rich, he will), then his teachers and fellow students will treat him as a Muslim; the child must take classes in Islam while the children of Christian families (if there are any) are sent to learn from a Christian priest. What guidance does the Church have for this child or his parents?

---

[10] For country by country numbers, see Duane Miller and Patrick Johnstone, "Believers in Christ from a Muslim Background: A Global Census," *Interdisciplinary Journal for Research on Religion,* 11 (2015): Article 10.

Liberation

In reading scores of texts by converts from Islam, I was able to identify what seemed to me a strain of liberation theology. Not the Latin American type, which is concerned with economics, but a variety that cries out against the injustice of the shari'a, which nullifies the human rights of ex-Muslims and treats them as non-persons.[11] How can the global Church join with ex-Muslim Christians still living under what they perceive to be the dehumanizing shadow of shari'a? And, related to our previous section, what can Christians in the West learn as their moribund civilization decays and is gradually replaced by a young, fecund Islamic society?

Shedding the Heritage of Dhimmitude

In Islamic Arabic, the name for a non-Muslim group living under a Muslim ruler is *dhimm*i. The dhimmi are subject to public humiliation and constant reminders that Muslims are benevolent and generous to allow the non-Muslims to live under Muslim rule. For excellent examples of dhimmi behavior, see any of the statements by Bush, Obama, Merkel, Trudeau, or Cameron on how wonderful Islam is and how much the USA, Germany, Canada and the UK are indebted to Muslims for enriching those countries; note their ceaseless insistence that Islam and terror have nothing to do with each other.[12] The prophet himself begs to disagree, as we have

---

[11] See Chapter 5 of *Living among the Breakage* or 'Your Swords do not Concern me at all' in *St Francis Magazine*, Vol 7(2), April 2011, pp 228–260.

[12] I am indebted to the Rev. Dr. Mark Durie of the Anglican Church of Australia for this insight. The complete book on the status of the dhimmi is Bat Ye'or's *Understanding Dhimmitude* (RVP Press, 2013). For a historical record of how dhimmitude led to the near elimination of Christianity in the East see her outstanding book *The Decline of Eastern Christianity under Islam* (Fairleigh Dickinson, 1996).

seen. But the indigenous churches in the Muslim majority world must shed this negative heritage. Dhimmitude has made a profound impact on the psychology of Christians. For centuries those Christians could not evangelize *dar al Islam* or critique Islam; in fact, they could not even teach their children about Islam. Every year the Christian elders had to be publicly humiliated in the presence of all as they paid the jizya. The *de jure* laws are no longer present in some countries, but the de facto tradition remains in place. What is needed is a large scale movement of public renunciation of dhimmitude by Christians, including those who have converted from Islam.

4. A PLACE FOR ANGLICANS

So let us ask now whether there is anything unique that Anglican Christians have to contribute in the coming decades? Let me also note that much of this applies to our sisters and brothers in the other magisterial traditions of that hodgepodge of reform movements started in the sixteenth century. (I mean Presbyterians and Lutherans, of course.)

We can offer a worldwide community. Yes, yes, I know, the Anglican Communion as a whole is in a tenuous position. But it's still here, there, and, if not quite everywhere, in much of the world. Belonging to a global community has a power to it that transcends simply belonging to this or that one congregation. Knowing that any time you visit a major city anywhere in the world, there is a good chance you will be able to worship in a manner and format you are accustomed to is, for some if not all people, attractive. We can offer a liturgy that is rooted in history. Some ex-Muslims are quite happy to do away with all forms and liturgies, but others retain a respect for what we call liturgy and common prayer. For those who do retain this attachment, I think we have a lot to offer in our prayer book tradition—though I must note that some of our prayer books used in the Muslim majority world are badly in need of updating. And this not for the sake of changing theology per se, but simply using language that people today understand.

Anglicanism has much to offer on the level of teaching resources. Countless Christians around the world have benefited from the apologetics of C. S. Lewis, the biblical scholarship of N. T. Wright, and the Alpha Course, for instance. I would even include as teaching resources the many novels of Madeleine L'Engle and the poetry of T. S. Eliot here. And so, I would hope that Anglican pastors, missionaries, and scholars would be able to provide some essential teaching resources, not only for the precarious body known as the Anglican Communion, but for the Church catholic.

Muslims often know little to nothing about Christianity. But even Muslims who are not devout often have been taught, from a young age, what is "wrong" with Christianity. They say, for instance, it is illogical to claim that one is a monotheist while also believing that Jesus is God, because that obviously means believing in two deities. Another argument is that it is illogical and contrary to justice to think that one person can pay for the penalty of another person, as Christians do in relation to the atonement. What just judge would allow for a just person to go to prison on behalf of a criminal? If our courts functioned like that there would be a great revolt, yet this is the centerpiece of Christian theology. Or consider the Christian's oft-noted difference between Jesus and Muhammad, that Jesus was peaceful and forgiving while Muhammad taught that paradise is in the shade of swords. Yet it appears that this disposition of Jesus is only temporary, because, as one Muslim friend answered when I asked him how many people Jesus had killed, "None yet, but when he returns who knows how many he will kill!" And I could easily extend this list another five pages.

Yet the truth is that very few Christians know how to answer even the most basic questions about the incarnation, the Trinity, or the atonement.[13] I could only wish that Christian children throughout the world were taught some simple, orthodox answers to these questions. I believe that Anglican Christianity has that fine combination of scriptural and historical insight, along with the theological depth and winsomeness in communication that are needed in order to provide such a resource. A possible pattern here would be the brief catechism in the American *Book of Common Prayer* (1979).

But let's be honest: As Anglicans, on the whole, we're failing. By this time in the chapter you should know that I like calling a spade a spade. I have told you to get used to terrorism and that the West is in a state of irreversible decline. And so let me tell you that Anglicanism, as a branch of the Great Tradition, is not doing very much. Yes, there are some things happening in sub-saharan Africa, and a few hopeful outposts elsewhere in *dar al Islam*. But almost all the money you spend on mission actually goes to helping poor Christians. That will never lead to Muslims putting their faith in Christ. The sad thing is that we have a proven historical way for balancing the ancient and the contemporary, the local and the catholic. And that is how missions form a diocese, and that diocese founds new ones or grows and divides into new ones. When there are enough dioceses, we have a new province. If that province grows enough, it can further divide into more provinces.

But what are we doing in *dar al Islam*? Very little, it turns out. Excuses are myriad: Our churches do not receive legal

---

[13] I note that Abu Daoud in *Sharing Jesus with Muslims in America* makes a beginning toward this effort.

recognition; we cannot build new church buildings; our clergy do not get clergy visas; and so on. If Anglican Christianity lacks the creativity to address these rudimentary problems, if I may be frank, it deserves to die.

We also focus way too much on the concept of partner dioceses. This tends to be unfruitful because the places where the Great Commission is yet to be fulfilled are places where there are no dioceses, or if there, they cater to non-indigenous congregations and rarely have any desire to share the gospel with local Muslims.

So let me put the ball in your court. What will you do? What will your parish do? What will you do as an individual? You, as a bishop, lay person, deacon, or presbyter? You, as a possessor of wealth? You, as a professional with valuable talents? You, as an intercessor?

FOUR PRACTICAL CHALLENGES FOR THE CHURCHES IN THE WEST

First, Christians must formulate a response to Islamization. I have already explained why I do not believe that discontinuing Muslim immigration is possible. So is it to be resisted? If so, on the political level? I don't believe this is viable because Islam is (incorrectly) conferred protection as a religion. Is explosive immigration to be accepted as a judgment on the West, as many Christians interpreted the triumph of Islamic imperialism in earlier centuries? Or perhaps it is true that since we didn't take the gospel to Muslims, God has brought the Muslims to us.

Second, Christians must be educated about Islam and encouraged to form Christ-centered relationships with Muslims. Whatever is possible in the political arena (and I'm not optimistic about that at all), relationships are most often in the context of Muslims coming to Christ. I am encouraged to see quality, practical resources available for individuals and churches like *Sharing Jesus with Muslims in America* by Abu Daoud (2016) and the DVD series *Journey to Jesus: Building Christ-Centered Friendships with Muslims* (2014), both available online. Mark Durie's *Liberty to the Captives* is likewise outstanding.[14] (I note that Abu Daoud and Durie are both Anglicans.)

The third challenge is providing pastoral care and catechesis for inquirers and converts. This is especially acute in parts of Europe where some refugees have sought out a new faith. As noted previously, many Muslims are asking questions, and some are coming to the conclusion that Islam is the problem. A colleague and friend working with the Assemblies of God in Europe made this astute remark: "I think the challenge is [for us to provide] deep, linguistically and culturally informed, Spirit-empowered discipleship, training, and shepherding of the growth."[15] I can't say it any better. Does your church website say that you welcome Muslim inquirers and Muslim background believers? Has your church taken any steps to equip your people to understand Islam and how to share the gospel with Muslims? During your prayers of the people, do you pray for Muslims to encounter the love of God in Christ? Believers who leave Islam for Christianity are usually estranged from their families. Is your church willing and able to be their new home and family?[16]

Fourth, put your money where your mouth is. Islam is the greatest challenge that the church has ever faced in its two millennia of life and ministry. Yet churches spend almost

---

[14] http://markdurie.com/books-dvds/libertytothecaptives
[15] Correspondence with author, February 2017.
[16] One of the most penetrating writings I have ever read on Christ's converts from Islam was written by Temple Gairdner, a pioneer missionary to Cairo with the Church Mission Society in the early 20th Century. The article is "The Christian Church as a Home for Christ's Converts from Islam" in *Moslem World* Vol 14, 1924, pp 235-246.

all of their mission funds helping other Christians. Does your church contribute any money to missionaries focused on sharing the gospel with Muslims? It was with this sort of ministry in mind that Anglican Frontier Missions was founded.

In summary, the future of the West will be an ever-increasingly Islamic future—migration patterns and Muslim fertility guarantee this. When witnessing to Muslims, we must have the conversation about miscategorizing Islam as a religion. Christians must think and talk about the repercussions of Islamization, which are inevitable. And above all, we must take practical steps to meet local Muslims, share the love of Christ with them in the context of personal relationships, and then make sure that we have mature, culturally aware, wise paths of discipleship and empowerment for them in place. Stop using all your mission funds to help poor Christians or making lousy Christians into devout Christians, and start using those funds to make disciples of non-Christians, especially Muslims!

10

INDIA HARVEST

by George Ivey

India is a nation that is "ripe unto harvest." In approximately 2025, its population will surpass the population of China, and India will be the largest country in the world. There has been a youth surge in India in recent years. Today, 41% of the population is below the age of twenty.

The diversity of people and cultures in India can make one's head spin! There are over forty-five hundred ethnic and tribal groups living there. Hindi is the official language, but the truth is that India has no national language. About 460 languages are in use today. English, of course, is widely spoken in India.

India's indigenous people are from a Dravidian extract and are the first recorded people group to populate India over three thousand years ago. Migrants and conquerors, known as Aryans, occupied the northern territory, as the Dravidians moved south, creating two distinct cultures.

Rev. Canon George Ivey serves on the staff of Holy Cross Cathedral in Atlanta, Georgia, and is Canon Missioner for the Anglican Diocese of the South. He has pastored five churches and has brought a strong focus on missions throughout the world including India, Western Europe, the Caribbean Islands and Latin America. He has worked in Christian TV and in healthcare. He is married to Paulette, and they have two adult sons and four grandchildren.

The tenets of Hinduism were brought to the culture through a fusion of tribal animism and imaginative concepts of mythical gods. This religion, which is at least twenty-five hundred years old, has prospered because it incorporates every religious concept that humanity wishes to bring under its umbrella. There is no creed or declaration of faith. It is utterly syncretistic and repels exclusivity much like the ancient Roman culture.

The propagation of Hindu beliefs is carried from generation to generation by a system that situates people based on their lineage into strata or castes. The engine behind this system is tradition attached to national identity. It is thought to have produced the most dominant and widespread form of human discrimination on the face of the earth, with over 250 million Dalits, or outcasts, who are not afforded human dignity in society. The gospel is welcomed news to them as they are delivered out of a fatalistic belief in reincarnation.

Alongside the influential presence of Hinduism in the history of this great county is the long and strong presence of Islam. Muslim conquerors invaded India in the second half of the eleventh century. From then on, the picture of India has shown both Hindu and Muslim traditions. Moghul influence has profoundly penetrated the arts, the government, and the culture of India.

These two major religions have lived side by side for over nine hundred years. Sometimes, there is peace and mutual respect, while at other times, there is open hostility and violence. The partition of India and Pakistan in 1949 is the clearest example of the violence. Another site of hostility is Kashmir, with both India and Pakistan claiming legitimacy.

William Carey (1761-1834) is considered the father of modern missions in India. At great personal sacrifice, he spent forty-one years in India without a furlough, publishing the gospel in over two dozen languages. After translating the

Bible into over thirty of India's languages, he had only seven hundred converts by the end of his life. His mantra was "Expect great things *from* God and attempt great things *for* God!" Carey planted much seed and laid a strong foundation for the harvest of today.

Interestingly, E. Stanley Jones (1883-1973) was born a year following William Carey's passing. E. Stanley Jones powerfully impacted India with his Christ-like spirit and proclamation of the gospel; he is famous for his Ashram movement. He initially ministered to the outcasts and lower caste of the Hindu culture, but God gave him great favor with the educated, upper caste Indians, as well.

Mahatma Gandhi was a close personal friend of Jones, who wrote Gandhi's biography after Gandhi's passing. Dr. Martin Luther King, Jr. said that it was this book that influenced him to promote non-violence in America.

There is no greater proof of God's love for the Indian people, apart from Calvary, than what is reflected by the sacrifice, devotion, and perseverance of multitudes of Christian missionaries.

If you visit the Indian State of Kerala today, you will be amazed to learn that seven million Christians reside there. History indicates that after the day of Pentecost, St. Thomas boarded a merchant ship, sailed through the Strait of Gibraltar, and rounded the Cape of Africa. After landing in what is today Kerala, Thomas planted churches. God has greatly rewarded Thomas' sacrifice, and gospel roots have grown deep in India through the centuries.

There is a mighty outpouring of the Holy Spirit through many ministries in India, although there are many states with no access to the gospel. Recently, an undocumented language (Koro) of a remote people group was discovered in the Northeast corner of India.

Forty years ago, an American minister named John Gilman had a vision of reaching millions of Indians for Christ through the use of film. He realized many Indians were illiterate and he also realized that most Indians loved movies! John was able to acquire a feature-length film of the life of Jesus, entitled *Dayasagar,* which means "Oceans of Mercy." It is the video portrayal of the Gospel of Luke by all Indian actors in sixteen languages of India. Today hundreds of film teams show this and other films of the gospel in remote Indian villages nightly. Film has become an important tool for church planting throughout the nation.

The great Anglican mission leader V. S. Azariah, speaking at the 1910 Edinburgh Conference, invited missionaries from the West to join his efforts. "But," he said, "come as friends. India will be evangelized by Indians."

The following two chapters are by Indian leaders who have helped the work of AFM in India. They describe strategic concepts and efforts to expand God's harvest in India.

11

REACHING THE HIGH CASTE

by Prem James

The nineteenth and twentieth centuries saw an unprecedented mission movement around the world. The call of God to minister to the needs of a broken world moves us with compassion. The realization that no one can do it alone encourages us to work together, and we are further challenged to do so by the astounding fact that this generation has the realistic potential of bringing the gospel to every man and woman on the face of the earth. This includes the unreached people groups of India as well, if only, under the mighty hand of God, we are willing to work together.

Some mission theologians have articulated the following as emphases for the twenty-first century, in contrast to what was perceived as the twentieth century mission paradigm:

- The old paradigm was about pioneering; the new paradigm is all about *partnering*.

Prem James is the Area Director, South Asia for Partners International. His wife, Rita, is founder and principal of Asha Kiran, Ray of Hope, a school for special needs children in Bangalore. Asa Kiran is also celebrating its 25th year. Prem is a vigorous promoter of cooperation in mission. All of the work of AFM in India has benefitted from his input and wisdom.

- The old paradigm was about resources; the new paradigm is about *relationships.*

- The old paradigm was about strategy; the new paradigm is about *synergy.*

Keeping the above in mind, let us look at what *network* and *partnership* mean. These words are often used interchangeably; most networks have an element of partnership in them while every partnership involves some degree of networking.

> NETWORK: A group of people who are linked informally and who communicate with one another to share ideas and information to meet their individual needs.

Some of the key characteristics of network are:

- Shared interests
- Communication
- Exchange of information

PARTNERSHIP: A close working relationship between individuals and/or organizations, who agree to work together for a specific purpose/goal because they can achieve more together than by themselves.

Some of the key characteristics of partnership are:

- Accountability
- Shared skills and resources
- Shared goals
- Synergy
- Increased strength

HORIZONTAL PARTNERSHIPS

A horizontal partnership consists of ministries located in the same area working together on projects, such as radio broadcasts, Scripture translation, or development. A horizontal partnership may be for one people group, city, or country, or across a number of people groups, cities, or countries.

Agency	People Group/Country/City									
	1	2	3	4	5	6	7	8	9	10
Personal Witness										
Visiting Teams										
Bible Translation										
Literature				➡						
Tracts										
Radio			➡							
Cassettes										
Jesus Film										
Development										
Medical					➡					
Relief										

Figure 5
Horizontal Partnerships

Some Examples:

- Four different literature ministries could work together on a distribution system.

- Five different radio ministries could work together to broadcast in the same language, each contributing different aspects, e.g. one providing the transmission facilities, another producing the programs, another contributing features to the programs, yet another focusing on the follow-up and one providing literature to be used in the follow-up.

- Three different medical ministries could work together on a hospital project, with one providing the building, another medical staff, and a third medical resources.

VERTICAL PARTNERSHIPS

A vertical partnership consists of different types of ministries working together to reach a particular people (or peoples), language group, city, or section of the population. So, we may have radio, Scripture translation, development, and church planting ministries all working together to reach the same group of people and intentionally linking their work together.

Agency	People Group/Country/City		
	1	2	3
Personal Witness			
Visiting Teams			
Bible Translation			
Literature			
Tracts			
Radio			
Cassettes			
Jesus Film			
Development			
Medical			
Relief			

Figure 6
Vertical Partnerships

Some examples:

- Radio ministry broadcasting programs, with tract and literature ministries developing materials, which are linked into the radio programs.

- Offering tracts and literature on air; program recordings distributed to those who can't listen to the radio.

- The *Jesus Film Project* working with medical, development, and relief ministries in an area where there has been war or a natural disaster, with short-term visiting teams coming in to help both practically and spiritually, linking with local churches in the area who are able to provide a personal witness to the affected.

- All the ministries working to reach a specific area, intentionally linking the various types of ministry to impact the work of evangelism and church planting.

Having looked at the different kinds of partnerships, let us look at some of the benefits of networking and partnering that we can apply to the work among the Adivasis, the minority but indigenous people of South Asia.

- We can be better stewards of the resources God has given us.

- We can focus on our strengths and not on our weaknesses.

- We can do more together than we can do on our own (greater synergy).

- When we work in partnership, we have more hope of having an impact.

- When we work with others, it's more encouraging for us.

- There are so few Christians in India, and we are scattered. On our own we can achieve little; we need to work with others.

- There is such a great need for Bible translation in India; we have to do it with others if we're going to get the job done.

- We can more effectively advocate for Christians who are being persecuted in remote areas.

Why are networks and partnerships important for developing Church Planting Movements (CPMs) among Unreached People Groups (UPGs)?

- There are a number of UPGs that are still not reached with the gospel of our Lord Jesus Christ.

- Geographic, cultural, linguistic and other barriers make it difficult for one person/agency to do all the work.

- Our resources are limited.

Some suggestions for how work among UPGs can become effective:[1]

- Producing a directory of those who work among them (security sensitive);

- Mapping the areas where the UPG live;

- Listing current strategies;

- Integrating the literacy, radio and development work with the evangelistic work;

- Meeting periodically with leaders of various agencies/churches who work among the people;

---

[1] S.D. Ponraj, *From Graveyard to Vineyard* (Chennai: Mission Educational Books, 2010), 91.102.

- Building local leaders through conscious leadership development;

- Listing tools that are needed for evangelism, church planting, and other social causes;

- Encouraging networking and partnership among the agencies/churches interested in working among a particular UPG.

Bihar Outreach Network (BORN) adopted a church planting project called "Bless Bhojpuri" for the twenty million Bhojpuri-speaking UPGs in four districts of western Bihar. It was a four-way partnership in face-to-face evangelism and church planting. The four partners committed themselves to a common vision: Go to the unreached people and bring total community transformation by working together. The partners shared their resources in equipping, supporting, and mentoring the grass roots church planters. International, national, and local partners were involved in the church planting movements among the Bhojpuri speaking people groups:

First Partner (International): Scripture in Use Ministries committed themselves to train the field workers through communication materials.

Second Partner (International): Pantano Christian Church, Tucson, Arizona, was committed to supporting the workers who were trained in oral methods in their seminars and in Oral Bible Schools. The partnership project was known as "Bless Bhojpuri" and covered the Bhojpuri-speaking people groups in four districts of Bihar.

Third Partner (National): Bihar Outreach Network (BORN) was committed to bringing different churches and missions together to focus on church planting movements among UPGs, and to bring a total community transformation, using oral communication as an effective method. BORN was made up of sixty-two churches and indigenous missions; it not only conducted training but also mentored the workers and monitored their activities in the field. It provided them with resources, such as picture books and audio/video cassettes in their native language.

Fourth Partner (Local): The local indigenous missions in Bihar State. There were seven indigenous missions actively involved in church planting movements in these four districts. They were formed by local Bihari leaders during the last five years. BORN helped them in the formation and establishment of these missions. The mission leaders recruited students and sent them for training. After the training they appointed them as church planters, and mentored them to lead the church planting movements among the UPGs.

What made the partnership effective? All of the four partners shared important values:

1. **Common Vision.** The partners' vision was to reach unreached people with the gospel and bring a total community transformation, with a special focus on the people of non-literate oral cultures of Bihar State.

2. **Common Values.** They believed in the oral Bible and in the power of oral communication. They believed that people of oral cultures do not need to be literate in order to become disciples and leaders in the local church.

3. **Common Mission.** Their final goal was to disciple all the people of the oral cultures in Bihar, bring them into a church fellowship, and plant churches that

would plant other churches and develop a church planting movement.

4. **Common Goals.** They put together a project called Bless Bhojpuri with a goal to plant two thousand churches and to baptize fifty thousand people between the years 2000 and 2010.

5. **Common Sharing of Resources.** They committed to sharing their resources among the partnering agencies and working together to fulfill their mission goals. This involved prayer, training programs, funds, mentoring, and field administration.

6. **Common Appreciation/Reporting.** They had common reporting. Each of the partners took equal credit for the final goal accomplished in terms of baptisms given and churches planted. They had a common appreciation for each partner's role in the project.

THE RESULT OF THE PARTNERSHIP IN ORAL EVANGELISM

Through the Bless Bhojpuri project, the partners have been able to train three hundred grass roots church planters in oral communication through the Bridges Seminars and the Oral Bible Schools, comprised of both full-timers and volunteers. These were under the supervision and mentoring of the indigenous mission leaders and BORN leadership. The result over the last four years: fifty-five hundred people baptized, two hundred churches planted, and three hundred small groups formed.

Case Study of the Lingayat Partnership

In 1986 there was a consultation that highlighted the need for reaching out to high caste Hindus. Traditionally, Christian work was mostly among the tribal and low caste people. As a result of this consultation, the Lingayat people group living in Karnataka was chosen for a pilot program. About twelve different agencies came together with a common goal to reach this people group. They had periodic meetings, prayer, and planning to see that this group would be reached with the gospel of our Lord Jesus Christ.

As a result of working together, the following was achieved:

- One-year radio program for Lingayats;
- Three different follow-up tracts;
- Periodic Lingayat conferences;
- Vision seminars for pastors.

The number of Lingayat believers is now five thousand, up from two thousand when the partnership began. Thus, we see the effectiveness of the united efforts through partnerships in oral evangelism. We know that working together works. May the Lord help us to partner with each other so that every UPG will be reached with the gospel of Jesus Christ.

12

CHURCH PLANTING MOVEMENTS
IN BIHAR

by S. D. Ponraj

After working for Friends Missionary Prayer Band for seventeen years, the Lord challenged me and my wife, asking us to begin a transformation movement in a difficult mission field—the North Indian State of Bihar. This state was known as the "graveyard of missions and missionaries." While praying, the Lord spoke to us from Ezekiel 37, which confirmed that "the dry bones of Bihar" will get new life through the gospel of Jesus Christ, and Bihar will be transformed into a "vineyard for missions." We obeyed and went to begin our work in Bihar in 1991. During a missions conference held in Patna in 1992, a network of churches and mission groups was formed called *Bihar Outreach Network* (BORN). I initially spent time mobilizing these groups toward united action.

In 1998 I took over the leadership of BORN with a team of leaders from various churches and missions. The Lord honored their efforts and the movement spread into a

---

The Reverend Dr. S.D. Ponraj began in Gujarat State with Friends Missionary Prayer Band. For twenty years he was Director of Bihar Outreach Network (BORN). The author of twelve books on mission, he now leads the Bihar Christian Church which has over four hundred congregations. AFM has collaborated with Ponraj and BORN in using and promoting the Strategy Coordination model.

number of unreached people groups of Bihar. By God's grace and the united efforts of the churches and missions, over one hundred thousand people have been baptized and five thousand house churches formed. BORN has trained about five thousand church planters, pastors, Bible teachers, volunteers and church elders through systematic seminars and training programs. The following are the factors that contributed toward the transformation movement in Bihar State.

EARNEST PRAYERS OF GOD'S PEOPLE OVER THE YEARS

People all over the world, and especially in India and South India, engaged in intercessory prayer for Bihar for several decades. In the 1990s, Prayer Through the 10/40 Window, initiated by the AD 2000 Movement, focused on Bihar. Later, DAWN Ministries mobilized prayers from different countries of the world and particularly from Latin America. The BORN movement established Bihar Prayer Network and published the *Bihar Prayer Guide.*

Thousands of people were mobilized to pray for Bihar State. Their earnest prayers have not gone without effect. God heard their cry and answered their prayers.

FAITHFUL SOWING OF THE GOSPEL IN THE PAST

From 1970 to 1990, several missions have been faithfully preaching the gospel in Bihar State. Missions like Gospel Echoing Missionary Society (GEMS), Friends Missionary Prayer Band (FMPB), Operation Mobilization (OM), and India Every Home Crusade (IEHC) have faithfully shared the gospel through literature, open-air preaching, and film shows as well as through personal contacts and correspondence courses. GEMS has been working faithfully in Bihar over the past forty-five years. The faithful ministry done by these pioneering missionaries and others has softened the hearts of the people.

UNITY DEMONSTRATED BY THE LEADERS OF VARIOUS CHURCHES AND MISSIONS

In 1992, the Lord brought the churches and missions together in Patna on one platform, demonstrating unity. Some 350 leaders representing the Church of North India, Baptist Church, Assembly of God, Brethren Assembly, GEMS, FMPB, OM, and others came together for the first time to consider working jointly for the evangelization of Bihar. The second such conference was held in 1995 at Ranchi, called by India Missions Association. And the third one was organized in 1998 at Patna under the banner of the AD 2000 Movement. These united gatherings resulted in the formation and strengthening of BORN. God honored the united efforts of his people.

FOCUSED TRAINING OF THE GRASSROOTS CHURCH PLANTERS

More than five thousand evangelists, missionaries, and volunteers have gone through various teaching programs through the efforts of BORN. Bihar is the most illiterate state in India. For many years, evangelists and church planters were struggling with how to effectively communicate the gospel. Many had failed and others were greatly discouraged with the poor results in their ministries. Into that desperate situation, the Lord brought a special course called "Gospel Communication Bridges for Oral Learners," which introduced by Scripture In Use Ministries. This training program brought a real breakthrough in the minds of the evangelists. Those who attended the seminars felt greatly encouraged for the task of communicating the gospel to the thousands of non-literate people in the villages. Special focus was given to communication with the village women, who have almost zero literacy. The result was marvelous. Hundreds not only understood the gospel but also decided to be baptized and reach out to other unreached people.

THE PRIORITY GIVEN TO TRAINING AND DEVELOPING LEADERS AT DIFFERENT LEVELS

Training was given not only to evangelists and church planters but also to prospective leaders. During the last ten years, mission consultations and unreached people group seminars have greatly helped the church and mission leaders in Bihar. Since 1999, BORN has been conducting the Nehemiah Institute for Strategic Mission and trained over one hundred leaders in Bihar. BORN also conducted the Esther Institute for Strategic Mission and trained several women as leaders for missions in Bihar. Many of these leaders have started new mission societies, adopted unreached people groups, and are leading church planting movements. These leaders are making the breakthrough a reality.

CONCENTRATED EFFORTS ON UNREACHED BUT RECEPTIVE PEOPLE GROUPS

Two people groups in India, "Backward Class" and "Other Backward Class," are unreached but receptive to the gospel. Fifty-two percent of India's population are in these two groups, whereas the number for Bihar is 63.5%. Therefore, if we are to reach India, we must concentrate on these people groups. In Bihar, when we focused on these people groups, we saw a breakthrough among them.

STRATEGIC INVOLVEMENT OF THE
LOCAL PEOPLE IN CHURCH PLANTING

In Bihar, the evangelists and church planters, including many of the church and mission leaders, consider mission in terms of church planting and not just evangelism. That means that every effort is taken to reach the unreached people with the gospel, baptize them, and form worship groups. Thus, every mission has set goals in terms of baptisms and church planting. Another important aspect of strategic mission is the "people group approach." Every evangelist and church planter adopts one or two people groups and focuses their efforts on planting churches among them.

EMPHASIS GIVEN TO STARTING AND SUSTAINING
CHURCH PLANTING MOVEMENTS

Bihar Outreach Network always emphasized that its main focus was not to plant individual churches but to start a Church Planting Movement (CPM) among all one hundred unreached people groups in Bihar. BORN leadership conducted five-day volunteer seminars on CPM and taught how to start a CPM in the Nehemiah Institute and Esther Institute for Strategic Mission. Tad de Bordenave participated in several of the BORN training sessions in Patna, especially the Nehemiah Institute. So far, during the past several years as a result of these teachings, CPMs have been started among a number of unreached people groups in Bihar.

HIGHLY-MOTIVATED EVANGELISTS,
CHURCH PLANTERS, AND MISSION LEADERS

Another reason for the breakthrough in Bihar State was that the evangelists, church planters, church leaders, and mission leaders were highly motivated by a series of district-wide consultations on unreached peoples with a focus on church planting. They found that the BORN leadership served as "Barnabases," who encouraged them. The BORN leadership took time to counsel, teach, motivate, and mobilize the local people for church planting efforts.

RESOURCES MADE AVAILABLE TO
EVANGELISTS AND CHURCH PLANTERS

Bihar's Outreach Network leadership worked hard and took efforts to mobilize the needed resources for church planters. BORN was not just an association or an umbrella organization. It was a movement with a vision, and it worked to achieve the vision through its member missions and churches. With this in mind, BORN provided support to about four hundred grassroots church planters, mission leaders, Bible teachers, ordained pastors, and office staff. Field equipment was made available, such as musical instruments, mass media equipment, vehicles, and power generators.

STRATEGIC MINISTRY PARTNERSHIPS
MADE BY CHURCHES AND MISSIONS

Bihar Outreach Network was committed to partnership at the local, national, and international levels. BORN worked with various evangelistic organizations in India and around the world to use the available materials and training programs to equip the people of God in Bihar for effective mission work. Some of the partnerships had tenures of eight-to-ten years. BORN partnered with different denominations to strengthen the newly formed churches in Bihar. BORN also worked with various funding churches and agencies to meet the needs of member missions.

THE BORN ORGANIZATIONAL STRUCTURE IN PLACE

Even though BORN Network was a movement, it was also a well-organized body with a strong board of directors, a team of well-trained leaders, a well-equipped staff, and an efficient office structure. This organizational structure did a fine job of collecting information, providing good documentation, and communicating with the field staff, sponsors, and prayer partners.

BORN was always a movement. The Lord raised it to fulfill his purposes at a desperate time when Christians were in need of one another. And the Lord blessed the united efforts. BORN's leadership and structure were designed so that it would flourish for an important season. Like many movements of God, the legacy of this one continues through numerous offsprings that further its purpose. BORN has given life to new manifestations of God's work among the people of God. For all this we thank God.

PART FOUR

ANGLICANISM, THE GREAT TRADITION, AND FRONTIER MISSION

13

MISSIONS THE ANGLICAN WAY
MINING THE TREASURERS OF ANGLICANISM FOR FRONTIER MISSIONS

by Chris Royer

AFM's vision can be deduced from our name, "Anglican Frontier Missions." We are not just "Frontier Missions." We are also not "Baptist Frontier Missions" or "Methodist Frontier Missions." Our name describes who we are (Anglican) and what we do (frontier missions). So, what is uniquely "Anglican" about our "frontier missions"? In what ways does Anglicanism intersect with frontier missions and drive our methodology as we share the gospel with the largest and least-evangelized people groups of the world?

One way we fulfill the Great Commission "Anglicanly" is by ministering alongside other Anglicans, collaborating with them to evangelize and disciple unreached people groups. For instance, AFM U.S. has been partnering with AFM Nigeria and its chairman, Bishop Nathan Inyom (Diocese of Makurdi), for twenty years to shine Jesus' love to unreached peoples in West Africa. And, as Rev. Canon Norman Beale and Bishop Kuan Kim Seng of Singapore wrote in Chapters 4 and 7, AFM collaborated with the Diocese of Singapore to found the Anglican Deanery of Nepal. Partnering with other leaders in the worldwide Anglican Communion to effectively identify and minister to unreached people groups is one way Anglicanism affects our approach to frontier missions.

A second dimension of our "Anglicanness" in missions is our partnership with biblically faithful Christians of other denominations and traditions to reach those for whom Christ died. Anglicans have never believed themselves to be the only expression of the one, holy, catholic, and apostolic Church. Thus, from our inception, AFM has actively initiated collaboration with other denominations and mission agencies to complete the enormous task of reaching six thousand Unreached People Groups (UPGs), believing that other biblically faithful organizations bring a unique calling and charism to the global body of Christ and thus play an indispensable role in world evangelism.

A third component of our "Anglicanness" in missions is that our missionaries are all commissioned by churches within the Anglican world. But truth be told, as I preach and teach in dozens of churches every year, I've observed that many Anglicans are unaware of Anglicanism's amazing transferability and applicability in pioneer mission fields.

MY MISSIOLOGICAL CANTERBURY CONVERSION

Twenty-seven years after I became a Christian, I became an Anglican Christian and then an Anglican priest. The biblical, historical, and theological record was part of the impetus for my Canterbury conversion, as well as my personal sense of divine calling. But I also embraced Anglicanism for missiological reasons that I discovered while ministering in the Middle East.

One day, a newly baptized Christian from a Muslim background (CMB) asked me, "Chris, now that I've become a Christian, would you tell me what our religious holy days are?" I knew exactly where he was coming from. Muslims have thirty religious holy days with Ramadan alone. True,

Muslims fast during the days, but Ramadan's nights, from sunset to sunrise, are filled with scrumptious spreads and frequent visits to friends—a festive and celebratory atmosphere. Add to Ramadan the three holy days of Eid al-Fitr[1] and the six-to-nine days of Eid al-Adha[2], and the total number of religious holy days is already at forty, not even counting the minor ones.

So what my CMB brother in Christ was really asking me was something like this: "Chris, as a Muslim, I had a religious calendar, with religious festivals, that I followed. There was a religious rhythm to life and a flow to time. That's what I'm used to. Now that I follow Christ, I don't want to use that calendar any more, but I do desire some type of religious tradition that regiments and celebrates time. So, what does Christianity have to offer?" Unfortunately, as a non-liturgical non-Anglican, the best I could serve up was Christmas and Easter Day. Just two holy days, compared with the forty-plus holy days in Islam. At this, my brother in Christ looked at me, almost incredulously, as if to say, "Is that the best you can do, just two?"

God used this brief conversation (among other things) to launch me into an examination of Anglicanism. The more I studied and the longer I lived in the Middle East, the more cognizant I became of Anglicanism's applicability and transferability to the largest and least evangelized people groups. While my experience comes mainly from the Turkish Islamic world, I contend that Anglicanism's treasures are

---

[1] Eid al-Fitr is the festival that marks the end of Ramadan. In Turkey, people celebrate by visiting family and close friends. Children often celebrate by going door to door, collecting candies and sweets, similar to what U.S. kids do during Halloween.

[2] This festival marks the completion of the *Hajj* (Pilgrimage). During this festival, Muslims also commemorate Abraham's faith (seen in his willingness to sacrifice his son Ismail) by slaughtering an animal (usually a sheep or a goat) and then dividing the meat among family members and the poor.

transferable into other non-Western cultures. By "non-Western cultures," I mean cultures that never experienced the Reformation or went through the historical processes that defined the Enlightenment, like scientific empiricism, the elevation of autonomous human reason, secularism, and the desacralization and dismissiveness of religious customs and tradition. Although many UPGs benefit from the technological and scientific achievements that are the fruits of the Enlightenment (e.g., automobiles, cell phones, electricity), these cultures are nonetheless markedly different from Reformation- and Enlightenment-influenced cultures in areas of rituals, practices, beliefs, and worldview.

And Jesus said to them, "Therefore every scribe who has been trained for the kingdom of heaven is like a master of a house, who brings out of his treasure what is new and what is old" (Matthew 13:52). My conviction is that Anglicanism contains a *storeroom of treasures,* new and old, treasures that frontier missionaries and indigenous Christians in newly formed churches should draw upon.

By Anglicanism, I don't mean a Christian denomination narrowly tied to a specific creed, person, or historical event with a singular and specific theological approach. Anglicans aren't Cranmerians[3] and the Thirty-Nine Articles don't function analogously to the Heidelberg Catechism or the Augsburg Confession. Anglicanism's tent has always been broad with room for Anglo-Catholics, evangelicals, charismatics, liberals, Arminians, Calvinists, and many more. So by "Anglicanism," "the Anglican way," and "the Anglican faith tradition," I denote our broad, ancient, and theologically orthodox tradition of faith and faithfulness, tied to the apostles' teaching through our episcopate. I denote a posture and corporate way of living, worshiping (through our

---

[3] Thomas Cranmer (1489–1556), Archbishop of Canterbury and leader of the English Reformation.

liturgy), speaking, and thinking about God, preserved, expressed, and anchored in the Word, the Spirit, and the sacraments. This Anglicanism contains unmined resources to reach and disciple UPGs. But before I delve into the colors, sizes, and textures of Anglicanism's treasures, I need to lay out a theological groundwork with the somewhat technical (but very important) missiological concept of context-ualization.

CONTEXTUALIZATION IN TWO SETTINGS

Henry Venn, preeminent Anglican missionary statesman of the nineteenth century, pioneered the three-self model as a guideline for effective church planting in cross cultural contexts. Venn proposed that all cross cultural church plants need to develop *self-evangelization, self-government,* and financial *self-support* to become sustainable and truly indigenized.[4] (Subsequent missiologists developed a fourth category, *self-theologizing.*[5]) But how exactly is this done? How do missionaries to frontier regions take the gospel, which they have received in their own cultural milieu, and translate it into another culture, sometimes vastly divergent from their own? The answer to this question is "contextualization." Contextualization has two phases.

---

[4] Henry Venn was the honorary secretary of the Church Missionary Society from 1841–1873 when he pioneered the three-selfs movement. Venn arrived at his conclusion inductively, after surveying the weaknesses of CMS church-plants that remained anemically dependent upon CMS resources and personnel, even years after the initial planting had occurred. Venn proposed that the goal of missionaries must be to wean their church plants from foreign influence as soon as possible, to avoid what he called "the euthanasia of mission."

[5] "Self-theologizing," a term coined by Paul Hiebert, indicates the ability of indigenous churches to read, interpret, and apply Scripture within their cultural contexts. I will develop this theme a bit later.

CONTEXTUALIZATION DONE BY THE MISSIONARY

The first phase is what AFM cross cultural worker Duane Miller calls "Directed Contextualization"—contextualization *directed by* the frontier missionary *into* the culture of an unreached people.[6] *Directed contextualization* is necessary because while the truths of the gospel are unchanging, the "human situation," that is, the cultural contexts within which individuals receive and grow in Christ, vary significantly. Contextualization theory assumes that no culture is completely evil nor completely good. All cultures contain strains of goodness due to common grace (Acts 14:17) and our creation in the image of God. But all cultures also contain the deep stains of evil due to the fall of humankind (Romans 3:23). As Ed Stetzer, executive director of the Billy Graham Center for Evangelism at Wheaton College, writes, "All people live in a culture of some sort. There is no neutral position that might allow a person to stand in a cultural vacuum and make objective pronouncements on the cultures of others."[7] Thus, a frontier missionary, who takes the gospel to an unreached people, must first identify the nonessential beliefs, rituals, stories, traditions, art, etc. that is attached to Christianity in the missionary's own culture. Then the missionary needs to gather information about the unreached culture in order to contextualize (that is, *translate*) the gospel from the home

---

[6] Duane Miller, *Living Among the Breakage: Contextual Theology-making and ex-Muslim Christians* (Eugene, OR: Pickwick, 2016), 14.

[7] E. Stetzer, "What is Contextualization? Presenting the Gospel in Culturally Relevant Ways." *The Exchange, A Blog.* Accessed April 13, 2017: www.christianitytoday.com/edstetzer/2014/october/what-is-contextualization.html.
  Stetzer is the Billy Graham Chair of Church, Mission, and Evangelism at Wheaton College.

culture into the new culture. For contextualization to be effective, it must occur on at least four levels:

1. The communication of the gospel
   (Bible translation, evangelism, and preaching)
2. Spiritual formation
3. Church worship forms
4. Christian ethics.[8]

CONTEXTUALIZATION DONE BY THE INDIGENOUS CHURCH

For the second phase of contextualization, I draw more deeply upon Miller's research. Miller notes that Shoki Coe was the first writer to use the term "contextualization."[9] Grounding his work on Coe's thinking, Miller labels the next phase in contextualization "Organic Contextualization." Vigorous *organic contextualization* is critical for the gospel to develop deep roots because *organic contextualization* is done *by* and *from* the younger church, not by the frontier missionary.[10] In order for the newly planted church to translate the gospel into its own culture so that it thoroughly permeates the culture, Miller contends that the new church must first discern its own local cultural context to identify its

---

[8] P. Hiebert, *Anthropological Insights for Missionaries* (Grand Rapids, MI: Baker, 1985), 188.

A. Tippet, *Introduction to Missiology* (Pasadena, CA: William Carey Library, 1987), 93-94.

[9] S. Coe, "In search of Renewal in Theological Education," *Theological Education* 9 (1973): 233-43;

S. Coe, "Theological Education: A Worldwide Perspective," *Theological Education* 11 (1974): 449-69

Duane Miller, *Living Among the Breakage*, 13-23. Miller's argument is much more nuanced and developed than I can present here. In his book he more fully develops and illustrates *organic* and *directed contextualization* as well as contextuality, contextualize, indigenization and their relationships with each other.

[10] Duane Miller, *Living Among the Breakage,* 14.

challenges and problems. As the newly planted indigenous church thinks through aspects of its own culture and how Scripture applies and relates to its culture, the church is engaging in o*rganic contextualization.* Miller emphasizes that in *organic contextualization,* the "questions, framework, and solutions come from the indigenous church. It is *theology by, theology from,* and *theology with*"[11] the local, newly planted church. And so, with this understanding of contextualization in hand, we proceed to discuss the relevance of Anglicanism on the frontier mission field, especially in the areas of spiritual formation and church worship forms.

CONTEXTUALIZING ANGLICANISM'S TRADITIONS

A few years ago, I talked with a colleague named Frank (alias name) who has labored for years in Kazakhstan. Frank arrived in Central Asia as a non-denominational, charismatically-oriented church planter with a big heart to see his people group come to Jesus. Some years after God had used him to plant an indigenous church, he returned from furlough in the U.S. to discover something shocking: The indigenous church leaders were dressed in an unfathomable manner—they were all wearing clergy shirts, with collars too! Stunned, the first question he managed to ask them was how in the world they had acquired the clergy shirts in this remote Central Asian region. His next question, though, was much more significant, "Why are you wearing them?"

They responded that they were incredibly thankful for his sacrificial lifestyle, leaving the U.S. and living as one of them, learning their culture and language. They were also grateful that he taught and modeled Jesus, and that he genuinely walked in the power of the Holy Spirit. But they explained

---

[11] Duane Miller, *Living Among the Breakage,* 20.

that when they decided to follow Jesus, Frank had unwittingly asked them to turn their backs on one thousand years of cultural-religious tradition without providing them an alternative. "Just Jesus and me" might appear to be enough for the new believer in the U.S, but these Christians from a Muslim Background (CMBs) clearly needed Jesus attached to some sort of cultural-religious tradition, appropriately contextualized into their culture. Thus, their response, "In our culture, religious leaders dress religiously. That's why we're the wearing clergy shirts, and the collars too."[12]

These CMBs from Central Asia, as well as the CMB I referred to earlier who wondered about Christian holy days, both understood that Jesus is the only way to the Father (John 14:6) and embraced him. But now that these individuals had accepted Jesus, they were looking for a religious tradition within which to serve and follow him. Unlike many in the West, they implicitly linked form with meaning, the symbolic with what it symbolized. Unwittingly, they were now engaging in *organic contextualization*, asking crucial questions regarding the socio-religious relationship between holy days and structure/rhythm of time and their new Christian reality. They viewed these questions of tradition as somehow connected to their spiritual formation, even if they couldn't quite articulate why. Because religion and religiosity were highly visible and functional in their society, they were searching for a kind of functional substitute for Islam's fasts, feasts, celebrations, and ceremonies to express their new faith and connect them to

---

[12] The clergy collars may not be these indigenous leaders' final decision on what dressing religiously means for that particular culture. Indeed, they may discover (or create) a more indigenized form of religious garb in the future. Adopting Western clerical forms was their first (and probably not only) attempt at organic contextualization.

the historic and universal Church.[13]   In short, they were asking for us to do *theology with* them, helping them to apply the traditions of the Bible and church history to their inherently tradition-rich culture. This is organic contextualization at its best.

Before my colaborer Frank and I became Anglicans, we had no answer for these types of questions. Our *directed contextualization* was insufficient: We were children of the Enlightenment, secularized missionaries raised on a secular calendar, ministering to innately religious people who viewed time religiously and elevated custom and ritual. But as I began to discover the Anglican faith tradition, with its seasons (beginning with Advent and concluding with Ordinary time), colors, rhythms, saints, vestments, and other traditions, I began to realize that Anglicanism's respect and reverence of church tradition is one of our strengths in the pioneer mission field. The "tradition of friendliness" of Anglicanism (as long as tradition does not contravene the Word of God),[14] is one of its treasures that makes Anglicanism uniquely suitable for *directed and organic contextualization* in Islamic and non-Western milieus.

---

[13] Missiologist Paul Hiebert uses the term "functional substitute," in part, to describe how the rituals of the Lord's Super and Baptism can serve as substitutions for certain rituals in a particular culture. More recently, Lim argues that Christian theologians in Asia should find deliberate, non-syncretistic functional substitutes for the socio-religious practice of venerating the dead. Hiebert, P. (1985). *Anthropological Insights for Missionaries.* Grand Rapids: Baker, p. 185; Lim, D. (2015). Contextual Ancestor Veneration: An Historical Review. *International Journal of Frontier Missiology*, 32(3) Fall 2015, p.113.

[14] Article XX, Of the Authority of the Church: "The Church hath power to decree Rites or Ceremonies, and authority in Controversies of Faith: and yet it is not lawful for the Church to ordain anything that is contrary to God's Word written, neither may it so expound one place of Scripture, that it be repugnant to another. Wherefore, although the Church be a witness and a keeper of Holy Writ, yet, as it ought not to decree anything against the same, so besides the same ought it not to enforce any thing to be believed for necessity of Salvation."

To be clear, I'm not asserting that Anglicans are the best at pioneer missions or that we have led the way. In truth, evangelical churches and parachurch mission organizations have been on the forefront of frontier missions since the conclusion of World War II. I'm also not claiming that we Anglicans excel in evangelism—our Pentecostal and charismatic sisters and brothers, as well as those in para-church organizations, seem to do a much better job. (However, the Anglican Church of Nigeria is a wonderful exception.) Finally, I want to avoid the impression that I am speaking about Anglicanism in a triumphalist and hubristic manner, or that we can go it alone without the global Church.

But what I am asserting is that Anglicanism, despite all its faults, is a deep mine from which *contextualizable treasures* can be extracted, refined, polished, and then offered to the global Church. The first *treasure*, which I've just written about, is the contextualizability of Anglican church tradition, much of which dates back to the apostolic and patristic periods. The discerning missionary or indigenous believer, aware of contextualization principles, can draw from the *treasure of church tradition* and, with the Spirit's guidance and vigorous theological reflection, create functional substitutes suitable for the indigenous culture that will serve to support and strengthen the process of spiritual formation.[15]

CONTEXTUALIZING THE ANGLICAN LITURGY

A second *treasure* of Anglicanism is the contextualizability of its worship. Anglicans call this the liturgy. When I first began church planting in a Muslim city, my de facto outline for our Sunday worship service was a distillation of the

---

[15] To be sure, there are other areas of Anglican tradition that can be contextualized: fasting, religious dress (vestments), the Daily Office, and commemoration of the dead are just a few.

smorgasbord of evangelical churches I had attended at Wheaton College. The "liturgy" I created went something like this: fifteen minutes of singing worship songs, twenty minutes of teaching based on whatever passage I felt God wanted me to share for that day, and individuals praying aloud for as long as the Spirit would lead (and our concentration allow). After the final "Amen" we fellowshipped over tea and light dessert.

One day after worship in our house church, an indigenous brother in Christ approached me and said, "Chris, I know that you are supposed to be the expert. I know you've been taught the Bible and probably know how to lead a church, but I have to tell you this: The way we're worshiping makes me feel like I'm treating God casually and lightly." These words disturbed me. This CMB brother was not trying to criticize my leadership style—he spoke very deferentially. And I knew he genuinely cared for me and respected me. But his underlying message was that he was not connecting with God in our worship service. Without calling it that, he was engaging in *organic contextualization*, and his words caused me to look afresh at worship forms in the early Church, in American culture, and in Islamic culture. Furthermore, he was inviting me to join him in that adventure!

I started with how the Church fathers organized worship service and then decided to spend time with Arab Orthodox Christians in Antioch, where "... the disciples were first called Christians" (Acts 11:26), and Syriac Orthodox Christians in southeast Turkey at the 1,700-year-old Mor Gabriel Monastery. In my research, I learned that the Arabic word for ritual prayers, *salat*,[16] comes from the Aramaic word for liturgical prayer, *salat*, both of which refer "precisely to liturgical prayer, a public worship of God in the form of

---

[16] In Turkish, the word *namaz* is used for the Arabic equivalent of *salat*.

audibly uttered words."[17] Both Syriac Christians (whose church predates Islam) and Muslims pray five times a day, and the Qur'an itself states that Muhammad was aware not only of Christians, but also of at least one Christian monastic community which (presumably) worshiped liturgically on a daily basis. Thus, Christian influence over the Islamic prayer form is highly probable.[18]

To be clear, many CMBs around the world enjoy the freedom, flexibility, and spontaneity found in non-liturgical worship services. But other CMBs (like the friend I just mentioned in this chapter), desire a worship style that is more seemly, reverent, and appropriate to their indigenous cultural and religious context. One CMB Turkish Christian pastor I talked with commented that the American independent church model has been foisted upon the Turkish Church.[19] According to this leader, the paucity of liturgical and ecclesiological resources translated into majority Muslim languages and the dearth of missionaries familiar with liturgical worship have caused the emerging CMB Church to naively assume that the American independent church model is the exclusive way to worship God.

I came to the conclusion that for many CMBs, liturgical worship is an intuitive, socio-religious form compatible with the Islamic cultural-religious prayer tradition. Anglican liturgy is embodied worship involving physical motion. Anglican liturgy (*liturgy* literally means "the work of the people") is also something the congregation does, corporately, all together. But the liturgy's value is not only in

---

[17] F. Peters, *Muhammad and the Origins of Islam (Albany, NY:* State University of New York Press, 1994), 164.

[18] J. Arthur, *The Foreign Vocabulary of the Quran* (Worcestershire, UK: Read Books, 2013).

[19] Email from a BMB, 14 Oct. 2006.

the proximity of its form to Islamic liturgical worship, but also in *what* and *how* it communicates. The liturgy is a pedagogical tool and an instrument for spiritual formation.

CONTEXTUALIZING ANGLICAN DISCIPLESHIP[20]

Effective discipleship is a critical topic for people ministering to CMBs. Missiologists Patrick Johnstone and Duane Miller note that we live in unparalleled times vis-a-vis Muslims coming to Christ.[21] Some ten million Muslims have put their faith in Jesus since 1960, and sixty-nine movements of Muslims to Christ have sprung up in just the first twelve years of this century.[22] So the challenge in our day is not only getting Muslims to "come in the front door"—they are more open to Christ than ever before in history. The challenge is also "keeping them in the house"—facilitating their growth in Christ-like attitudes, behaviors, affections, and worldviews, both individually and corporately, through the efficacy of the Word, the Spirit, and the sacraments,[23] all of which we experience in liturgy.

Christians ministering to CMBs know they have a brief window of time to grow disciples because as soon as CMBs come to faith, spiritual warfare intensifies. Some of the assaults CMBs are immediately confronted with are familial rejection, employment termination, sickness, loneliness, depression, social ostracism, and for many, the palpable feeling that they have betrayed their family, their nation, and

---

[20] I first heard the term "liturgical discipleship" from Duane Miller.

Interdisciplinary Journal of Research on Religion 11(10), 2015. Available online at http://tinyurl.com/gw5k4km.

[22] D. Garrison, *A Wind in the House of Islam.* (Monument, CO: Wigtake, 2014), 5 & 18. Garrison defines a movement of Muslims to Christ as "at least 100 new church starts or 1,000 baptized believers who have comet to Christ in the past two decades (p. 5).

[23] More about Sacrament later.

their honor by accepting Christ.[24] The challenges faced by CMBs are instantaneous, exposing the paramount need to ground them deeply in Christ as quickly as possible. Without deep roots, "...they have no root in themselves, but endure for a while; then, when tribulation or persecution arises on account of the word, immediately they fall away" (Mark 4:17). And without deep roots, "...the cares of the world and the deceitfulness of riches and the desires for other things enter in and choke the word, and it proves unfruitful" (Mark 4:19).

The beauty of Anglican liturgical worship is its usefulness and suitability as a garden tool for cultivating the spiritual soil of the heart. Through regular participation, I contend that the liturgy has the potential to cultivate deep roots greater than other forms of worship for those in a non-Western milieu. For instance, the lectionary ensures (if followed) that most of the Bible is read during a three-year period. For illiterate people, Sundays may be the only chance they'll ever have to hear the entirety of biblical revelation. And for others who can read, church still may be the only place they're exposed to the Bible because they won't read it on their own. True, Jesus said, "But when you pray, go into your room, close the door and pray to your Father, who is unseen" (Matthew 6:6, New International Version). But for many in the Muslim world, they have no individual room in which to pray and read Scriptures because their dwelling is bursting with relatives.[25] So if a new CMB isn't in the habit of reading for leisure or work, or if the person is not living in an environment conducive to reading, Sunday may be the

---

[24] Ziya Meral, *No Place to Call Home: Experiences of Apostates from Islam, Failures of the International Community* (Christian Solidarity Worldwide, 2008).
Survey: Christian Solidarity Worldwide, 2008. Available online at: https://www.academia.edu/2462595/
No Place to Call Home Experiences of Apostates from Islam Failures of the International Community.
[25] Many other Muslim peoples have not acquired the habit of reading.

only opportunity for hearing and reflecting upon the Word of God.

Much like the pagans streaming into the early Church, unreached peoples coming to Christ today need to understand the entirety of biblical revelation. In the early Patristic Age, the lectionary (based on Jewish elements of worship),[26] began developing as a response to the inability of new Christians to read God's Word for themselves (either they couldn't read, or Scriptures were not readily available). Thus, biblical revelation was regularly and systematically read and explained to them on Sundays during the liturgy.[27] So also today, many new Christians need *to hear* the biblical metanarrative read and then explained (the sermon) in order to inculcate the truths of Scripture. The lectionary is the catechetical instrument for this, a conduit through which the Spirit can imprint the stories and truths of Scripture into new believers' hearts and minds so that they can grow ever deeper roots of faith. *Growing deep roots quickly* is imperative

---

[26] "After the reading of the Law and the Prophets the synagogue officials sent to them, saying, 'Brethren, if you have any word of exhortation for the people, say it' "(Acts 13:15).

[27] In the mid-2nd century A.D., Justin Martyr wrote, "And on the day called Sunday, all who live in cities or in the country gather together to one place, and the memoirs of the apostles or the writings of the prophets are read, as long as time permits; then, when the reader has ceased, the president verbally instructs, and exhorts to the imitation of these good things" (*First Apology*, 67). Toward the close of the 4th century, the Author of *Constitutions of the Holy Apostles* wrote, "In the middle let the reader stand upon some high place: let him read the books of Moses, of the Kings and of the Chronicles, and those written after the return from the captivity; and besides these, the books of Job and of Solomon, and of the sixteen prophets. But when there have been two lessons severally read, let some other person sing the hymns of David and let the people join at the conclusions of the verses. Afterwards let our Acts be read, and the Epistles of Paul our fellow-worker, which he sent to the churches under the conduct of the Holy Spirit: and afterwards let a deacon or presbyter read the Gospels" (2.57.9).

due to the intensity and swiftness of trials that new CMBs face after conversion.

The Nicene Creed is another catechetical tool in the liturgy. At the mosque, Muslims always recite their creed, the *Shahada*: "There is no God but Allah and Mohammed is his prophet." Thus, for CMBs, weekly recitation of their faith with a historical formulation is nothing novel. However, the Nicene Creed is more than a functional substitute of a formulary to recite core beliefs. The Nicene Creed is also their (and our) scriptural and doctrinal anchor, safeguarding contextualization from morphing into syncretism and heresy and ensuring that their faith continues to be the same faith "that was once for all entrusted to God's holy people" (Jude 3).

The liturgy includes the fundamental components of spiritual formation: singing, confessing sin, praying for purity, hearing God's law, hearing the entirety of Scriptures, sermon, creed, praying, offering, the Peace (opportunity for reconciliation between humans), Eucharist (our communion with God), commissioning, and dimissory blessing.[28] The liturgy was developed in a milieu *by and for* people who valued tradition, ritual, ceremony, community—the same milieu that much of the non-Western world lives in today. Abu Daoud, friend of AFM, writes, "In fact, ritual is and always has been a key element of human identity; this is why MBB's [Muslim Background Believers][29] often flounder and feel lost if the old rituals of the mosque and holy days are not replaced with the new rituals ordained by Christ and his

---

[28] J.K.A. Smith, *Desiring the Kingdom: Worship, Worldview, and Cultural Formation* (Grand Rapids. MI: Baker, 2009).

[29] In this chapter I refer to Muslim Background Believers (MBBs) with the more contemporary nomenclature, Christians from a Muslim Background (CMBs), but both terms denote the same thing.

church."[30] The liturgical rituals of Anglicanism, based in Scripture and developed by the church, are a gift and *treasure* of inestimable value that we Anglicans can offer to the Church as she reaches out to UPGs in frontier missions.

CONTEXTUALIZING THE HOLY EUCHARIST

Anglicans have always believed that matter matters, that God has chosen to impart his power, grace, and blessings through physical and material things: Moses' staff (Exodus 7:14-21), a bronze snake in the desert (Numbers 21:9), the Jordan River, as opposed to the rivers of Damascus (II Kings 5)—and ultimately, the body and blood of Jesus Christ: "...by his *wounds* you have been healed" (I Peter 2:24), and "...we have redemption *through his blood*, the forgiveness of our trespasses..." (Ephesians 1:7). The God-man Jesus Christ is the foundation for the sacraments, which Anglicans have defined as "outward and visible signs of inward and spiritual grace, given by Christ as sure and certain means by which we receive that grace."[31] Although Anglicans believe baptism and the eucharist are the "two great sacraments of the gospel"[32] and that there are five sacramental rites (confirmation, ordination, holy matrimony, reconciliation of a penitent, and unction),[33] I will focus my remarks here on just one sacrament, Holy Communion.[34]

---

[30] *St Francis Magazine* 4, no.3 (2008). *St Francis Magazine* was an online publication about Christian witness in Arab and Islamic contexts and was published by Interserve and Arab Vision. The website is no longer functioning, but all of Abu Daoud's articles are available at:
https://independent.academia.edu/AbuDaoud.
[31] *Book of Common Prayer* (New York: Church Publishing Company, 1979), 857
[32] *Book of Common Prayer*, 858
[33] *Book of Common Prayer*, 860
[34] For a treatment of how the liturgy at baptism can be used in a BMB setting, see "Mission and Sacrament, Part IV" by Abu Daoud at:
https://independent.academia.edu/AbuDaoud.

Anglican divine Richard Hooker listed numerous benefits from regular participation in Communion, some of which are the mystical and the real participation in Christ, the Holy Spirit's sanctifying power, and the strength of Christ's glorious power, which will fulfill what is promised in the sacrament.[35] Both the Articles of Religion[36] and the 1662 *Book of Common Prayer*[37] articulate that Christians participate in Christ's divinity and his glorified humanity through partaking in Holy Communion. Although Muslims also look at the world sacramentally, they cannot grasp the foundation of Christian sacramentality because they do not accept the foundational sacrament, the God-man Jesus Christ. Nonetheless, Muslims understand that practicing certain pillars of Islam and performing certain rituals (physical actions) can in some way release the mercy, forgiveness, and blessings of God—though they can never be 100% sure of when, if, or how mercy is imparted.

When I lived in the Middle East, I had a neighbor downstairs who owned a construction company. At the groundbreaking ceremony for every project, his family sacrificed a sheep and sprinkled its blood over the unbroken ground, believing that the blood would bring blessing and protection to the project. One evening. I watched a news report about a Turkish pop star who totaled his car by

---

[35] R. Hooker, Of the Laws of Ecclesiastical Polity, V. 67. 7.

[36] "The Supper of the Lord is not only a sign of the love that Christians ought to have among themselves one to another; but rather is a Sacrament of our Redemption by Christ's death: insomuch that to such as rightly, worthily, and with faith, receive the same, the Bread which we break is a partaking of the Body of Christ; and likewise the Cup of Blessing is a partaking of the Blood of Christ." Article 28

[37] Mascall argues that Christ's "real and essential presence" (and not his "corporal or material presence") is signified in the 1662 *Book of Common Prayer*'s Eucharistic service. Mascall, E. L. (2017). Christ, the Christian and the church;: A study of the incarnation and its consequences. Peabody, Ma: Hendrickson Publishers

accidently driving it into a lake. (He was probably drunk.) The reporter asked him if he had sacrificed a sheep and sprinkled its blood on the car at the time he purchased it. The pop star answered yes, but then added that he'd be sacrificing two sheep (not one) as soon as he bought his next car!

Examples of sacramental thinking abound in the Middle East: The stories of *The Arabian Nights*, the custom of wearing the *mavi boncuk* (blue bead) amulet for protection from evil, and shrines and tombs of holy men all speak to how Muslims believe that divine power flows through natural and physical objects. And yet, since many missionaries to Muslims come from non-sacramental backgrounds, the Muslim-background churches that they plant put little emphasis on the sacramental significance of the Eucharist. For instance, in a four-page survey sent to church leaders in Turkey, not a single question addressed the local church's sacramental theology or frequency of taking communion.[38] The sacraments were not even on the radar of this ecumenical ministry. But if matter and ritual are truly instruments of divine grace and blessing, if Islamic cultures de facto recognize this, and if Anglicanism's historic formularies and common worship celebrate this, then Anglicans have a *treasure* of inestimable value to share with the church as we reach out to frontier areas.

CONCLUDING THOUGHTS: ANGLICAN-CENTRIC MISSIONS

I now return to the questions I asked at the beginning of this chapter: Where does Anglicanism fit into what AFM does? In

---

[38] Silas 2005 Report. That most Turkish churches possess a low view of the Eucharist is understandable because most missionaries to Turkey come from non-liturgical backgrounds. These missionaries, then, are merely replicating in their church plants the theology they have inherited from their own Christian traditions.

what way(s), if any, are we uniquely Anglican in our approach to frontier missions?

First, Anglicans have always acknowledged that we are not the only Christian church but one among many expressions of the catholic and apostolic faith. As such, we at AFM humbly admit that we do not have the corner on missiology or ecclesiology. We also recognize that multiple factors contribute to fruitful discipling and church planting movements. Therefore, under the leading of the Holy Spirit, we joyfully partner with other biblically faithful Christians in frontier missions but prioritize partnership with the Anglican Communion in recognition of our common theological and liturgical heritage.

Second, since we believe that particular characteristics of Anglicanism—liturgy, sacramentalism, and reverence for tradition—are inestimable *treasures* God has given us, we inculcate them into our pre-field and ongoing missionary training. We advocate fulfilling the Great Commission "Anglicanly" to church mission committees, rectors, and bishops. And we speak humbly, yet boldly, at the appropriate times and settings, to non-Anglicans about the contextualizability of Anglicanism in the frontier mission field. To conclude, liturgical worship, veneration of tradition, and a sacramental worldview should not be regarded as *de facto* foreign incursions of Western preferences into non-Western cultures, but as contextualizable treasures. These can become inherently meaningful and intuitively grasped by people within their own indigenous cultures and traditions. Thus AFM will humbly, judiciously and strategically continue to share Anglicanism's amazing applicability with the global church and unreached peoples.

14

THE CHINESE CHURCH AND THE GREAT TRADITION

by Joshua Wu

China is a huge country with a vast and rich culture. Nearly anything one can say about China is probably true in a certain place at a certain time. The future of the Chinese Church is in God's hands, and I trust he will continue to work and move in this great country, which he loves dearly, and continue to establish and expand his Church there. As a missionary in China, I have come to the following conclusions and deep convictions: one, that there is still a great need for continued frontier missions in China; and two, that the Anglican tradition is uniquely positioned to address the deep longings and needs of the Chinese Church. As I reflect upon my time in China, what I have learned and what I see as future opportunities, it brings me back to a particular breakfast I had in a Dong minority village in Southern China.

It was the morning after the patriarch of the family had come to faith in Jesus, and he and his son were discussing their newfound faith in Christ. They then asked me a

Joshua Wu has been involved in church planting in China and South-East Asia for over ten years, with a specialty in coaching church planters and translators. He also teaches oral storytelling. He has an MA in Linguistics and has done doctoral work in missiology. Joshua is an AFM partner.

question I will never forget: "Is there anyone around today who knew Jesus when He was on earth? We have a lot of questions we would love to ask them, like 'what did He look like?'" I was surprised by their question and simply responded, "Jesus lived on earth nearly 2000 years ago..." At this they seemed very confused and disturbed, then they said something that would change my life forever, "If Jesus lived and died and rose again for us 2000 years ago, why are we and our people just hearing about this now?" I had no answer. I simply said, "I don't know. I am just so glad you are hearing now!" And by the grace of God, that was enough for them, and they resounded, "We are glad too, and as long as we live, we will make sure the rest of our people will hear this good news too!" And so we ended breakfast, with a painful realization seemingly averted. However, this question still haunts me and has forever ingrained in me the profound need for frontier missions. The sad reality is that after all these years there are still millions upon millions of people around the world who have yet to hear the gospel because of cultural, geographic, and linguistic barriers.

That same Dong patriarch later took me aside one evening to look at the stars and his rice field ripe for harvest. He told me to look up and look around at the beauty of creation. He told me that he had worked that land his entire life and had known from his youth that there is a Creator. He also said that their people group had stories of how they used to worship the Creator God, the maker of heaven and earth, but how in their disobedience they had forgotten about him and forgotten his name. He explained that this belief echoed in a ritual they did every time they drank wine: They would dip a finger in the cup and flick it to the sky and down to the ground to thank "whomever" created heaven and earth. He then pointed out their household altar and how in the middle of it there was the encryption, "To the God We Have Forgotten." He then looked me in the eye and said, "But now, I know his name!" This Dong patriarch showed me that even though he and his people had forgotten the name of their Creator, a longing to know and honor him echoed in their rituals and ceremonies, and had been waiting a long time to see this longing fulfilled in Christ.

This Dong patriarch set me on a quest not only to see the unreached reached, but also to see what it would look like to truly equip these local believers with the tools they need to reach their own people. And I began to ask the questions, "How might the gospel take root in this people group in a way that it becomes so much a part of their lives that it remains an enduring witness? How might the Dong people see the fulfillment of their culture in Christ?" Those questions would lead me down a path to understand and nurture indigenization, and help give birth to indigenous churches. Over the next several years it would lead me deeper into indigenous expressions of the faith through ethnomusicology, ethnoarts, and ethnodoxology. When I set off on this journey, I did not know it would lead to the historic liturgy, and I did not know that in this journey I would end up becoming an Anglican priest. However, I now see that the future of frontier missions, especially in China, is remembering the past and translating the past into the present.

During my time in China I learned that it was very important to listen to and discern the needs of local believers and not just impose on them what I thought they needed— or even what the most recent book on missions said they needed. I needed to listen to them, and together we needed to listen to the Word of God and discern the leading of the Holy Spirit. As I started to listen and observe the needs of new believers and the churches being planted, and as we sought the Spirit together, something started to take shape that was beautiful but oddly familiar.

One day I asked some local translators of an unreached and bibleless people group that we worked with, "What is the first thing we should translate for your people from Scripture?" I was thinking it might be an oral Bible story set, or maybe the Gospel of Luke, or other typical starting points. However, as we prayed together and asked the Holy Spirit to reveal to us where we should start, I realized that they were praying in the trade language, not their native language. I gently inquired about why this was and to my surprise, they said, "Because we don't know how to pray to God in our language yet."

This hit me like a ton of bricks, and I realized that my Western, goal orientated, product driven, production-oriented worldview was making me blind to the immediate need right in front of me: These brothers and sisters did not yet know how to pray and worship God in their own language. Thus we mutually came to the decision to start by translating the Lord's Prayer into their language, and use it as a gateway to indigenous mother tongue prayer and worship. This served as a tool to give them a voice for prayer and worship, the building blocks for personal devotional life. At the time I vaguely remembered reading in the *Didache* how the early Christians would pray the Lord's prayer three times a day (*Didache* 8:2-3). So after we translated the prayer, I encouraged them to pray it verbatim three times a day. I then told them that once they felt like they had internalized it, to then use that prayer and its movements as an outline to their own prayer, like a prayer tutor, teaching them how to pray in their own language with their own words, with the help of the Holy Spirit.

This went so well that soon we were exploring what other prayers were in Scripture for us to start learning. Soon our eyes were open to all the prayers that Paul prayed, and Moses prayed, and even Mary prayed, and then we realized: Wow, the Psalms! In the Psalms, God already gave his people a prayer book to teach them how to pray! This lead to us exploring what it would look like to incorporate the Psalms into our worship gatherings (Ephesians 5:19).

As we explored singing the Psalms, we realized that as we translated portions of Scripture into their language, and as people started to learn how to read, we could designate these newly literate people as "readers" in the church, and they could publically read the Scripture during worship (1 Timothy 3:14). We then realized that we had all these components in our worship times, but we needed some way to structure it so that it made sense and embodied the gospel message. So we started to find Scripture that spoke of God's holiness and our sinfulness and we said, "Why don't we start our worship times together by saying how holy God is, realizing we are sinful and that we need to repent, and why don't we just repent and confess our sins right there, and then be reminded of God's great love and forgiveness to us in Christ Jesus. Oh, I think there is a Scripture that speaks about that in 1 John 1:9."

We then realized through Acts and the writings of Paul that eating together and Holy Communion were important, so we added that to our worship, too. And so it went on, as we started to form an indigenous liturgy without really knowing what a liturgy was, and without knowing we were reinventing the wheel. What the Holy Spirit was doing among us, and how he was leading our small groups, was the same way he had been leading the Church for two thousand years. However, we did not realize that yet; we were just delighted to be swimming around in the lovely tide pool we had created, completely oblivious to the great ocean from which that water came. However, soon the Holy Spirit would cause a great wave to hit my little tidal pool. This happened to me one Sunday morning during my first experience of Anglican worship in Asia.

One Sunday while in Malaysia for a doctoral seminar, I realized that it was Pentecost Sunday, and I was filled with a deep desire to celebrate Pentecost. After spending years in the underground house church movement in China and Southeast Asia, I really wanted to experience what it was like to worship in a traditional church building again. I found an Anglican cathedral that followed the liturgical calendar and was going to be celebrating Pentecost. It was there that I experienced the beauty of the Anglican Liturgy. In that moment I realized that for the past couple years I had been intuiting from the mission field and my personal journey what the Spirit of God has already developed and preserved in the historic Church. I realized that that Anglican Liturgy was not dead ritual or vestiges of a bygone era, but alive and active. It was an embodiment of a living tradition that in its very nature was missional; it embodied Scripture and the gospel in powerful ways that spoke to the whole of a person, mind, body, and soul.

It was here that it all clicked, and I realized how my journey of discerning the work of the Holy Spirit on the frontier mission field had lead me to what the Holy Spirit had been doing in the Church for the past two thousand years. I then became aware that I was digging and playing around in a tidal pool, when there was an entire ocean bidding me to come and swim.

As I entered into the vast ocean of the great tradition of the Church (East and West), I was struck by the profound realization that many of the issues I was dealing with in frontier missions were the perennial issues the Church had already encountered in history, and the Church had already addressed the questions I was asking. What was needed was for those answers to be indigenized and translated into local contexts. I started to realize that so much of my formation as a Christian and the tools I drew from as a missionary came from a relatively new and limited toolbox; that toolbox was greatly limited because it drew from only a sliver of the greater Christian tradition. I was trying to provide Western answers to Eastern problems.

This was a turning point in my life. It changed the way that I viewed ministry and missions. I had previously viewed missions as a task to be completed, and I had ignored so much of its relational and devotional components. I started to realize that seeking the worship of God among the nations meant not merely changing people's minds about Jesus, but also inviting people to love and honor him. Truth was not merely something to know about, but a person to be known and loved, namely Jesus Christ (John 14:6). The Chinese taught me that, for them, worship involved their bodies and a way of devotion that I was not familiar with.

Through all of this I realized that much of my missional practices were trying to offer Western answers to Eastern questions. This is not to say that my Western answers were wrong, just that they were often unintelligible to the vast majority of the people I was seeking to serve. As I studied how the Church throughout history interacted with issues that arose among them, I saw that they handled things in ways that was not intuitive to me but was intuitive to so many of the people I served in China. For a long time, I did not know why my intuition sometimes differed from that of my Chinese brothers and sisters. Something that helped me to understand this difference in intuition was a helpful little worldview exercise that I learned while leading orality and storying workshops in Asia.

In this exercise people were shown pictures of three-to-four objects side-by-side. They would then be asked, "Which one does not belong?" For example, one picture showed a saw, an axe, a log, and a hammer.

We would let the participants know that there was no "wrong" answer, but we wanted to see which one they picked. Interestingly enough, nearly all the Westerners who had spent less than a year on the field would almost always immediately respond, "The log does not belong," the reason being that is not a tool like the others. However, the Asian participants (from China, Thailand, Malaysia, Burma, Vietnam and other countries) would answer "The hammer does not belong because it cannot be used to cut the log." Missionaries who had been on the field for one year or more would seem to waffle between the two possible responses of the hammer or the log, though neither response would be the typically Asian one.

This activity showed the important worldview divide between "traditionally Western" thinking and "traditionally Eastern" thinking. Obviously Western and Eastern ways of thinking are nuanced and complex. Not to oversimplify this complexity, generally Western ways of knowing are greatly influenced by Greek philosophical systems, especially Aristotelian logic, which focuses on *abstract and categorizational thinking*, while many Eastern (and agrarian) cultures seem to focus on *concrete and relational* ways of knowing.

This contrastive way of knowing between East and West, is written about by Richard Nisbett,[1] who references the work of developmental psychologists Anne Fernald and Hiromi Morikawa. Fernald and Morikawa went to the homes of several Japanese and American families with children of the same age groups. They set up a test where they introduced several toys for the mothers and their children to play with: a stuffed dog, a stuffed pig, a car and a truck. They asked the children to play with these toys as they normally would. What they found fascinated them. Across the board, regardless of the age of their children, the American mothers used twice as many object labels as Japanese mothers

---

[1] Richard Nisbett, *The Geography of Thought: How Asians and Westerners Think Differently... and Why* (New York, The Free Press, 2003).

("piggie," "doggie"), and Japanese mothers engaged in twice as many social routines of teaching politeness norms (empathy and greetings, for example). They further observed that an American mother's pattern might go like this: "That's a car. See the car? You like it? It's got nice wheels" A Japanese mother might say: "Here! It's a vroom vroom. I give it to you. Now give this to me. Yes! Thank you." The two psychologists concluded, "American children are learning that the world is mostly a place with objects, Japanese children that the world is mostly about relationships" (Nisbett, pg. 150). This is profound and rings true to me after over a decade in Asia, marrying into a Chinese family, and raising kids there. I have noticed this pattern even with my own wife in her interactions with our children and by the way she is helping to shape their worldview.

This realization of the philosophical underpinnings and their effect on how people interact with the world led me into a doctoral program in missiology at an Asian seminary in Malaysia. During my studies, I came to realize the profound implications of the findings of Nesbett, Fernald and Morikawa, and that most, if not all, of the world's cultures have an intuitive default in how they interact with the world around them. Their intuition has lead them to interact with their surroundings as a place of things and objects in an *abstract-categorizational way,* or as a place of relationship in and subjects in a *concrete-relational way.*

Many cultures around the world are shaped by intuitive connections based on their agricultural and agrarian roots, as well as religious and philosophical systems, which in China have been predominantly Animism, Daoism, and Confucianism. This way of knowing deals with reality and concepts of god/gods/spirits as realties to be interacted with and honored/appeased, and the world as a subject to be interacted with. This is why so many Asian religions are heavy on ritual and ceremony, but lacking in clear dogma.

Greek philosophical tradition viewed reality as something to be understood and categorized in its internal reality. It focused on the intellectual understanding of complexities; interaction with the nonmaterial was something to be understood and dealt with in judicial terms. Thus, Western expressions of religion had a heavy emphasis on philosophy and dogma, but were often minimalist with ritual and ceremony. This is, in part, because the philosophical children of the Greeks and Aristotle (like myself) are inclined to view faith in terms of doctrine, dogma, and intellectual assent forms of *inward and disembodied* devotion. In contrast, philosophical children of Confucius or Daoism or tribal beliefs view faith in terms of ritual, ceremony, and relationship as a way of *outward and embodied* devotion.

However, the interesting thing about this is, as the saw/axe/log/hammer exercise shows, neither the West nor the East exclusively has the "right" answer. They are each viewing the same thing from two different angles. It is profound that the wisdom and foreknowledge of God would cause the incarnation of Jesus Christ to happen at one of the first times that these two ways of knowing interacted in human history. In many ways the Hebraic way of knowing fits into the *concrete-relational* way of knowing. First century Judaism focused a lot on ritual, liturgy, ceremony and relationship with God through fidelity to a community that practiced these things.[2] In contrast, first century Greek philosophy embodied more of an *abstract-categorizational* way of knowing focused on the intellect, theory, and personal responsibility. But we see Jesus interacting with both of these frameworks, addressing *truth* as both intellectual

---

[2] This is a complex issue as there was still a part of personal faith within this framework, too. These issues have been debated, but a fair and thorough treatment of this this can be found in the writing of N.T. Wright, such as in *The New Testament and the People of God*.

information *about* God, but also as a subject, namely himself, who needed to be trusted, received, and honored.

We see in Jesus not only the perfect embodiment of both God and man, but also the perfect synthesis of West and East. It is also worthy of note that God called Paul, a Hellenized (Western) Hebrew (Eastern), inspired him to write much of the New Testament, and set him apart and sent him on the Gentile mission. Thus, the Christian faith is truly the only faith in the world that has a native bandwidth for Eastern and Western ways of knowing. It is the only truly catholic (universal) faith. This allows Christianity to speak prophetically to all cultures. To Eastern ceremonialism, it can fulfill people's desire to *honor* "a higher power" through embodied ritual, but it also shows them the importance of orthodoxy (worshiping "rightly" the True God). To Western scholasticism, it can fulfill a desire for truth, but also show that this desire must end with real and embodied devotion, not merely disembodied knowledge. The gospel in this way is truly transcultural. Yet, despite this transcultural appeal of the gospel, David Bosch reminds us that, "the gospel always comes to people in cultural robes."[3]

This really impacted me because, in Scripture, I saw both of these ways of knowing, especially in worship. In Scripture it is not just *what* we say about God, it is also *how* we say it. This is reminiscent of Christ's words to the woman at the well that one day worshipers will be worshippers in *Spirit* and *Truth*. Together, this means saying "truthful" things *about* God as inspired by an active relationship *with* God through the indwelling Holy Spirit. I started to realize that not only was the gospel itself transcultural, although coming to us in cultural robes, but the worship was also transcultural, needing to be dressed in cultural robes. For me as a

---

[3] David Bosch, *Transforming Mission: Paradigm Shifts in Theology of Mission* (Maryknoll, NY: Orbis Books, 2011), 304.

Westerner, becoming a worshiper is all about the mind. However, my Chinese brothers and sisters helped me realize that worship is also about the body, tradition, symbols, and ritual. I now realized that if I am not supportive in helping them cultivate worship that incorporated this, then their worship would be unnatural and in foreign garbs instead of native and beautiful robes.

It was here that I started to bring the questions I was encountering on the field to the historical saints and scholars of the Church for answers. I found that many of the cultures that produced great saints and scholars mirrored, or had deep connections with, a frontier missions context! Through the eyes of these saints, I could see things in Chinese and Southeast Asian culture that I had not previously seen. It was then that I fully understood the importance of the liturgy and the need to see it localized.

These cultural concepts have helped me see that Anglicans have a lot to offer the future of frontier missions in places like China. We can become tour guides and mediators and translators of the treasures of the Great Tradition to the local church. This will not only help prevent the local people from reinventing the wheel; it will also allow them to benefit from the wealth of wisdom that many saints have passed on to us and to them. As I helped local believers connect with the great treasures and traditions of the Church, I was amazed at how it gave a voice to many of the emotions they intuitively felt and were struggling to articulate. They began to realize how Christianity was the fulfillment of their culture and truly addressed the deepest longings of their heart. They saw that the faith is not, as many once believed, "a Western God for Western people." They started to realize that God indeed spoke their language and culture in ways that are deeper and richer than they could imagine.

The value of embodiment permeates all parts of the Chinese culture. The Anglican Church can help Chinese

Christians live out their faith in embodied ways. This value of embodiment has only seemed to intensify with the communist revolution and rise of materialistic Marxism. Restaurants and homes alike are always marked with some visible representation of their hopes, dreams, desire for success or wealth, or auspicious markings or images that they hope will bring blessing or "luck." However, so many recent Western missions in China have been iconoclastic and disembodied, seeking only the conversion of the mind, instead of presenting the faith as a way of life, in which all of life is lived in reference to Christ.

I was blind to the significance of this for a long time. However, one day while at my local teahouse, several locals got into a discussion about their Buddhist prayer beads and the amulets they were wearing. I was utterly amazed at how much money they spent on these things; in fact, they spend more on these religious items than most people spend on cars or even some houses. Nevertheless, I was even more shocked at the fact that they were displaying and bragging about these physical embodiments of Buddhism while eating pork buns! "Aren't devout Buddhists supposed to be vegetarian?" I thought to myself. However, I finally realized that for them, this was how they showed allegiance to their religious belief, and to them this *how* of embodied allegiance was more important than the *what* of the Buddhist doctrine. I then looked at myself and saw that I did not display or embody my belief and allegiance to Jesus in any physically discernible way. I then remembered how missionaries, priests, and monks throughout history often wore a cross or some type of distinctive clothes that communicated their Christian faith to those they met. I thought that might be something to test in my context. Thus, I went home and ordered a very simple wooden cross to wear around my neck, much like how they wore their amulets. When it arrived in the mail, I put it on and went back to the teashop to see my friends there.

As I stepped into the teahouse, those same Buddhist friends saw me, pointed to my face, then to the cross, and then back to my face. They exclaimed, "Oh, you are a Christian!" Then pointing to their prayer beads and amulets, they said, "We are Buddhist! We have much we can talk about." I was shocked. Had they really only just realized that I am a Christian? I had been trying to tell them about Jesus for the past year and a half, often being extremely explicit about my faith and about Jesus. I sat down with them and explained that fact to them. Their response spoke volumes about their worldview—and their value of embodiment and allegiance.

They told me they had understood that I believed in the philosophy of Jesus, but they did not know that my personal allegiance was to him. They just assumed it was a matter of private opinion that had the same impact on my life as my favorite TV show. All that was because I did not take the time, or care, to embody this allegiance in a visible way. They went on to say "We used to know that Jesus was your teacher, but now, because you are wearing that cross, we see that he is also your Lord (your allegiance is to him). Now we want to take your words about Jesus more seriously because we see how important he is to you." From that day forward I made it a spiritual discipline to always wear a cross. There are countless other stories from my time in China that came about because I was wearing a cross. I then started to realize that for many Chinese Christians (including my own wife), wearing a cross was about showing their true allegiance to Jesus; it was not just a fashion choice.

When I understood the Chinese desire for embodiment and allegiance, I finally understood why so many people I had shared the gospel with over the years were hesitant to get baptized. I started to realize that the Chinese seemed to know more about what baptism really is than I did. I also came to understand how much baptism was understood by Christians and non-Christians alike as a change of allegiance. Before China, I did not really focus on conversion as a change of allegiance, and when I did think in terms of allegiance, it was more about an inward change of allegiance in the realm of the mind. Thus, for so many years, I focused on getting Chinese folks to change their mental allegiance and verbally affirm certain important and Scriptural truths. However, I was blind to their need to also change their allegiance in an embodied way. This outward and embodied change in allegiance is one of the things that baptism does. This is why so often parents of Chinese believers would be OK with their children "believing" (in their heads) the teachings of Jesus, but they would become infuriated, and sometimes, disown their children if they showed their belief in Jesus through embodied water baptism.

The importance of baptism in the life of a Chinese Christian was made very real to us through our Chinese friend Shelby.[4] Shelby came to faith and spent several years being discipled in China by foreign missionaries, yet had never heard of baptism and the Lord's Supper. When she finally heard about baptism and decided to be obedient to Jesus through receiving baptism we told her the minimal requirements: (1) to be baptized with water, and (2) in the name of the Father, Son, and Holy Spirit. We also showed her the baptism liturgy in the *Book of Common Prayer*. We explained its components and their symbolism. We then asked Shelby how she would like to receive baptism. She

---

[4] This is not her real name; it has been changed to protect her identity. A fuller version of her story can be found in my article, "Desiring the Kingdom in Missions: An Application of James K. A. Smith's 'Liturgical Anthropology' in a Cross-cultural Context," which can be found in the July 2015 edition of *Global Missiology*.

http://ojs.globalmissiology.org/index.php/english/article/view/1810.

emphatically said she wanted the tradition and the ceremony. Two weeks later, in our little apartment on Easter morning, Shelby was baptized and received her first communion.

However, what happened afterwards was remarkable. The following week we met with her to debrief about her baptism and first communion. Her eyes lit up and she expressed to us that it was the most special day in her entire life; she realized that day that she was "really a Christian." She then explained that previous to that day, she felt that she was believing in Jesus only with her mind. After the sacraments of baptism and the communion, she felt for the very first time that she was really and truly a Christian with her heart and body, her whole self. She then went on to say that she also realized that her allegiance was now to Christ and that had implications for every aspect of her life. She then went on to talk about her newfound zeal for sharing the gospel.

A year or so later, she endured horrible persecution from her family for her allegiance to Christ. She contacted me about how to keep the faith while being beaten and locked in her room by family for her faith. I reminded her of her baptism and the creed she confessed, which spoke about the communion of the saints. I reminded her that even though she was alone in her room, when she came to God in worship and prayer, she was joining in the worship of God with countless saints around the world and in heaven. I told her that her baptism was an outward sign of this inward and spiritual reality, that she was part of the family of God, and nothing could separate her from that reality (Romans 8:35-39). This encouraged her greatly and gave her the encouragement she needed to press on. I also taught her *lectio divina* and digitally sent her small sections of Scripture to read and practice it with. I saw how baptism, the communion of the saints, the divine nature of worship and prayer, and *lectio divina* were tools I was now able to offer her—that I previously had been completely ignorant of. This dear sister was not experiencing anything new or surprising to the Holy Spirit. Christians have suffered for the faith since the beginning, but God has given the Church wisdom and tools to help those who are persecuted for righteousness sake.

The more I serve in China, the more I have come to see how much the historical and liturgical treasures of the Church speak to the deep longing of believers there. One such example concerns dear friends of mine who were also missionaries in China. The wife was Chinese and the husband American. They later moved to America and joined a highly liturgical church. I was intrigued by their choice of a liturgical church. I came to find out that the husband had a journey similar to mine during his time in China, and it had also lead him to see the importance of the historical and liturgical heritage of the Church. However, the wife had an even more personal reason for joining a liturgical church. She told me that she was born and raised among a Buddhist people group. However, when she became a Christian, in many ways she felt that she had to give up her birth culture. She had become Christian, but in doing so, she lost her home culture. She went on to tell me that worshiping God in a liturgical way changed this for her. She said that for the first time in her life, she now feels that she is fully Christian. She feels that her culture had found its fulfillment in Christ and the liturgy. She told me, "When I worship God in the liturgy, my body understands what I am doing. It is not like I am getting confused and think I am worshiping Buddha or some idol. I know I am worshiping the true God; it is just that I understand the language of liturgy. This is my language, and I am finally able to speak it in worship."

That heartfelt explanation from my friend encouraged me but also broke my heart. I thought to myself, "How many other believers have had their worship heart language muted because of a failure to cultivate indigenous liturgy that speaks to their hearts and bodies?" And also, how many people were turned away from the gospel because they felt that Christianity was the rejection of their culture instead of its fulfillment.

In the last century, Chinese culture has undergone a lot of change and many people are talking about the future. Many have talked about China's identify crisis and the new culture wars among modernization, individualism, consumerism, innovation, and westernization on one side, and on the other side, the Confucius values of harmony, collectivism, tradition, and fidelity to a culture with over five thousand years of history. Many have commented on China's search for an identity that has the bandwidth to bridge the past and the future. I have seen firsthand how the Anglican tradition serves as a gateway to the historic Church; the Anglican tradition gives people the connection between an ancient-future and a future-ancient *church.* This type of church can be wholly indigenous, yet radically catholic (connected to the whole of the Church).

We as Anglicans can serve the local church in China by opening to them the imagination and permission to translate the gospel into their cultural context so that truly indigenous worship can emerge and endure. For this is the historical nature of a *local rite*, the intelligible and meaningful expression of the Great Tradition in a local culture and context. It is the synthesis of the Great Tradition in conversation with local culture that gives birth to a local rite. This is also what we could call the phenomenon of *indigenous liturgy*. Indigenous Liturgy is as old as Christianity itself. The very fact that Christians worship on Sundays instead of Saturdays is a form of indigenous liturgy. Early Christians took the tradition of the Jewish Sabbath and its meaning of setting apart a day of rest and worship and translated it to a practice of worshiping Jesus on Sunday as a way to remember, celebrate, and honor his resurrection. We as Anglicans can appreciate local rite and indigenous liturgy because our very prayer book is the culmination of the ancient catholic faith expressed in Anglo-Saxon language and cultural ways. Thus, there is an ancient precedent for indigenous liturgy. Christians need to stay true to this heritage and see the cultivation of a truly Chinese (or Sino-Catholic) rite.

I hope I have shown the treasures of the Prayer Book and the Anglican liturgy itself, along with the sacramental theology of the liturgy. These speak powerfully to our Chinese brothers and sisters, yet so many of them have never been gifted this wonderful life-giving treasure. The rich and precious traditions, ceremonies, rituals, and sacramental theology that we have in the Great Tradition were forged by the Church and her saints and martyrs, who understood the importance of embodying and giving witness to the faith. This historic witness to the faith gives the Church zeal in evangelism and endurance in persecution. As all signs point toward a new wave of persecution in China, I think a huge opportunity for Anglicans doing missions in China is to help point local believers to this storehouse of treasures. Local believers have a need to express and embody their faith in ways that are meaningful not only for themselves, but also for those with whom they share the gospel. I think our goal should be the emergence of truly Chinese catholics,[5] not just Asian Anglicans. Our Anglican heritage is indeed a treasure and speaks powerfully to Chinese culture. What is even more powerful is when local Chinese use the Anglican Tradition as a gateway into the Great Tradition of the Church and create a truly Chinese expression of the Christian tradition and catholic faith locally.

---

[5] Not Roman Catholics, but the traditional Catholic and universal faith.

15

PLANTING THE ONE HOLY, CATHOLIC, AND APOSTOLIC CHURCH

by Yee Ching Wah

In this paper I will share some principles and practices of what we have attempted to express in the planting of one holy, catholic and apostolic Church in the deaneries in which the Diocese of Singapore works. First, let me mention two models that are unsatisfactory and why that is so.

The Great Commission is about making disciples of all nations. Unlike Genetically Modified Organisms (GMOs), which promote quick growth, we should not pursue GMO church expansion that emphasizes growth by modifying the genetics of the church. Such rapid church growth movements bring temptations to overlook weaknesses, but they pay no serious attention to biblical and historical ecclesiology. This is growth at the expense of the biblical and historical essential attributes of a church. Neither is the Great Commission about economic efficiency. We often hear

---

The Reverend Canon Yee Ching Wah serves as the Dean of Thailand, the Associate Director of Missions for the Diocese of Singapore and an Honorary Priest at St James' Church. He and his wife Siew Ling were missionaries in Thailand for fourteen years. They live with their three sons in Singapore. Canon Yee continues to travel monthly to Thailand to coach teams in planting new churches. He is an AFM international partner.

voices that raise the objection, "Wouldn't it make more sense to redirect our resources to support 25-30 indigenous workers for the same amount it takes for one American family to go?" According to *Christianity Today*, back in the year 2000, over 140 mission agencies in America alone were operating with this "economic" mission philosophy, which reduces missions to a matter of economic logic, building on the premise that mission is about gathering and sending money to support more economically viable workers. Is Christian mission being reduced to the "employment" of workers to grow a work rather than nurturing the witness of Christ through a discipleship journey?

Discipleship must be incarnational. Discipleship is not merely an impartation of pure doctrine, or formation of new spiritual discipline, or commitment to personal purity. All these are important aspects of discipleship, but the orientation is still personal in nature. If we stop there, we have stopped short. We have stopped far short. If discipleship of an Anglican church is confined merely to a personal commitment to follow Christ in doctrine, discipline and purity, we have watered down who we are as Anglicans.

We have a benchmark, one that serves as correction to all false ways. We declare that we believe in the one holy, catholic and apostolic Church as in the Creed of Nicaea that Constantinople affirmed after the Council of Constantinople in 381. These creeds are derived from the teaching of Scripture that we are a body of Christ; we are the temple of the Holy Spirit. The Church is not merely a collection of like-minded people given to a common cause. It is the body of Christ, "...growing up in every way into him who is the head, into Christ, from whom the whole body, joined and held together by every joint with which it is equipped, when each part is working properly, makes the body grow so that it builds itself up in love" (Ephesians 4:1-16).

The Church is the temple of the Holy Spirit. "So then you are no longer strangers and aliens, but you are fellow citizens with the saints and members of the household of God, built on the foundation of the apostles and prophets, Christ Jesus himself being the cornerstone, in whom the whole structure, being joined together, grows into a holy temple in the Lord. In him you also are being built together into a dwelling place for God by the Spirit" (Ephesians 2:19-22).

The Church is made up of persons being built into a community of citizens in the kingdom of God. And in the context of the Great Commission, they are striving to make disciples of all nations, baptizing them and teaching them; this creedal declaration means that discipleship must be both personal and communal in nature. Disciples are baptized into a body and built into a temple. We believe that the creedal declaration is not a nebulous spiritual ideal, but a very visible expression on earth, imperfect though it may be. This is one important reason why discipleship must be incarnational—life to life impartation and interaction in the context of a community, rooting ourselves in the long heritage of God's kingdom on earth as it is in heaven. Our Anglican ecclesiology demands discipleship to be incarnational. We are not merely gathering numbers to worship one Name. We are planting one holy catholic and apostolic Church.

WHAT IS THE ONE HOLY, CATHOLIC AND APOSTOLIC CHURCH?

First, what is the one holy catholic and apostolic Church? Or against the backdrop of Reformation, what is the true Church? In the thrust of mission, how is the one holy catholic and apostolic Church expressed?

The early Church positioned the four marks of the Church against those given to various divisive teachings. In his work, "Against the Donatists," Augustine emphasized the worldwide universality of the Church in addition to its sanctity. Augustine also stressed the authority of the Church evidenced in its miracles, nourished by hope, increased by love, and confirmed by age, then the episcopal succession and finally its undeniable epithet of catholic.[1]

The Roman Catholic Church claims authenticity by viewing these four words historically and apologetically. "By the 1400s the Roman church believed that the gifts of unity, holiness, catholicity, and apostolicity were to be celebrated as its exclusive property. The ultimate function of the four words became self-justification rather than self-examination. Numerous apologists used the four classical attributes primarily as support for the authenticity of the Roman church."[2]

The reformers rejected historicity as the Roman Catholic's claim to authenticity and pointed to something behind and beyond the four attributes, namely, the center, Jesus Christ, through whom the Church owed her life and nature.[3] The authenticity of the Church is measured by how near she is to the center, Jesus Christ, in terms of the preaching of the Word, right administration of the sacraments, and the exercise of church discipline. Unfortunately, the dogmatic manner in which each church was measured and differentiated destroyed the very attributes they wanted to uphold. The Church was divided rather than unified. Instead, apostolic followers aligned themselves to teachers and theologians of a particular distinctive, which led to the proliferation of denominations.

---

[1] Augustine, Contra Manichaei; PL 42, 175.
[2] Charles Van Engen, *Mission on the Way: Issues in Mission Theology* (Grand Rapids, MI: Baker Books ,1996), 117.
[3] Charles Van Engen, *Mission on the Way*, 118.

Hans Kung and G. C. Berkouwer approached the four attributes as both gift and task. The unity, holiness, catholicity and apostolicity of the Church are gifts from Christ. It is the task of the Church to grow into these attributes and be authentic. It is a movement of growth from faith to life.[4] Kung understands that the four attributes are not objective and unchanging facts defining the nature of the Church. Rather, the Church must realize anew in each generation the need to discover a changing form to express the same essential attributes:

> It is impossible to simply preserve the Church for all time in the original form it enjoyed as a primitive Church. Changing times demand changing forms. Yet in spite of all changes in form the basic structure of the Church given to it in Christ by God's saving act must be preserved, if it is to remain the true Church.[5]

Kung showed how the four attributes are interrelated and inseparable:

- What is ecclesiastical unity without the breath of catholicity, the power of holiness, and the original impulse of apostolicity?

- What is ecclesiastical catholicity without the links of unity, the distinction of holiness and the vitality of apostolicity?

- What is ecclesiastical holiness without the binding power of unity, the generosity of catholicity and the long roots of apostolicity?

- What finally is ecclesiastical apostolicity without the brotherhood of unity, the diversity of catholicity and the spirit of holiness?[6]

---

[4] Charles Van Engen, *Mission on the Way,* 120
[5] Hans Kung, *The Church* (New York: Burns and Oakes, 1968), 263.
[6] Hans Kung, *The Church,* 359

However, what was starkly missing from Kung's exposition was the missional perspective. Jurgen Moltmann enriched that understanding and brought it forward with dynamism. The four attributes are not meant to be inward activities of the Church, but the witness of the Church to the world. The missional perspective of these attributes means that the four words are not meant to be adjectives that qualifies the Church, but a description of the missionary activities of the Church in engaging the world:

> The "one" church of Jesus Christ would be seen as a unifying force. It would seek to invite,   gather,   and incorporate the world.... The "holy" church of Jesus Christ would be understood as a sanctifying agent in the world. It would work toward forgiveness,   healing, and the presence of the holy in the midst of the people... The "catholic"   church of Jesus Christ would be understood as a reconciling event in the world. It would build bridges to gather fractured, alienated humanity into a common, renewed, changed fellowship of believers... The "apostolic" church of Jesus Christ would be seen as a proclaiming event in the world, the basis of truth and certainty, the offer of   structure   and   stability,   the fellowship of disciples who know, love, and serve each other because they know, love and serve their Master.[7]

The Church is not merely one, holy, catholic and apostolic; she is *unifying, sanctifying, reconciling and proclaiming.* True authenticity of the Church is seen in how missional she is to impact the world. It has roots, but it is also advancing the kingdom of God. Stephen Neil wrote:

> Until the end of the eighteenth century the missionary effort of the Anglican Churches had been few, weak, and intermittent, and mainly carried on through the agency of those who were not themselves Anglicans. When a small group of Evangelical clergymen met in 1799 to found the Church Missionary Society, they gave a new dimension in

---

[7] Van Engen, *Mission on the Way*, 123-124

the Anglican world to the words "I believe in one holy, catholic and apostolic Church."[8]

These four attributes shall be addressed in two related pairs as follows: *one catholic*, which is to hold together unity and universality within the faith, and *holy apostolic*, which is to hold together the faith lived out today from the faith received.

ONE CATHOLIC, THE UNIFYING AND RECONCILING MISSION

In every deanery where the diocese of Singapore has begun indigenous church planting, there already exist some established denominations and agencies. It is very common to perceive the Anglicans as another denomination. To accept this perception is to betray our identity. On the other hand, broadcasting our uniqueness may be perceived as arrogance in the eyes of other Christian institutions. The fact of the matter is that none of the existing Protestant Bible Schools in all the deaneries understand or teach Anglicanism. What must we do to remain faithful without appearing arrogant? Let me share three principles that may help us: unity within, faithful learning, and openness to embrace.

Unity Within

Before we can be a witness of unity, we must display unity within. There are at least three Methodist groups working independently in Thailand. They are not alone. Other denominations, such as the Pentecostals and the Baptists, also have multiple groups, depending on the sources of their support. The same scenario is observed in the other countries of our deaneries.

---

[8] Stephen Neill, *Anglicanism* (A R Mowbray & Co Ltd, 1982), 323.

It would not be a surprise to the Evangelicals if there were multiple Anglican groups within the same country because such stories are common. But it is very surprising to them to learn the pain we endure to maintain just one Anglican Church. Our failure to be one would mute our declaration that we believe in the one holy, catholic and apostolic Church.

The Anglicans arrived in China in the fourth wave of mission endeavor after the three previous waves entered for a period and were expelled subsequently—Nestorians in the eighth century, Franciscans in the thirteenth century, Jesuits in the fourteenth century. Bishop Boone arrived in Shanghai in 1844, leading a team of missionaries from America. The British, based in Hong Kong, established a Diocese in 1849, went on to form the second Diocese at Ningpo in 1872 and the third in North China in 1890. Stephen Neil wrote:

> The British and the Americans worked without any common plans or consultation, without clear delimitation of dioceses. Further complications were added when the Anglican Church of Canada entered the field. Almost every diocese have their own Prayer Book, depending on their affiliations and some with features peculiar to the Chinese books.[9]

There were fourteen Dioceses in China. Of the fourteen, twelve had these affiliations:

- Five had connection with the Church Mission Society, United Kingdom (CMSUK);

- Two with United Society for the Propagation of the Gospel;

- Three with the American church;

---

[9] Stephen Neill, *Anglicanism,* 332.

- One with the church in Canada;
- One with China Inland Mission.

The Anglican Church in China became more unified only after Lambeth in 1930, when China was recognized as one independent province within the Anglican Communion and the various streams began to converge. The first Chinese chairman of the House of Bishops, Bishop Lindel Tsen, was present in Lambeth 1948 as diocesan bishop of China. However, there still existed multiple versions of the Prayer Book.

Anglican Missions in Japan experienced similar problems as China in the initial years. The Americans came in 1859, CMS in 1869; SPG and the church in Canada came after 1869.

But the Anglicans in Japan converged much sooner because Bishop Edward Bickersteth of South Tokyo (1886-1897) saw that the only remedy was to form one national Anglican Church of Japan. Further unity was forged in 1878 with the first conference of Anglican missionaries, which adopted a common prayer book. In 1887, the first joint synod of British and Americans convened and adopted the first constitution.[10] This came about fifty years before China's alignment.

The work expended rapidly. The Synod of 1911 was attended by seventy-four delegates. In 1916, there were:

- 2 Bishops
- 53 Priests (20 Foreign, 33 locals)
- 15 Deacons (2 Foreign, 13 locals)
- 413 Workers (79 Foreign, 334 locals)
- 125 Mission Stations
- 49 Schools

---

[10] Nippon Sei Ko Kai, *The Japan Holy Catholic Church*, Literature Department (New York: Church Mission House, 1946), 4-5.

- 2 Hospitals
- 3483 local communicants

We have a situation in Nepal where a bishop from Korea consecrated a retired clergyman from America as bishop together with a local pastor from a non-Anglican church. They subsequently began ordaining priests and deacons. It has sown much confusion on the ground because the clergy in our Anglican Church in Nepal are acquainted with those ordained by the retired American bishop. If they too are Anglican, why the differing standards of qualifications and preparations? This situation is still unfolding and we hope that it can be resolved soon.

The Missions Consultation Roundtable, held every three years by the Diocese of Singapore of the Province of South Asia, is a significant witness of our common root. Anglican mission partners from diocesan structures and mission agencies participate in the Roundtable because we believe we reached a common page of our unifying witness sooner than the Japanese Anglican Church. We demonstrate the various parts of the body working together as one in a mission field, with each part playing the respective role of sending, facilitating, deploying, monitoring, and harvesting.

In Indonesia, Thailand, and Cambodia, the four dioceses within the Province of Southeast Asia also work closely together to plant churches in the deaneries. Our desire is to pass on a united deanery when it becomes an indigenous diocese, not one fragmented diocese, by being aligned to one or another of the various sources of the pioneering mission.

We serve these deaneries well by bearing a common witness expressed in our house order; within the deaneries, there are existing differences in the society, for which our catholic faith needs to bring healing and reconciliation. There are tribal differences, dialect differences, regional differences, and denominational differences. Our one catholic declaration is an aspect of obedience to unite across these divides—through teaching, modeling, reconciling, and celebrating through our one Lord, one faith, one baptism, one God and the Father of all. Our witness is strengthened and substantiated by the unity within.

Faithful Learning

The second principle for humbly sharing our one catholic Church is the faithful learning of our common heritage. Anglicanism does not have a founder who wrote volumes of theology to define what we believe, nor does Anglicanism expect a confessional allegiance to a certain statement of faith. Our Articles of Religion are not an attempt to provide a comprehensive statement of faith; their purpose "...is to make clear the position of the Church which set itself the aim of being Catholic, avoiding on the one hand the late Medieval traditions of Rome, and on the other the excesses of the Anabaptists."[11] Our reformer fathers sought to restore catholic orthodoxy by returning to the nourishment of the Word and sacraments through liturgical worship.

Theological education in our region rarely includes church history from the perspective of returning to our pre-medieval heritage. The resulting ecclesiology is denominationalism that does not have roots deep enough to penetrate the Reformation stratums, or individualistic pioneers who do not grow roots beyond their idealistic crust. It is imperative that the Anglican missions expound orthodoxy the way our reformer fathers searched to go beyond Roman Catholic teaching. Otherwise, Anglicanism would be just another denomination with limited distinctive contributions to offer to the body of Christ.

---

[11] Stephen Neill, *Anglicanism,* 81.

Openness to Embrace

Being united and rooted in our identity puts us in a humble and secure position to embrace the wider body of Christ and to share what we have. The emerging Anglican churches in the deaneries must not be isolated from the wider body of Christ. We may be the late arrivals in every one of these mission fields, but we have much to share for the sake of Christ who loves his whole Church. A question was asked as to why must Anglicans plant churches in these countries since many churches of other denominations already exist? The simple answer is that the gospel has not reached the ends of the earth.

The more substantive answer is: If we Anglicans know who we are, we will realize how much enrichment we can humbly bring to the wider body of Christ. We cannot undo history, or turn back the clock to become the one catholic church structure as in the pre-Schism age, which was the pre-Vatican II presumption of the Roman Catholics. Neither can we abandon the expression of the one catholic Church by spiritualizing it, which is the predisposition of denominations and independent churches. Either of these positions will not lead us back to the one catholic Church with theological, biblical, historical and pastoral integrity. Anglicans' commitment to the creeds and the unique position of reaching both spectrum of expressions, places upon us a sober responsibility to steer the drifts and to close the gaps. If Anglicans can serve the ocean vessels to flow and form a fleet, rather than merging into one mighty ark, that will be our offering of worship that pleases our One Lord and Father and a faithful exercise of the episcopacy. Let me quote Cyprian Bishop of Carthage on the unity of the Catholic Church:

> The episcopate is a single whole, in which each bishop's share gives him a... responsibility for the whole. So is the Church a single whole, though she spreads far and wide

into a multitude of churches as her fertility increases. We may compare the sun, many rays but one light; or a tree, many branches but one firmly rooted trunk. When many streams flow from one spring, although the bountiful supply of water welling out has the appearance of plurality, unity is preserved in the source. Pluck a ray from the body of the sun, and its unity allows no division of light. Break a branch from the tree, and when it is broken off it will not bud. Cut a stream off from its spring, and when it is cut off it dries up. In the same way the Church, bathed in the light of the Lord, spreads her rays throughout the world, yet the light everywhere diffused is one light and the unity of the body is not broken. ... Yet there is one head, one source, one mother boundlessly fruitful. Of her womb are we born; by her milk we are nourished; by her breath we are quickened.[12]

These words were written long before the emergence of denominations. The proliferation of denominations and independent churches does not make Bishop Cyril's charge on the episcopate any less true. In fact, it is a solemn charge to us who believe our roots trace back to the historical Church and the apostolic trust. In that sense, ecumenism based on common scriptural faith is part of our mission as Anglicans. This leads me to the next two related attributes, *Holy* and *Apostolic*.

HOLY APOSTOLIC

Let me first deal with the attribute of apostolicity before coming back to the attribute of holiness. What does being the *apostolic Church* mean? Scriptures and the writings of the early fathers do not produce evidence that apostolic succession is the unbroken chain of laying on of hands. There was no replacement after the death of the last apostle,

---

[12] Cyprian, Bishop and Martyr of Carthage, d 258, On the Unity of the Catholic Church 5: CSEL 3 pp. 213ff. Tr. Early Latin Theology, ed. Greenslade (Library of Christian Classics) V, 1956, pp.126-7

the way Judas was replaced by Matthias. Paul's use of the title "apostle" was more of an ambassador commissioned by Christ to witness to Christ. Therefore, the prerequisites are of those who have witnessed the risen Lord, and those who have been commissioned by the Lord for missionary preaching. [13]

In the writings of numerous Church fathers, such as Ignatius, bishop of Antioch around 107 A.D., the orders of bishop, priest, and deacon were established soon after the era of the apostles. There was no reference to the method of appointment, such as the laying on of hands, nor was any reference made to the bishop of Rome.[14]

Hans Kung, the Roman Catholic theologian who was one of the architects behind Vatican II, sees the real continuous link with the apostles as twofold. First, agreement with the apostolic witness. The Church does not hear its Lord and his message by direct inspiration, but only through the witness of the apostles, through their witness of listening to the Lord himself. Second, continuing the apostolic ministry. The Church can only remain true to the apostolic witness, the witness of the Bible through service. Together with the apostles, the Church must serve the Lord, the Lord of the Church and of the apostles.[15]

This view developed after Hans Kung's rejection of papal infallibility, which unfortunately earned him punishment by the Roman Catholic Church. Nonetheless, his study was a thorough piece of biblical, historical, and theological work that we can draw from.

Coming back to the attribute of holiness, is the Church a *communio sanctorum* or a *communio peccatorum*? Meaning,

---

[13] Hans Kung, *The Church* (New York: Burns and Oaks,, 9th Impression 1986), 348

[14] Colin Buchanan, *Is The Church Of England Biblical?* An Anglican Ecclesiology (London: Darton, Longman and Tord Ltd, 1998), 153.

[15] Hans Kung, *The Church*, 356-357

is the Church the communion of saints or the communion of sinners? How do we understand the holy Church amidst the undeniable reality of sinful members of the Church? Two main excuses were common in church history. One was an attempt to make the Church holy by the exclusiveness of "holy members" as the true Church and the exclusion of sinful members. Some early examples were the Donatists, the Montanists, and the Cathars. In modern times, we observe similar tendencies in churches such as the Exclusive Brethren. Another attempt was to distinguish between the holy Church and sinful members. But this division is unreal. What is a church with no members, a holy nation with no citizens? What is the body if only the head is holy?

> Men cannot make ourselves holy. Believers are "saints" in so far as they are "sanctified" in Christ (1 Corinthians 1:2) by the Holy Spirit (Romans 15:6). There are no self-made saints, only those who are "called to be saints."[16]
>
> It is God who distinguishes the Church, sets it apart, marks it out for its own and makes it holy, by winning power over the hearts of men through the Holy Spirit...This is why we do not simply believe in the holy Church, but believe in God who makes the Church holy."[17]

Thus the Church is not a community only for holy people. It is a community of people being made holy. Neither is it a community of sinners who are content to remain sinners, presuming on the grace of God: casual with sins, uncomfortable to challenge the fragile human ego, and fearful to illuminate the judgment of the Holy God. In the holy Church, sinners find a safe home to be open, to repent, to be forgiven, to be reconciled, to be empowered—always fixing our hope in our sanctified destiny.

---

[16] Hans Kung, *The Church,* 324.
[17] Hans Kung, *The Church*, 325.

The holy apostolic Church holds in tension faithfulness to the proclamation of Scriptures as received through the apostles, with the sanctifying journey of the set apart people of God. Holy apostolicity goes far beyond transmitting a static codex or the gathering of those who have attained a certain standard of holiness. It is the faithful proclamation of the heart of God as received from the Scripture that influences the world through Spirit-empowered, forgiven saints who are being sanctified. The aim of the holy apostolic Church is more than the faithful teaching of Scriptures. The teaching has a Spirit-filled missional thrust to transform the sinful world, by being a reconciling home to deeply nurture sinners to saints.

The one holy catholic and apostolic Church is missional. The deep understanding of our heritage compels us to go beyond merely establishing churches in the deaneries. Our purpose cannot be any less than the purpose of God: "Your kingdom come, your will be done, on earth as it is in heaven" (Matthew 6:10).

HOW DO WE WORK OUT THE PLANTING OF THE ONE HOLY CATHOLIC AND APOSTOLIC CHURCH IN PRACTICAL TERMS?

Allow me to share with you four principles guiding our learning in this process. They are:

1. The Principle of Commonality
2. The Principle of Contextualization
3. The Principle of Sustainability
4. The Principle of Relativity

I believe these four principles, first applied to the financial aspect of missions, can also guide us in our ecclesiastical development.

1. The Principle of Commonality

The episcopacy of the Bishop of Singapore covers seven countries. Although these deaneries are of different political entities and national boundaries, our *ecclesia* responsibility must surpass these differences to recognize our commonality in the kingdom of God, just as we promote our provincial commonality albeit the differences of the four Dioceses. Although each country presents cultural, linguistic, ethnic and historical differences, our common identity in Christ must express some similarities in the way we relate within and across the deaneries. However, commonality does not mean equality. This is where the following three principles of contextualization, sustainability, and relativity provide some wider coordinates to help us find an equilibrium for each deanery.

2. The Principle of Contextualization

While we work toward commonality in the specific area of clergy benefits, the immediate contextual consideration is the vast economic differences amongst the various deaneries. The Gross National Product (GDP) of the countries in the diocese ranges from USD 697 per capita for Nepal to USD 56,268 per capita for Singapore. The highest GDP per capita after Singapore is Thailand, which stands at USD 5,519.

The salary and benefits of the clergy in each of the deaneries will conform to the economics of the respective countries. Other contextual factors relevant for reference are the benefits enjoyed by other similar Christian organizations of the respective deaneries, and the common benefits enjoyed by the private and public sectors.

3. The Principle of Sustainability

The Principle of Sustainability is to recognize the realistic financial capacity of a deanery when it attains the basic constitutional features of a diocese, namely, at least six self-supporting parishes with mature clergy and lay leadership. The clergy benefits desired for the deaneries must be sustainable at that level of financial capacity. If the desired benefits care well for the clergy but are beyond the capacity of the emerging diocese, it would push back the timeline to attain the self-financing criteria. We must also be careful not to impose benefits that the local leadership of a future diocese may think unnecessary.

4. The Principle of Relativity

We must also be mindful that the current level of benefits that Singapore clergy are enjoying were not there forty years ago when the diocese was financially weaker. Good benefits were developed over time as the society and the financial capacity of the diocese developed. Therefore, the level of benefits derived for each deanery must be relative to the development of the society and the financial health of the emerging diocese.

Let me now attempt to apply these principles to the ecclesiastical development of the deaneries.

APPLYING THE PRINCIPLE OF COMMONALITY

A planted Anglican Church must become recognizably Anglican. This is not to say that there is only one fixed form to be duplicated in all places at all times. But Anglicans from any part of the world should be able to identify with the planted indigenous church, despite the linguistic and cultural differences because of our Anglican commonalities.

I suggest that our commonality must be recognizable through forms of worship; reading of Scriptures; attention to the sacraments, the Articles of Religion, and our episcopal ministry of the threefold order; and internal governance. These practices all grew out of the subterranean roots of our common identity, history, and mission.

We do not pursue commonality for the sake of being uniform but for the passing down of the faith received and the manner in which they are received.

APPLYING THE PRINCIPLE OF CONTEXTUALIZATION

While commonality is espoused, the *Thirty-nine Articles* and the Preface to Cranmer's *Book of Common Prayer* affirm the importance of contextualization, evident first by the vernacular movement. There are contextual expressions that enrich the expressions of the common faith. Songs written with the vernacular, enriched by local music, speak to the hearts of the indigenous people in a way that translated material could not.

In all our deaneries, vestments and order convey a fitting worship of the king of Kings. Missionaries from America, the United Kingdom, and Australia have diverse attitudes toward vestments based on their context. Care must be exercised not to import such issues to confuse the indigenous church because those issues are irrelevant to their context. Contextualization forces us to understand broader and think deeper in order to adopt practices leading to higher devotion.

Six years ago, the Anglican Church in Thailand ordained the first Thai priest using the vernacular order of service. Church leaders of various denominations were invited to witness that historic day. On the same day, there were two important events of other Christian institutions in Bangkok, which required the presence of their leaders. Some Christian leaders who came had intended to make a brief appearance out of courtesy and move on to their other obligations. But they stayed until the end of the service. They stayed on for the reception. They stayed talking among themselves in awe of our Ordination Service that they had just experienced. They told me how struck they were with the depth of our ordination; the undeniable presence of the Holy Spirit, the well-ordered fashion of worship, which was fit for the King. They had no problem with our bishop's cope and mitre. For these veteran Thai pastors, half of whom were from independent churches, this was most fitting for the context in Thailand.

APPLYING THE PRINCIPLE OF SUSTAINABILITY

The Principle of Sustainability emphasizes practices and ethos that would and could carry on beyond the pioneering missions. Care must be exercised not to introduce ministry and practices that would be thrown out the moment the pioneering missions leave. The purpose of practices and ministry must be clear. They may also be good initiatives for a season, and they must not evolve into a sacred cow that no one dares to slaughter. The introduction of good practices must be shared, deepened with an understanding of why we do what we do, and accepted by the church's members for it to be sustainable. Directives alone would not sustain good ministries.

The Book of Common Prayer has now been translated into the local languages of five of the six deaneries. Its usage is adopted variously in the different locations of the deaneries. It has been so helpful that the Bishop of Singapore entrusted Rev. Canon Dr. Michael Poon to travel to the deaneries to train the leaders. He spends one-to-two weeks in each deanery to train the national clergy and pastoral staff on the wealth of heritage we are connected to in worship through the *Book of Common Prayer*, the Lectionary, etc.

A good proportion of our staff are from other Christian traditions, and native Christians do not know Anglicanism because it has not existed for long in their country. Therefore, these local trainings are essential. They enrich our worship. They secure our identity. They give us understanding to innovate. They build in us confidence to pass it on.   And they result in sustainability.

APPLYING THE PRINCIPLE OF RELATIVITY

As you travel to the deaneries, do not be surprised to find churches that do not quite resemble the Anglican Church with which you are familiar. We must not expect a fledgling church to have the full expression of what is common Anglicanism.

Question: Do we launch a new church plant with a full "perfect" liturgical Sunday service? Should that be the aim at all? The Principle of Relativity helps us gauge the type of feeding at the different seasons of growth. Planting a church is like nurturing a baby, providing the right food at the right time in the child's development.

Let me close with a story to illustrate what I have been sharing in our consideration of planting the one holy catholic and apostolic Church.

Last year marked a quarter of a century of the Anglican missions among the people of Thailand. In twenty-five years, Anglicans planted thirteen congregations, pioneered four kindergartens, and launched two community service ministries. Most of the pioneering staff are still present. We took a year to compile our stories of what the Lord has done in every place. After the articles were edited for a final round of proof reading, all of us sat around the table. Each read their story out loud for all the others to hear. At the end of the exercise, I led them to identify three values that represent what God has sown among us that we would like to pass on to future generations. The three values our Thai pastoral workers identified from our short heritage were: family, rootedness and mission.

We are not mere partners in an organization; we are a secure *family* that gives fatherly care and brotherly love to one another in the Lord. Our *rootedness* in Scripture, history and customs gives us balance, stability and wholeness in our ministry approach. It has carried us through many crises. It was *mission* that brought us into being. We shall not let achievements blunt our pioneering spirit to preach the gospel and plant churches. Mission is the purpose for which this rooted family is living. I am proud of their observations. Looking at the three words, isn't this the one holy catholic apostolic Church developing?

Conclusion

PRESSING ONWARD

by Chris Royer

Not that I have already obtained all this, or have
already arrived at my goal, but I press on to take
hold of that for which Christ Jesus took hold of
me. (Philippians 3:8, New International Version)

Max Warren, general secretary of the Church Missionary
Society from 1942 to 1963, wrote these words about the
importance of understanding the institutional history of a
mission organization for its future missionary endeavors:

> I am deeply convinced that only a right attitude to the past
> provides me with any possibility whatever of a right
> attitude to the future. And by a right attitude to the past
> I mean a genuine conviction that the Holy Spirit was
> operating in the past, that he guided our fathers before
> us, and that he was all the while at work taking up the
> cross-treads of human ignorance and failure and sin and
> using them to weave a pattern whose full revealing awaits
> the future.[1]

As I have been reading the previous chapters of our
twenty-five-year anniversary book, and listening to countless
testimonies of AFM missionaries, board members, staff,

---

[1] F. Dillstone, *Into All the World: A Biography of Max Warren* (London: Hodder
& Stoughton, 1980), 80.

prayer partners, volunteers, and donors, I have observed the power and presence of the Holy Spirit operating through this unique band of Christians. I have seen the Spirit move "in the cross-threads" of AFM's human weaknesses, insufficiencies, and mistakes. With our inauspicious beginnings in 1993 at an exceptionally inopportune time—during the precipitous decline and then implosion of the Episcopal denomination in 2003—it is truly miraculous that AFM survived the early years. I am convinced that God sustained and preserved AFM because missions to unreached peoples lie deep within his heart. Missions to unreached peoples began with the call of Abram to reach the nations around him (Genesis 12:1-3) and crystalized with Jesus' Great Commission (Matthew 28:18-20). Missions to unreached peoples will be consummated in heaven when a great multitude from every nation, tribe, people, and language will be standing before the throne, shouting, "Salvation belongs to our God, who sits on the throne, and to the Lamb" (Revelation 7:10). Thus, as Hudson Taylor, pioneer missionary to the interior of China, reminds us, "The Great Commission is not merely an option to be considered but a commandment to be obeyed."

Therefore, AFM's laser-like focus on unreached peoples, which has grounded and guided us in the past, will continue to be our singular focus in the future. Accordingly, AFM will continue to ground our methodology in sound empirical research and the Strategy Coordination method (exemplified in Chapter 6). AFM will also continue to send short-, mid-, and long-term missionaries to areas and peoples where the Church does not yet exist. AFM will continue to engage in the pioneer phase of missions (discussed in the Introduction). And finally, AFM will continue to work cross-denominationally, strategically, collaboratively, and insofar as circumstances on the field allow, "Anglicanly." (See Part 4, Chapters 13-15).) I'm optimistic about the future of AFM and the contribution Anglicans can make to frontier missions because, as Paul writes, "If God is for us, who can be against us" (Romans 8:31)? The Father's passion and plan is for every nation to know him and He's called us to be his hands and feet in this endeavor.

And yet, meaningful Anglican involvement in frontier missions over the next quarter century cannot be taken for granted. Now, more than any time in the last two centuries, the *raison d'etre* for frontier missions is being questioned not only from outside the church but more startlingly, from within.

SOME CONTEMPORARY OBJECTIONS TO MISSIONS

I often talk with American Christians who believe that the American Church should quit sending missionaries overseas, expressed in words like, "The needs are greater in the U.S.," "Local indigenous Christians can minister more effectively (and at a lower cost) than sending American missionaries," and "Let's just send money, not more people." It is worth noting that these statements reflect that the Western- and American-centric missions thinking, which permeated much of the nineteenth and twentieth centuries, has abated significantly. American Christians, by and large, understand that missions today is not just "from the West to the Rest," but "from Everywhere to Everyone," and that God has given the global Church the responsibility and privilege to reach the nations.

However, American Christians seem increasingly skeptical and uncertain of the role we should play. Due to waning confidence in the uniqueness of Christ, the rapidity of change in our global and ever-globalizing world, a guilty conscience stemming from the abuses of American power, and the sheer hostility to Christians in many regions of the globe, American Christians seem uncertain and hesitant about the role we can and should play (if any at all) in global frontier missions.

Missiologist Paul Borthwick writes compellingly about the strengths American Christians can bring to the table.[2] One strength of American missionaries is the optimistic belief that change really is possible. Peter Kuzmič, a Croatian theologian and missiologist, labels this "naïve optimism," by which he means that Americans are "optimistic, future-looking, and change-oriented."[3] The downside of our naïve optimism is that American Christians can dismissively and subconsciously oversimplify problems and cultural issues, underestimate the privilege and power that our affluence affords us, and undervalue the perspectives, contributions, and gifts that other Christians from the global Church can provide. American missionaries should be vigilant in these areas. But the benefit of our "naïve optimism" is that, while many cultures and nations are irretrievably stuck in past feuds, karma, fatalistic ideologies, and the rigid thinking that emanates from hierarchical and tightly classed, caste, and kinship societies, American Christians can often bring new ideas, innovation, and a "can do" spirit to missions. The entrepreneurial and optimistic spirit in American Christians has been invaluable in birthing countless ministries around the globe and the need continues today. The vast bulk of unreached peoples live in nation states that do not offer religious or missionary visas. Thus, acquiring and maintaining residency and then ministering effectively in these areas with no (or limited) Christian presence requires

---

[2] P. Borthwick, *Western Christians in Global Missions: What's the Role of the North American Church?* (Downers Grove, IL: Intervarsity Press, 2012). Borthwick (pp. 64-69) mentions five strengths of the American Church: Generosity and economic wealth, optimism and the belief that change is possible, experience in and resources for training, multiculturalism, and our long mission's history. I discuss two of these five strengths in this chapter.

[3] P. Borthwick, *Western Christians in Global* Missions, 66

resilient entrepreneurialism, a quality that American Christians can humbly contribute to the global church.

A second strength of the American church is our economic wealth and a deeply generous spirit. This combination enables American Christians to finance global initiatives, like the "Third Lausanne Congress on World Evangelism" in 2010, of which Americans gave some sixteen million dollars (80% of the total budget).[4] We should also use our wealth to strategically and comprehensively train our missionaries before sending them to unreached fields. We must also provide effective member care and professional development for our missionaries while on the field to minimize their premature attrition.

To be clear, I am not advocating that American missionaries do what can be done by local, indigenous Christians in areas where churches have already been planted.[5] Allocating resources and personnel in this manner not only stunts church growth but is also poor stewardship of resources. What I am arguing for, however, is that the American church still has the privilege and calling to engage in strategic frontier missions to reach the least reached people groups.[6] Indeed, thousands of unreached people groups still are waiting for the gospel to enter their culture. Vast swaths of real estate on our globe are still devoid of churches. Reaching the 29% of our globe that has no (or extremely limited) access to the gospel requires tens of thousands of new cross cultural missionaries to go and live among them, learn their language and culture, and share

---

[4] P. Borthwick, *Western Christians in Global* Missions, 65.

[5] Nearly a century ago (1927) Roland Allen provided a powerful critique of how extended non-indigenous missionary presence can actually thwart the growth of the Church. Allen, R. (1997). The Spontaneous Expansion of the Church and the Causes which Hinder It. Eugen, OR: Wipf and Stock Publishers.

[6] Alan Johnson, "A Model for Understanding the Missionary Task," *International Journal of Frontier Missions, 18, no.3 (2001):* 137-138.

and model the gospel. Frontier missions is not only our Lord's last command but also, as missiologist Andrew Walls asserts, the "lifeblood of historic Christianity."[7] We must not abdicate this high and holy calling.

AFM'S VISION FOR THE NEXT TWENTY-FIVE YEARS

As AFM moves into our second twenty-five years, we are acutely aware that our structures and methodologies are not sacrosanct nor set in stone. As Samuel Escobar writes, "John Wesley and Count Zinzendorf, as well as William Carey, Billy Graham and Mother Teresa, were ready to revise the old way of carrying on mission and to develop new structures adequate for the new times, because they were open to the movement of the Spirit."[8] As we at AFM strive to remain sensitive to the movement of the Spirit, we realize that our practices and processes may have to change. However, the values and vision that have undergirded us in the past will continue to guide us in the future as we follow the Spirit's leading to evangelize the more than six thousand people groups still unreached with the gospel.

During the nineteenth century, thousands of Christians launched out from Western Europe and North America to share the love of Jesus in Africa. Many died from malaria upon their arrival. Others endured countless hardships. But their labors were not in vain. The vibrant African church today is comprised of the descendants of *once unreached peoples*. In 1800, less than 1% of Africa was reached with the gospel, but as of 2010 some 504 million Africans (48.8% of

---

[7] Andrew Walls, *The Cross-Cultural Process in Christian History: Studies in Transmission and Appropriation of Faith*. (Maryknoll, New York: Orbis Books, 2002).

[8] Samuel Escobar, *The New Global Mission: The Gospel from Everywhere to Everyone* (Downers Grove, IL: Intervarsity Press, 2003), 126.

the continent) call themselves Christians.[9] Due to the prayers, sacrifices, and ministries of thousands of missionaries who went to Africa during the nineteenth and twentieth centuries, Africa is now an epicenter of vibrant Christianity!

Today, the frontiers of missions lie with India, China, Southeast Asia, and the Islamic world, areas our authors have written about in Part 3, Chapters 7-12. AFM's vision is that when Christians in 2100 look back over the twenty-first century, they will remark with deep gratitude that these areas have also become centers of vibrant Christianity due to the missionary efforts of Christians in the twenty-first century!

And so, AFM's vision remains unchanged from our founding days: to mobilize the Church to pray for and send missionaries to the largest and least-evangelized people groups and geographical regions, that churches might be established among all the 16,833 ethnolinguistic nations on our planet. Before this became our vision, it was Christ's vision. And human history is marching forward toward the fulfillment of this vision: "With your blood you purchased for God persons from every tribe and language and people and nation. You have made them to be a kingdom and priests to serve our God, and they will reign on the earth" (Revelation 5:9-10, New International Version). Hallelujah! Amen!

---

[9] J. Mandryk, *Operation World: The Definitive Prayer Guide to Every Nation* (Colorado Springs, CO: Biblica Publishing, 2010), 29.

ABOUT
ANGLICAN FRONTIER MISSIONS

AFM's Vision is to plant biblically-based, indigenous churches among the largest and least reached people groups still waiting to hear the gospel for the very first time. Partnering with members of the worldwide Anglican Communion and other Christians who live near or among unreached peoples, AFM equips and sends short-term, mid-term, and long-term missionaries.

CONTACT US!

Anglican Frontier Missions
P.O. Box 18038
Richmond VA 23226
804 355 8468
https://anglicanfrontiers.com/
info@afm-us.org
Twitter: afm_us
Facebook: Anglican Frontiers

More Resources from AFM

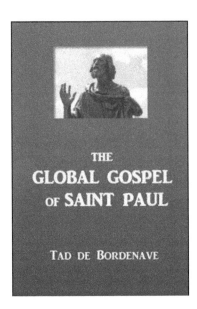

AFM Founder and first director Tad de Bordenave argues that the proper and primary filter for reading St. Paul is seeing his determination that the grace of God be extended to all nations. This was his foremost teaching and the centerpiece of his ministry. Alongside the many outstanding emphases that guide the church, this should be out front—as teaching and as clarion call.

AFM cross cultural worker Duane Miller compares the crucial elements in Christianity's and Islam's story— creation, fall, salvation, and final judgment—to each other, revealing new insights on how Islam, Christianity, and modernity both interact and clash.

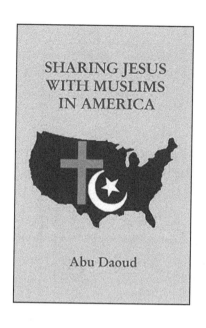

AFM cross-cultural worker Abu Daoud provides a theological backdrop alongside practical advice for sharing the Gospel with Muslims in the U.S.

Tracing the year that begins with the debates with Stephen in the Synagogue of the Freemen and moving past the encounter with Jesus near Damascus, AFM founder and first director Tad de Bordenave outlines how we see Paul moving from the leading stalwart for Jewish exclusivism to the apostle to the nations. In this history we see the same controversies that divided the early church continuing today. Following Paul's spiritual journey will move us today to embracing the call to frontier mission.

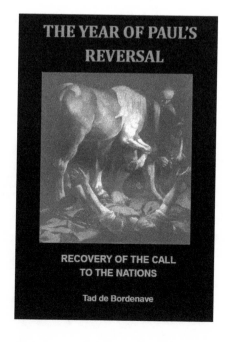

This series by Tad de Bordenave follows the lectionary year with comments on the lessons and scenes related to frontier missions. This book brings missionary insight to the Sunday readings as well as stories of God at work among the least evangelized peoples.

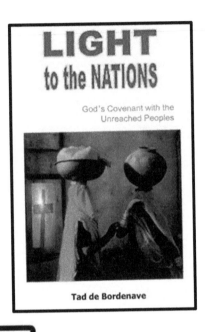

A four-chapter DVD series on the metanarratives of Islam and Christianity, covering the topics of creation, humanity, Israel, Muhammad, the Umma, Jesus, the church, and salvation. Excellent for adult education on the differences between Islam and Christianity.

SUGGESTED DONATION
Books: US $12
Video: US $15

Name: _____

Book/Video	Quantity	Suggested Donation
Additional Donation:		
TOTAL ENCLOSED DONATION:		

Address: _____

_____

Telephone: _____

Email: _____

☐ **I would like to receive E-Newsletters from AFM** (prayer requests, updates from missionaries, etc.)

Privacy policy: **Under no circumstances** will AFM sell or share any of your information with anyone other than the webmaster and co-workers on this web site.

Mail this form to:

P.O. Box 18038

Richmond, VA 23226

Please make all checks payable to Anglican Frontier Missions.

CPSIA information can be obtained
at www.ICGtesting.com
Printed in the USA
BVHW070748130119
537711BV00001B/73/P